Mathwise

Mathwise

Teaching Mathematical Thinking and Problem Solving

Arthur A. Hyde
National-Louis University

Pamela R. Hyde
Willard Elementary School

Heinemann
Portsmouth, NH

Heinemann Educational Books, Inc.
361 Hanover Street   Portsmouth, NH 03801-3959
Offices and agents throughout the world

Various figures and problems in this book have been reprinted from
*Thinking in Context: Teaching Cognitive Processes across the
Elementary School Curriculum* by Arthur A. Hyde and Marilyn Bizar.
White Plains, NY: Longman, 1989.

Library of Congress Cataloging-in-Publication Data
Hyde, Arthur A.
    Mathwise : teaching mathematical thinking and problem solving /
Arthur A. Hyde, Pamela R. Hyde.
        p. cm.
    Includes bibliographical references and index.
    ISBN 0-435-08311-2
    1. Mathematics—Study and teaching (Elementary).   2. Problem
solving. I. Hyde, Pamela R.   II. Title.
QA135.5.H93 1991
372.7'044—dc20   90-47046
                                                      CIP

Designed by Maria Szmauz
Printed in the United States of America
91 92 93 94 95   10 9 8 7 6 5 4 3 2 1

contents

1

$$\cdots\cdots\cdots\cdots\cdots\cdots\cdots\cdots\cdots\cdots\cdots\cdots$$

Problem Solving— Linking Mathematics and the World

Most of us have had many experiences with mathematics—some enjoyable, some terrifying. We remember the dreadful ones vividly. Nearly everyone can recall a moment (often many moments) as a student when abdominal tension lurched into hyperdrive during the mathematics lesson. Whatever the teacher was saying, doing, or showing seemed incomprehensible. Meaningless scribbles of chalk danced on the board like crazed hieroglyphics. Our only thought was, please God, don't let her call on me!

Our society grants mathematics a measure of deification; we are regularly persuaded by the validity of numbers. My new six-cylinder Cheetah gets forty-eight miles to the gallon. The election eve polls project a landslide victory of 62 percent for Senator Twaddle. Hurry on down to Igor's Emporium where prices have been slashed: at least a third off every item in the inventory. Various statistics are used effectively to convince us of society's truths.

Many of us believe that mathematics is important but beyond our capability. It is an area of life in which few of us feel competent. Yet ironically, many adults who readily express their own inadequacies in mathematics have developed ways of doing mathematics very effectively in situations of importance to them. On these occasions, they are able to devise a mathematical approach that accomplishes their purposes. Research studies have shown that adult shoppers can do flawless calculation and problem solving in actual stores, but perform dramatically less well on schoollike tests of identical material. Furthermore, these adults frequently dismiss their own personal ways of doing the mathematical operations as not being "real math."

For instance, when figuring out how much wallpaper to buy, we might not calculate exactly the square inches of paper we need to cover a computed area, but might rather estimate the number of rolls, allowing extra for cutting and matching. When deciding which size box of laundry detergent is the "better buy," we might not calculate the unit price of each, but instead use our sense of proportionality (e.g., if one box is 20 ounces for $1.40 and the other is 48 ounces for $2.75, the bigger is cheaper because it is more than twice as big and less than twice the price).

The way we use the mathematics we know and understand is analogous to the way young children operate. We know from research studies that when children begin schooling, they have some simple but sound ways of doing mathematical problem solving. Individual children invent their own methods for dealing with important situations that require calculation, reasoning, or problem solving (e.g., subtracting by holding out fingers for the total and pulling back the number to be taken away). However, children readily abandon their personally derived ways of thinking in favor of those taught by their teachers: mechanical procedures, usually devoid of meaning to them.

Both children and adults, then, are able to use mathematics in situations that matter to them. All of us are more capable of doing mathematics than we have been led to believe in school. Some educators have become critical of the pronounced discontinuity between the "school math" and students' lives.

Negative experiences with "school math" make many students anxious and lead them to avoid mathematics in later life. The panic students feel when being called to the blackboard to do a problem or when taking a test causes their minds to shut down. Problems flawlessly worked out the previous night are swept away with the morning tide, utterly vanishing from recollection. Schools should consider the exhortation to the physician: First, do no harm! At the very least, schools should avoid whatever creates bad feelings and attitudes toward mathematics and about the students as learners.

Among the many factors in our schools and society that have contributed to students' negative feelings toward mathematics are mathematics curricula that consist primarily of "skills." The reduction of mathematics to ever smaller and separate skills and subskills is a tragically mistaken notion, the misguided application of behavioral psychology to education. This conception has trivialized children's work in mathematics (and in reading and writing as well) into memorization of bits and pieces with little meaning.

Consider how much time in mathematics is spent on learning arithmetic facts. In many schools, the results of arithmetic operations on pairs of the first twelve integers must be memorized to be repeated on a timed test before children are allowed to do any other form of mathematics. Although arithmetic computation is only one small part of mathematics, children spend most of their mathematics time in elementary school learning about arithmetic operations in increasingly complicated forms. Skim most mathematics textbooks and you will see page after page of arithmetic drill exercises in which students must calculate various sums, differences, products, and quotients with paper and pencil. These numbers are disembodied—they refer to nothing; to many children, they mean nothing.

Students have a right to experience more in mathematics than merely memorizing mathematical facts. They should be actively experiencing and grappling with mathematical *ideas* as they come to understand and use them in their lives. Mathematical ideas give meaningfulness to mathematical facts. Memorizing that 3 times 12 equals 36 is meaningless without a *conception* of what multiplication is. Experiences are needed to build rich understanding of the concept of multiplication so that it can be powerfully used.

. . . .

A Problem-solving Approach to Building Understanding

How, for example, might the concept of *area* be taught so that students truly understand what area means? Most textbooks give a brief explanation of the concept and a few examples of how to calculate it; then the students apply the concept in a set of exercises. The emphasis is on the *procedure* to calculate the area, and students develop a very narrow understanding of area. ''Area is what you get when you multiply the length times the width of a rectangle and say 'square feet' [or inches] afterward.'' They may get the right answer, but what is their conception of area? Do they really understand what it means?

A more meaningful approach would be to start with materials or ideas within students' experiences—for instance, square floor tiles and a rectangular room, such as the classroom. Then a question is posed: How many tiles would be needed to retile the entire floor? The task requires students to make a conceptual shift away from one-dimensional, linear measurement to two dimensions, thinking in squares instead of lines (like inches or feet). They may actually count squares or some might use their knowledge of multiplication to figure out how many tiles would be needed. After this simple introduction, students are given samples of a new square tile, one foot on each side, made of heavy cardboard. The teacher then asks, ''How many of these new tiles will be needed to retile the classroom floor?'' The students can use this basic measuring device to determine work on the task.

Next, they should discuss, with the teacher's help, how the linear measure of the length and width is related to the number of tiles. The teacher might have to show them how measuring the length and width of the rectangular room (with a ruler or tape measure) is easier than (though perhaps not as much fun as) placing their sample tiles on the floor. Then students determine how many tiles it would take to cover some absurdly large rectangular area, like the gym or the playground. The value of the procedure of length times width will be apparent. Notice that working with the procedure comes after the basic sense of what the concept is all about.

The students are now ready to move from concrete experiences to the more abstract notions of area. Just as a foot is a standard (and familiar) measure of distance, their tile is a standard measure of area: a square foot. So instead of saying it would take 450 tiles to cover the classroom's floor (15 feet by 30 feet), we can say the floor is 450 square feet. This is a simple conceptual change, not a big leap, because of the experiential groundwork that has been laid. Finally, they can move to the symbolic and procedural aspects of 15 feet $\times$ 30 feet $=$ 450 square feet, or the formula, length $\times$ width $=$ area ($l \times w = A$). These representations should be last, not first, as often happens in texts. They are ways of abstractly representing a concept.

This example gives a basic understanding of the concept of area, introducing it in a meaningful way, by building on students' existing ideas. Many examples and activities are needed to broaden this concept in the students' minds. For instance, the *shapes* of the areas being measured and the units of measure (square inches, square centimeters, square meters, square miles, etc.) may be varied. Students could profit from representations and drawings, such as on graph paper. These additional experiences all help build a more generalized and abstract concept of area.

The curriculum should be filled with realistic situations, phenomena, and interesting, relevant problems. The initial understanding of mathematical concepts students gain through these activities can become the "launching pads" for meaningfully expanding and generalizing these concepts to greater levels of abstraction.

The general approach used for introducing the concept of area, as well as other mathematical concepts, can be seen in figure 1.1. The domain of mathematics includes particular kinds of knowledge and thinking. The students' experiences with everyday situations foster ideas, conceptions, beliefs, attitudes, and so on. The teacher can arrange problem-solving activities—questions, tasks, investigations, and inquiries—that will bridge these two spheres, that will stimulate the flow of experiences from one sphere to the other. Such activities can originate in either the domain of mathematics or the lives of the students; they may be posed by students as well as by the teacher. Student-initiated inquiry can be exceptionally beneficial for constructing meaning.

We are not merely suggesting that problem solving should be the culmination of learning a mathematical idea, the application of a known concept. Problem solving should not be a set of problems at the end of a chapter. Because problem solving is a way of thinking and doing mathematics, it can be a major vehicle for helping students truly understand and use mathematics. Problem-solving activities can introduce students to new mathematical ideas, provide exciting experiences that develop deeper understanding, and also help students apply what they understand to their lives.

Problem-solving activities start by stimulating students' thinking about words they already know so that the teacher can make connections between the new ideas that will be addressed and students' existing conceptions. The teacher uses the language, terms, and ideas that students have already

. . . .

Figure 1.1

Domain of mathematics	Problem-solving activities	Students' lives
Mathematical Knowledge	Questions	Experiences
Concepts	Tasks	Events
Procedures	Investigations	Phenomena
Interconnected Ideas	Inquiries	Ideas
Mathematical Thinking		Conceptions
Reasoning		Beliefs
Communicating		Attitudes
Problem Solving		Schemata
Abstracting		
Generalizing		

encountered. Students should talk about their thoughts with the teachers and one another. As humans, we are capable not only of articulating our ideas, but also of reflecting upon and playing with our ideas through oral and written language. Thought and language are intimately related and mathematical ideas are refined as we communicate them to each other.

Psychologists who have studied how people think and understand ideas tell us that we actively construct our own meanings of what we perceive. New information may be assimilated into existing *schemata* or these may have to be modified to create new structures and relationships among ideas. Some psychologists use *schema* to mean specific knowledge and how it is structured, while others understand it as both the way the information is organized and how it is habitually used. In either case, we use our schemata to interpret our experiences, including ideas, words, and terms we have heard.

We need to make students aware of what they do know and how they know it. We need to be aware of what these conceptions are. We need to be sure the schemata they bring to mind are appropriate, so they will understand as richly as possible the new ideas we are asking them to consider.

Students can gain a strong conceptual understanding of arithmetic operations from physical representations, before the teacher introduces procedures. Notice how the following problem-solving activity we've used many times with third graders blends multiplication and division into their reciprocal relationship.

Arrange the students into groups of three or four and give each group 12 large Lego blocks or Unifix cubes. Ask the students, "Can you arrange the blocks into stacks (straight up, one completely on top of another) so that there are the *same* number of blocks in each stack?" If they find one possibility, they should try to create others. Give them a sheet of paper with a two-column list of the following headings to record what they find:

How Many Stacks?   How Many in Each Stack?

When they have found all they can, ask them to discuss what they found. Make sure they realize that 1 stack of 12 blocks is different from 12 stacks of 1 block. Some students may argue that these two arrangements do not fit the instructions of the problem. Have the class discuss the underlying assumptions of the problem. Does the phrase "the same number of blocks in each stack" imply there must be more than 1 stack? Can a stack contain only 1 block? These answers depend on one's conception of "stack." In mathematics, we adopt some conventions and conceptual definitions in order to proceed. Students should be helped to see that it is important to define terms and recognize assumptions behind our concepts and conventions. Suggest a "tentative" definition of stack that allows a stack of 1. Similarly, 1 stack of 12 should also be allowed.

When each group has generated a number of possibilities, write down the students' answers on the board in any order they offer them. At some point you should ask them, "How do you know if you have found them all?" To find out, reorganize their answers into an organized list on the board such as

How many stacks?	How many in each stack?
1	12
2	6
3	4
4	3
6	2
12	1

Notice how this organized list illustrates the pattern of possibilities. The list helps students see a key idea. Some numbers are missing from the left column. Can we have 5 stacks of equal size? Or 7, 8, 9, 10, or 11 stacks? None of these is possible if each stack must contain an equal number. Similarly, we cannot have these numbers in each stack either.

You may want to discuss with them that they were *dividing* up 12 blocks into equal stacks. Depending on their prior knowledge, some may have realized that they could find possibilities by *multiplying* two numbers together to obtain 12.

In discussing the different stacks of 12 blocks, we usually ask students if they have found all the possibilities and how they would know for sure. We also ask them to describe what they see in this organized list. Do you see anything special or unusual? Most students see something like "As one side goes up, the other goes down." Some say that "there are three pairs; one stack of twelve is like twelve stacks of one."

In responding to students' ideas and expressions, the teacher must juggle two often competing concerns: nurturing expression of ideas and building accurate explanations. For instance, the two comments above are not very sophisticated in a mathematical sense; they could be stated more precisely. However, students need to develop their ability for mathematical precision, logic, and thought in a nonpunitive environment. We encourage students' attempts to express mathematical ideas, no matter how haltingly they come out, in the same way a parent encourages a child's early attempts at talking. The teacher can always gently help students refine and clarify ideas that have been expressed. However, a teacher cannot clarify an idea that a student never expressed for fear of being corrected in a demeaning fashion.

Three standard ways of helping students articulate their ideas concerning patterns are (1) simply having them express their ideas orally, (2) writing their ideas on the board, or (3) having them write on paper what they conceive. Early in the year or when starting a new topic via problem solving, oral discussion allows the most latitude and encouragement. We have found that several students will see the same pattern, yet express their conception differently. The teacher then should point out the similarities between expressions. For instance, "As one side goes up, the other goes down" and "The more stacks, the fewer there can be in each stack" are different expressions of the same idea, even though the second is more precise. When the teacher focuses the students' attention on the fact that both are talking about the same idea, most students will also see the difference. The teacher may also point out that one side "going up" is referring to the number of stacks becoming greater, and so on. Nonjudgmental responses can establish the idea without demeaning the student. Clarifying, refining, and summarizing are key aspects of teacher response.

As students become more willing to share their thinking, the teacher should record their ideas on the board. We suggest this recording format be used after students have begun to see that an idea or pattern can be expressed in several different ways. Then the teacher should pose some clarifying questions before writing down student's ideas, asking if the idea could be expressed a different way or if that idea has already been stated (but in a different form).

The most formal of the three ways for expressing ideas is for students who have been working in small groups to discuss their ideas (inferred patterns) and then write down what they have concluded. This small group discussion mirrors the other two forms of expression. Students help group members clarify what they mean. The group has to reach consensus when writing down its conclusions. Then one person from the group can read these aloud.

Next, take one block away from each group and ask them to repeat the task. Have each group record its answers. When asked to stack 11 blocks, the significance of the decision about what is a stack becomes apparent. If stacks of 1 and 1 stack of 12 are not allowed, there are no possible stackings with 11 blocks.

Next, take another block away, and repeat the process with 10 blocks. Continue removing 1 block and having students find all the possible stackings until only 1 block remains. You can provide special recording sheets that will make the distinction among the total blocks they are stacking easy to see. Some students may catch on to the idea of carefully checking for patterns. Some may realize that they don't have to work out all the stacks physically; they can imagine the possibilities.

When the teacher removes successive blocks and requires students to find all the different arrangements, the board will contain 12 organized lists such as the ones in figure 1.2.

With the 12 lists on the board, the teacher can discuss students' inferences: "What patterns do you see across these lists? What similarities exist? What differences?" The previous conjecture that the greater the number of stacks, the fewer in each

. . . .
Figure 1.2

12			**11**			**10**	
1	12		1	11		1	10
2	6		11	1		2	5
3	4					5	2
4	3					10	1
6	2						
12	1						

9			**8**			**7**	
1	9		1	8		1	7
3	3		2	4		7	1
9	1		4	2			
			8	1			

6			**5**			**4**	
1	6		1	5		1	4
2	3		5	1		2	2
3	2					4	1
6	1						

3			**2**			**1**	
1	3		1	2		1	1
3	1		2	1			

stack seems to hold in each case. Of course, 1 stack of 1 is a special case. The "pairs" mentioned earlier illustrate that although 2 stacks of 6 blocks are not identical to 6 stacks of 2 blocks, they both can be made from the total quantity of 12 blocks. These arrangements illustrate a family of facts: $6 \times 2 = 12$, $2 \times 6 = 12$, $12 \div 6 = 2$, and $12 \div 2 = 6$.

Another pattern students notice is that the lists are "flipped." Students often say that the top half and the bottom half are the reverse of one another, where one half of each "pair" can be found. Such an inference allows the teacher to develop several different ideas.

A clarifying question should be used: Do all 12 lists show the same flipping of top and bottom halves? Not exactly. Those with an even number of arrangements do. However, with totals of 9, 4, and 1, there are an odd number of arrangements. In the middle of these lists one can see the only cases in which there are the same number of stacks as blocks in each stack. Thus, 9, 4, and 1 are special numbers, the square numbers.

Finally, there is a set of numbers that has only one pair of entries—that is, only two possible arrangements. These numbers are 11, 7, 5, 3, and 2, the prime numbers. Note how a strong, concrete, experiential basis for the concept of prime is now possible: a quantity that can be arranged in stacks of equal size in *only* two ways. With a gentle nudge into division, it can be made clear to students that this fact means that such a number can be divided only by itself and 1.

Sometimes students are tempted to infer an idea concerning the odd numbers, such as "All the odd numbers have only two ways to arrange them." This is an occasion for gentle, nonjudgmental clarifying: "Let's look carefully at all the odd numbers and then at all the numbers that have only two arrangements to see if we can say that."

This activity can be extended to larger numbers to see if the patterns continue or if others emerge. The teacher can ask students to predict what will happen with numbers up through 25. Will we find any square numbers or primes? Depending on their level of experience, students may or may not need to make the actual arrangements with blocks to continue to explore patterns.

With this activity, the teacher thinks about the key concepts of the curriculum such as multiplication, division, and prime numbers, then considers the students' knowledge. The activity allows the students to wrestle with and experience what they need to build a deeper understanding of these concepts.

This activity can be done with students who have never been introduced to multiplication. For them, the emphasis would be on *finding* the appropriate stackings experientially. They will come to conceive of multiplication as a concept, not merely as a set of memorized facts.

For students who have some initial understanding of multiplication, the activity could give an opportunity to work concretely and experientially with multiplication facts and start to think about division. The concept of prime numbers can be introduced through a tangible and understandable physical model that embodies its essence. ●

Is it really possible to go through the entire curriculum creating problem-solving activities for every concept? Yes, and it is not as mammoth a task as one might imagine. First, the number of fundamental concepts to be taught in a year is large but not enormous. Second, some concepts require less experiential problem-solving activities than others, for two reasons: (1) students may already have good conceptions or accurate schemata to build upon, and (2) many concepts can be related to one another (as in the above example of multiplication, division, and primes).

We want students to develop substantial mathematical knowledge and make sense of the world around them. We want students to be engaged and motivated, to become self-reliant, to feel competent and capable in generating and investigating questions, collecting and analyzing information, and solving problems in school and in life. When properly balanced, teaching problem solving can enable us to accomplish all of these mutually compatible goals. Consider another problem-solving activity.

G ive each student in the class a banana, an orange, or a bag of peanuts. The fruits are unpeeled, the peanuts unshelled. Tell the students that these are their snacks and that you expect them to eat them. When they begin to remove the peels and shells, you should jokingly ask them what they are doing and why. Aren't they going to eat *all* of the nice snack you have given them? Why not? Aren't they wasting a lot of the food? Are they throwing away more than they are eating?

In this activity, students investigate the relationship between what is eaten and what is discarded. In social studies class, cultural differences in eating habits could be discussed. For instance, various cultures consume parts of animals that other cultures throw away. We can also look at such relationships mathematically.

Students can use a scale to weigh an entire banana (or orange or a fixed number of peanuts), then remove the peel (or shells) and weigh again. What mathematical concepts might be invoked?

We have posed this activity in a general form, applicable to a range of students and grades. For younger students (second or third graders), a highly structured form would probably include only one type of food, such as bananas. Students would need to think through carefully what is involved in weighing an object (e.g., understanding weight as a concept, the action of measuring on a scale, the type of scale and its sensitivity, the units of measure, and so forth). Some teachers and curricula use such an activity to help students understand the importance of a standard unit of measurement.

For younger children, this activity also introduces key concepts involving the part/whole relationship. The total weight is made up of the weight of the peel and the weight of the inside, edible portion. Weighing all three builds up such an understanding. Then a concept such as "half" can be used: "Is the edible part more than half of the total weight?"

You can choose the concept(s) for the students to converge upon in this activity, depending on their level and prior understanding. If the students already understand part and whole, you can readily use this activity to explore fractions, percentages, decimals, and ratios. Similarly, you may vary the difficulty of the computation involved by choosing the scale and units of measure.

For instance, when trying to develop their understanding of fractions, you might choose a scale using ounces and let the students round off the actual weights so that the numbers are easy to work with. Thus, the total weight of 100 unshelled peanuts would be about 10 ounces, with the shells about 4 ounces and the "meat" 6. The resulting fractions are $\frac{4}{10}$ and $\frac{6}{10}$, which constitute the whole, $\frac{10}{10}$. If you were interested in developing an understanding of ratio, you might ask, "Will a four-to-six ratio always be found with each bunch of one hundred peanuts?"

Students might also address the question of comparable "waste" among these three foods. What fraction, percentage, or decimal of each is discarded? The interconnectedness of these concepts can also be addressed. For instance, how does a 4-to-6 ratio for peanuts compare to a 7-to-20 ratio for bananas? In which case is more being wasted? Should we convert both these ratios into a ratio of 1 to some number? Should we convert the two fractions ($\frac{4}{10}$ and $\frac{7}{27}$) to common denominators? Or should we use percentages or decimals?

Related follow-up activities might involve looking at the weights of nuts and their shells; peanuts are legumes, not nuts. Are there wide variations in the "shell/meat" weight ratio among various nuts? ●

There are several important similarities between these two examples of stacks and foods. In both cases the problem-solving activity contains basic concepts for the students to wrestle with. In both, you as the teacher set the stage with the proper materials and engaging questions. Both activities have a fair amount of structure while allowing a certain exploration. You can vary the amount of time students explore. Similarly, you can focus the students' attention directly on the key concepts through the way you pose the questions. You decide at what points in the activity your cogent explanations of major concepts will be most helpful.

Yet there are some important differences between these two examples. In the stacking activity, students who have used many manipulatives in mathematics classes realize at once that they are being asked to do mathematics. The question initially posed is obviously mathematical in nature, even without signaling an operation or a concept. In contrast, the set-up for the foods activity is not obviously mathematical; it emerges from everyday experience. Especially if part of the initial explanation of the activity draws on students' schemata of cultures or eating habits, it is not obvious where you are leading them. They are motivated to investigate before they realize the essential mathematical features of the inquiry.

Both activities encourage the flow of thinking between the domain of mathematics and the lives of the students. In both, students must use their existing schemata and wrestle with the questions posed; in both they come to realize the value of mathematical ideas and their usefulness in understanding and interpreting experienced reality.

In the stacking activity, the students are aware that mathematics is involved. Notice that the initial set-up, however, deemphasizes the mathematics: the students are asked simply to arrange the blocks into stacks. The language of set theory is absent. We want students to experience the task and materials and let the mathematical concepts develop out of their thinking. There are always some students who question the validity of having 12 stacks of 1 block. They assert that 1 block is not a "stack." This assertion provides a great occasion for the class to discuss and debate what constitutes a stack. We deliberately chose a nonmathematical term (instead of group or set) so that students can see how mathematics is created by people.

Throughout both examples there are many opportunities to help students shift their thinking back and forth between the concrete materials and the mathematical ideas, between their common conceptions and the fundamental concepts from the curriculum. In a concluding discussion of each activity, you should ask students if they can think of other relevant situations or materials that are similar to what has been investigated. For instance, stacking cans or boxes (one deep) will involve a consideration of multiples. Similarly, you can ask students, "When someone buys a steak from the butcher, how much is actually fat and bone?" How would the key concepts help illuminate these situations? Other related investigations might be planned and executed.

· ·

The Changing Mathematics Curriculum

We want students to understand that we strongly favor mathematical ideas so that they can be powerfully used. Mathematical knowledge should not merely be a compendium of facts, concepts, and procedures that lies dormant in one's head. How we think and what we think about are intimately connected. Mathematical thinking and mathematical knowledge should be intertwined.

Today some profound changes are happening in mathematics education. We are in the midst of a major rethinking of what should occur in mathematics classrooms. In April 1989, the National Council of Teachers of Mathematics (NCTM) published the *Curriculum and Evaluation Standards for School Mathematics* (hereafter referred to as the *Standards*), an exciting document that encourages people to see mathematics in a new light. The general goals for all students are clearly stated:

1. That they learn to value mathematics.
2. That they become confident in their ability to do mathematics.
3. That they become mathematical problem solvers.
4. That they learn to communicate mathematically.
5. That they learn to reason mathematically. (NCTM 1989, 5)

These goals are addressed continually throughout the *Standards* in ways that truly redefine the content of school mathematics. Alongside strong statements encouraging conceptual understanding, meaningfulness, real world problem solving, thinking, manipulating materials, discussing, collaborating, and writing about mathematics, there are equally strong admonitions for decreasing rote practice and memorization without understanding, worksheets, and tedious and isolated paper-and-pencil computation.

These same themes are also prominent in the 1989 NCTM Yearbook,

New Directions for Elementary School Mathematics (Trafton 1989). Various chapters elaborate on mathematics as problem solving, communication, and reasoning and on the importance of students' developing thinking strategies, using natural language, and realizing the sensibleness and power of mathematics. Furthermore, several chapters explain a new role for computation that stresses an understanding of the meaning of operations rather than a memorization of facts. Students will have to decide which mode of computation is appropriate for a given problem or situation. Is an exact answer required? If not, some form of estimation will suffice. If so, then can an answer be found with mental arithmetic? Should paper and pencil be used? Or is the calculation sufficiently complex that a calculator would make most sense?

In these two important documents a strong message emerges: students can become powerful users of mathematics. Teachers should help students *do* personally meaningful mathematics. It is ironic that the common verbs in our language for doing mathematics are *computing* and *calculating*, which have rather narrow arithmetic connotations. Notice how active and engaging the terms *reading* and *writing* appear. Some educators actually use terms like *mathing* or *mathematizing* to convey a similar sense of action. The *Standards* pervasively uses words like *investigate, explore, describe, discuss, develop, use, construct, apply, invent, predict, relate, model, explain, represent, validate*, and so on.

For students to value mathematics and believe that they are capable of truly understanding and powerfully using it, they must experience mathematics that makes sense. In "It's Time for a Change," Mary M. Lindquist states:

At present, students perceive mathematics as a set of rules to be learned and practiced. Yet children come to school with a sense of mathematics, for they have been using it to solve problems they understood. We have failed to capitalize and build on this understanding as we teach more abstract procedures. We must help children construct meaning and sense by approaching *mathematics as problem solving*. They must see that mathematics is created by us and that it can make sense. (Trafton 1989, 2) (Emphasis added.)

· ·

Focusing on Problem Solving

Today problem solving means much more than trying to get an answer to the somewhat artificial word problems or story problems of yesteryear. Problem solving can be the heart of the mathematics experience for children, allowing them to wrestle with materials and ideas that mean something to them, to ask questions that they want to answer. Students have to understand the problem or task at hand, determine how to attack it, work through a process to get an answer (or possible answers), and be able to evaluate its (their) reasonableness.

Unfortunately most textbooks still have a long way to go. In the last ten years, many mathematics educators have been urging, pleading, and cajoling schools and publishers to enliven the mathematics curriculum with problem solving. The 1980 NCTM Yearbook was devoted to problem solving in the curriculum. By the mid-1980s, several publishers had begun to insert more problem solving into their textbook series.

Most new textbooks series have included more problems in each chapter. However, many of these are not particularly "good" problems; contexts are artificial and irrelevant, with insufficient attention paid to mathematical concepts and connections among concepts. Many of the problems are merely opportunities for arithmetic computation in a contrived situation. The only thought required of students is deciding which operation to perform.

Most textbooks offer the teacher a very meager sense of what is involved in problem solving. Teachers' guides have a list of problem-solving strategies that coincide with those that appear about four times each in the students' texts. Some common strategies are draw a picture, make a list, look for a pattern, and so on. A set of problems is supposed to be worked on using a particular strategy. However, it is unclear how these strategies relate to one another or how they add up to what problem solving is. Merely giving students problems to work on is insufficient.

Students should experience problems that fit with the curriculum in order to initiate and deepen their understanding of key concepts. Simultaneously, students should be developing their repertoire of problem-solving strategies based on sound mathematical thinking. In order to establish a productive, dynamic relationship between students' schemata and mathematical ideas, the teacher must carefully consider what kinds of problems make the best bridge. Some criteria of good problems are the following:

- There is no obvious way to work on the problem.
- The problem is set in a meaningful context for the students.
- The problem provokes students' interest in pursuing it.
- Working on the problem should use mathematical thinking and knowledge that is developmentally appropriate.
- Discussion of solutions should allow the teacher to build on the problem to explore mathematical ideas.

The absolute level of difficulty of a particular problem is not the issue. What is a problem for some may not be for others. For instance, consider the problem: "Betty bought three doughnuts for $1.20. How much did each doughnut cost?" Although it may require appropriate thought for one group of students, another group may see it as an obvious division operation. For the second group, this is not a problem at all; it is merely a thinly disguised computational drill. Meaningful problems can provide opportunities for doing or practicing computation; drill exercises for computation involving minimal context and thought should be limited.

We realize that creating meaningful contexts and student motivation is not necessarily simple. A classroom of children contains a wide diversity of interests and prior knowledge. It is unlikely that any one problem or context will be equally appealing to all the students. However, your attempt to create meaningfulness through a variety of activities and problems will produce the positive climate necessary for students to be willing to engage in substantial thought.

For example, one year we taught a fourth-grade class of twenty-eight students. When doing problem solving, they usually worked in seven groups of four. One day, when two students were absent, instead of telling the students how to form groups, we asked them to work in pairs to figure out some possible ways we could arrange the class into groups of three or four students. After a number of false starts (''We could have thirteen groups!''—Thirteen groups of two were not what we wanted), they did find the two possibilities: six groups of three and two groups of four, or two groups of three and five groups of four. Then they decided to use the latter setup because it had more groups of four (their usual arrangement).

This spontaneous problem is an example of what we are after: problems that mean something to the students, that they are motivated to attack, and that they can ''get their minds around.'' But also notice that the answer is not obvious. It requires some substantial thought.

For most students, the problems of their texts do not require much thought. They are ''routine''—occasions merely to figure out what operation to perform. Students have concocted some fairly outrageous methods for solving such problems. They don't really read the problems, they look for the two numbers and then automatically follow a procedure such as ''If one number is a lot bigger than the other, I divide the smaller one into it.''

In contrast, the problem of arranging 26 students into groups of 3 or 4 does not have obvious computations for most students. What operation would you do with the three numbers 26, 3, and 4? Problems of this kind can get students to stop and think. They can be attacked with various problem-solving strategies.

Teachers should step back from the textbook, workbook, and handouts and determine the key concepts of the curriculum at their grade level. Next they must similarly analyze the knowledge, abilities, motivations, interests, and schemata of the children they are teaching. Then, the vital step: inventing good problems or problem-solving activities that bring together the two entities: the domain of mathematics and the world of the students.

Distinguishing among types of problems

As you think about problems for your students to address, consider the three broad types prevalent in current textbooks. Each type can vary greatly in complexity. Each may be appropriate for your students. They are

- translation problems
- process problems
- real-life problems or situations

Translation problems require students to translate the words of a story problem into some kind of mathematical sentence or operation. These problems may require simple, one-step operations (e.g., apples sell for 25¢ apiece; how much would 4 cost?) or, multiple steps as in the following problem:

> A case of soda has 24 cans. A truck will hold 10 cases on each rack and there are 20 racks on the truck. If a store sells 20,000 cans each month, how many truck loads should be delivered each month?

Clearly, the student would have to understand what is going on in this problem before going through a series of steps or calculations. Adequate conceptualization would be very difficult for some children and simple for others. Simple conceptualization that leads to obvious calculations would mean it is not a good problem for some students.

Process problems describe situations or actions that cannot be readily translated into a mathematical sentence. Students must create a process for working toward a solution that uses some strategy like drawing a picture or making a chart.

Recall the process problem of arranging 26 students into groups of 3 or 4. There is no way to translate these three numbers directly into a mathematical sentence (without algebra). Students have to derive an effective process for working on the problem. Figure 1.3 illustrates one group's solution.

Process problems can vary greatly in their complexity and underlying mathematical concepts. Some books refer to them as nonroutine problems because there is no obvious computational procedure to solve them. Process problems encourage students to understand and represent the conditions and goal(s) as well as to work toward a solution.

Another excellent feature of process problems is that there may be more than one correct answer, depending on the assumptions one makes. In the previous problem there are two legitimate answers because the constraints precluded groups of sizes other than three or four. Consider the following problem.

Figure 1.3

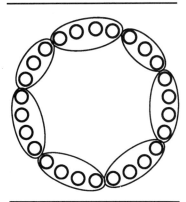

> Imagine that the pet store has just received a shipment of kangaroos and dingoes from Australia. You want to know how many of each has arrived. The store is closed, but you peek through the glass door—at the bottom, below the shade. You see 24 feet. How many dingoes and kangaroos are there?

Think about the situation and try to answer the question.

Immediately you must make several assumptions, such as 24 feet refers to animals' feet rather than to seeing 24 feet into the room. We might assume that none of the animals is obscured from view or, more facetiously, that none is leaping into the air at the moment you peered in. Also, kangaroos walk on 2 feet. But are dingoes part of your schemata of the animal kingdom? They are wild dogs that walk on all 4 feet. Did all 24 feet belong to these 2 kinds of creatures? Let's assume that they did. We probably would assume that there is at least 1 kangaroo and 1 dingo from the wording of the first sentence (although some might argue that there must be at least 2 of each). Make sure you try the problem.

What is the right answer? Did you assume that there was only one right answer? In fact, there are a number of possibilities:

Kangaroos	Dingoes
10	1
8	2
6	3
4	4
2	5

Multiple-answer problems are rare in mathematics textbooks. However, life is full of situations in which several answers are possible, depending on our assumptions. Furthermore, the process of thinking through our assumptions about a problem, situation, or question is essential in life.

It is fair to question many of the implied ideas in this problem. Student should be asked to imagine novel alternative assumptions. Students have come up with: What if some of the kangaroos were hopping at the moment we looked in the window? What if half of the kangaroos were females, each with a joey in her pouch? Varying assumptions can lead to markedly different solutions and processes of solving a problem. This kind of creative thinking can be stimulated readily through most process problems.

Real-life problems or situations cover a lot of territory. They are powerful contexts for using mathematics to understand, organize, and make sense of information from the world. Some good sources of ideas for such real-world problems are almanacs, books of world records and amazing facts, and even the newspapers.

A word of caution is in order. Some textbooks include what appear to be real-life problems but are actually rather narrow questions, such as extracting information from a table, schedule, map, or menu and using it in computations. The table may have some interesting numerical data, but the cognitive processes involved in extracting specific information rarely meet the criteria of a good problem.

In contrast, consider the following information that can be the start of a good real-world problem:

> People in the United States consume vast quantities of soft drinks. According to *Beverage World* magazine, in North Carolina 40 gallons of soft drinks a year are sold for every person. That is the high for the fifty states; the low is about 20 gallons in Wyoming.

The teacher can use this actual information to create a problem-solving opportunity by asking students the following kinds of questions:

- What do these statistics mean? What does "for every person" mean? How were they calculated? How might the information have been collected?
- Are there some people who never have soft drinks? If so, then how does this idea influence the "for every person" notion? Are there people who drink more than the given amounts? What might be the absolute most gallons of soft drinks that a person might drink in a year?
- What are all the different kinds of soft drinks on the market? What is included in these data?

These questions are fairly open-ended, calling for students to think carefully about what is being stated and to realize what is implied.

Students usually have a host of questions themselves about this kind of data. And some of their questions are actually translation problems such as: How much is 40 gallons in terms of 12-ounce cans? What do these work out to in months, weeks, days?

Students will be motivated to work on these self-generated questions because they are inherently meaningful. And even more importantly, their own questions will lead to other questions. In real-life problems, teachers should definitely encourage students to ask their own questions about the data. The teacher can usually get things rolling by asking what is going on here and why? Students will ask follow-up questions such as:

- Do I drink 40 gallons of soda pop each year?
- What are the high and low figures in our class?
- What are the different preferences in soda pop among the class?

Although some of these questions (either from the teacher or the students) could be worked on in class, others might require research or data collection. What are the types of soft drinks that different types of stores stock? What are their big sellers? In assessing the actual consumption of the students, they could keep journals of everything they drink during a week or month. These data could be tabulated for individuals and for the class, and consumption of various beverages could be compared. The data on soft-drink consumption of the class for a week could be projected to a year's worth to see how they compared with the high and low state figures. And so on.

The best real-life problems offer students opportunities to collect as well as analyze data from real situations. They are *investigations*. Students can keep records, take measurements, make graphs and charts, perform estimates and calculations—experience the value of mathematics to understand their lives and the world around them. The teacher can carefully use these examples and illustrations to help students build a solid, conceptual understanding of key aspects of mathematics as well as appreciate its usefulness, blending mathematical problem solving and many areas of students' lives.

In addition to these three major types of problems—translation, process, and real-life—you will occasionally run across problems that are based on spotting the hidden assumption or trick. Often these are called *puzzle problems*. Exercise caution in using these with students. Look at the problem to see if it involves mathematical thinking or concepts. When discussing the problem with the class after they've worked on it, will you be able to extend their understanding of mathematics? For example, consider the following variation of a problem that frequently appears in textbooks:

When Reggie went to the hardware store, he paid 5¢ for 3 and 10¢ for 21. If all were the same type of item and no item was damaged or on sale, how are these prices possible?

You may try many different calculations in frustration. Reggie was buying numerals for his house, a 3, a 2, and a 1, each for 5¢. The value of this problem lies in helping students examine assumptions and beware of ministerpretations. Because their mathematical content is often meager, the other types of problems are usually more valuable than puzzle problems.

Translation, process, and real-life problems each have a somewhat different emphasis. Translation problems can lay a good foundation for equations and algebraic representations of information. Process problems cause students to refrain from rapid computation and carefully think through what is going on. Real-life problems can illustrate the value of mathematical knowledge in understanding the world around them. Even an occasional puzzle problem can enliven a mathematics class by provoking unusual ways of thinking and a sense of levity. Given the abundance of translation problems in most textbooks, it makes sense to seek good process and real-life problems from resource books to supplement the curriculum.

Developing True Conceptual Understanding

Students do not learn concepts in an all-or-nothing fashion. It is not true that you either know it or you don't. Through a good problem-solving activity, a student develops a tentative understanding of each concept. With additional activities, a more sophisticated and elaborate web of thoughts evolves. More connections are seen; more aspects are appreciated.

The stacking activity, for instance, can be the start of truly understanding the reciprocal nature of multiplication and division. One is the inverse of the other. More experiences are needed to continue the development of these ideas. Similarly, the food-measuring activity can facilitate understanding of several interrelated concepts. And many such experiences are necessary.

Each experience with a concept in a particular activity or context can be valuable but it is rarely sufficient in itself. Lesh and Zawojewski (1988) use the term "local concept development" to describe how one problem-solving activity, properly accomplished, enriches a student's understanding of a concept in a particular way, a kind of "local" understanding. For a more powerful, general understanding of a concept to develop, many varied local developments must occur and be related to one another. Each may be valuable, each may assist in a more complex and general understanding of the concept, especially when the teacher directly helps the students see the connections among the experiences.

Richard Lesh and his colleagues have studied what happens when students face complex, real-life problems and situations. Their studies show the complex interplay of students' schemata, mathematical ideas, cognitive processes, and problem-solving strategies. While working on realistic situations, students go through cycles of conceptualizing and reconceptualizing that can enrich their understanding of mathematical concepts. Each conceptualization of a problem influences the way students select, organize, and interpret information. Students successively refine their understandings. For Lesh, the goal of teaching problem solving is for students to learn to think with mathematical ideas and to think about their own conceptualizations of problem situations.

To help you rethink your curriculum in terms of key concepts and problem-solving activities, we offer in the next chapter some suggestions for "mapping" your curriculum. Such a map, based on some important distinctions of mathematics, will help you in what you are doing.

2

Mathematical Knowledge
and Thinking

· ·

The Concepts of the Curriculum

In the mid–seventeenth century, a French nobleman and gambler was puzzled by his consistent losses on a particular bet in a dice game. He asked mathematician Blaise Pascal why the seemingly reasonable bet was not. Intrigued by the problem, Pascal corresponded with his colleague Pierre Fermat and the two men laid the foundations of modern probability theory.

Throughout the history of mathematics, one can see the essential features of this story repeated many times. A person looking at a phenomenon in the world and trying to make sense of it through the known mathematics of the day. A combination of skillful analysis and insight led to the creation of a new and original form of mathematics to deal with the particular situation. Then this new approach or conception was elaborated into highly abstract and general formulations to address many other problems or situations.

We can see two main aspects of the discipline of mathematics: pure and applied. The beauty of pure mathematics lies in its abstractions, generalizations, symbolic language, concepts, theories, and principles. Conversely, the power and utility of applied mathematics stems from its ability to explain the world around us. Though quite different, these twin aspects of mathematics help each other. Mathematicians frequently find new applications for the marvelous abstractions of mathematics. The problems in the fields of science, medicine, technology, art, and architecture have been the genesis of conceptual breakthroughs in mathematics.

The complementary aspects of pure and applied mathematics are analogous to the dynamic relationship we hope to establish between mathematical ideas and the schemata of the students. We want to help students to become comfortable in coming to understand their world through mathematics and to understand mathematical ideas through investigating their world.

Let us begin by considering what mathematical ideas are especially important to include in the curriculum. We will then discuss the kinds of thinking and problem solving in relevant, meaningful contexts that will help students appreciate these ideas.

We see three important distinctions about these concepts of the curriculum. Some, like the four arithmetic operations, are especially central to understanding and working with numbers. Related concepts involve measuring physical matter. We will refer to these topics as "numbers and measurement." In contrast, another group of concepts and topics in mathematics does not rely on numbers for understanding. These concepts may be visual, spatial, logical, and so forth; we will refer to them as "noncomputational mathematics." Students need to realize the distinction between these two areas of mathematics; they need to see that mathematics is more than the computation of numbers.

The final content area includes concepts that involve understanding relationships among two or more quantities. A student must understand each concept being used as well as the nature of the relationships among them. Such understandings are not only numerical but also logical.

Numbers and measurement

We believe that one of the best ways for students to deal with numbers and to understand arithmetic operations conceptually is to measure. Our world is filled with things and ways to measure them. We count quantities; we tell time; we determine price, distance, temperature, and so on. All these offer children marvelous opportunities to understand numbers by operating on real things. Measurement activities also can utilize estimation and various representations (graphs, charts, maps, etc.) to enhance thinking. This part of the mathematics curriculum includes the following:

- Quantity, counting, and computation.
- Units for measuring.
- Estimation.
- Part/whole relations.
- Computational geometry.

These five aspects of numbers and measurement contain important, interrelated concepts. Younger students should be learning about quantity by counting and manipulating objects. As they develop, students may work with statistics—collecting, organizing, and analyzing data. In later grades, students can learn what units are and why we need them by measuring physical objects and more complex phenomena. All students can use estimation to find reasonable answers to questions and problems appropriate to their levels. Throughout, students should be developing "number sense," understanding of place value concepts, and building "operation sense."

The curriculum and our lives are filled with part/whole relations that we think about and express in a variety of ways (e.g., as fractions, decimals, percentages). Conceptual understanding of these ways of thinking is crucial. We include them here rather than with other relationships because they are central to measurement and can form a basis for understanding other relationships and proportional reasoning.

Geometry includes both computational and noncomputational aspects. For instance, concepts in computational geometry include angular measure, area, and pi (π). Similarly, the Logo computer language prominently features powerful yet easy-to-learn graphic displays based on computational geometry.

Noncomputational mathematics

It may surprise and delight some students to learn that much of mathematics is not based on computation at all. This area relies heavily on visual and spatial thinking: concepts come from topics within the geometry of the plane (two dimensions) and space (three dimensions).

Students need to experience sorting, classifying, arranging, and arraying. Many of the manipulative activities of early childhood education help young children experience relationships among objects and the conceptual labels our culture uses. Much of geometry involves wrestling with these key concepts. Whether Euclidean, non-Euclidean, plane, or spatial, each geometry and its key concepts can be experienced in a variety of ways. Even the field of topology, often called "rubber-sheet" geometry, can be included. We need not emphasize the formal and the computational aspects. Substantial experiential, creative play should be encouraged. For example, here is a simple game created by a mathematician that your students can play in pairs. It is called "Sim."

Make 6 dots on a paper as the vertices of a regular hexagon. Any 2 dots may be connected with a straight line. Fifteen different straight lines are possible (see figure 2.1). The two students playing Sim should have different colored pens. Alternating, each student must connect 2 dots (not previously connected) with a straight line. The object is to *avoid* making a

Figure 2.1

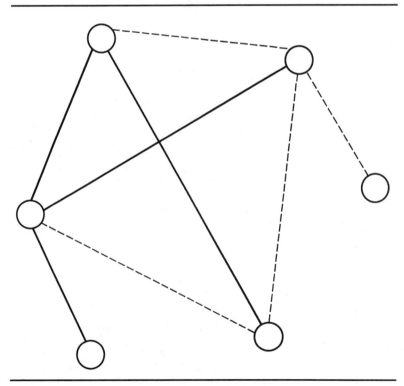

triangle by connecting 3 vertices. A game of Sim will not end in a tie because the 15 lines cannot be drawn with two different colors without forming at least 1 triangle. Someone must lose.

One person can try an analogous task: Find a way to draw 14 lines (7 in one color and 7 in another) connecting vertices without forming any triangles of the same color.

How might this game be modified? Ask students to make up a different set of rules or playing field. For instance, perhaps a player would win if he or she were the first to form triangle. How would the game differ if players were required to connect 4 from a set of 6 vertices into a convex quadrilateral (not a criss-cross)?

Drawing lines to connect pairs of the 6 dots may seem simple, but this game can relate to students' lives. Ask students to imagine that 6 people are waiting for a train at the station. Some are friends and some are strangers. Assert that there must be at least one group of 3 people who are mutual friends or one group of 3 who are mutual strangers. Is this assertion true? By connecting 6 dots with either red lines or blue lines (e.g., 2 dots connected by a red line means the 2 people are friends), students can represent the problem. When they have indicated all the relationships with either red or blue lines, at least one triad will appear—3 people connected in pairs by the same color. ●

Relationships

Mathematical relationships exist in many different forms. There are four main aspects of this area of the curriculum that should be considered for problem solving:

- Proportion and ratio.
- Arrangements and probability.
- Functions and equations.
- Graphing relationships.

Proportion and ratio are special relationships between entities. For instance, "population density" refers to the relationship between two quantities: it is a ratio of numbers of people to land area. When we say that the United States and Guinea-Bissau in Africa have the same population density (67 people per square mile), what does that mean? Consider the richness of conceptual understanding necessary to make sense of that statement.

In our lives, our experience of phenomena, objects, and things is often subject to constraints, conditions, or rules. For instance:

> You have to transport five little boys in a car for over an hour. Two can sit in the front seat with you and three in the back seat. You know from past experience with these children that there are two particular boys who should not sit next to each other because they will squabble and disrupt the trip. In what seats might you place these two?

Several answers satisfy the conditions, depending on assumptions you might make (e.g., that you must be the driver). One solution is to put one of the potential troublemakers (Cain) in the front seat and the other (Abel) in the back, in any one of several different positions. You could also put them both in the back seat, on the left and right sides with another child in between them.

We can make this problem more obviously mathematical (and a bit more difficult) by varying the question somewhat. What are all the different positions in the car in which the two potential troublemakers might sit and not be next to one another? Here is an important question: How would you know that you had found *all* the different possibilities? In combinatorial mathematics, we systematically consider possible arrangements of things under a variety of circumstances. From activities requiring simple sorting and arranging in the early grades, the curriculum can proceed to very complex arrangements that lead students to probability theory.

We want to help students move from understanding patterns and relations concretely to representing them abstractly. The mathematical concept of function can assist this understanding. For example, the amount of garbage produced by a city is a function of (depends on) the number of people in the city. In this case, the more people, the more garbage.

In examining functions, it is more important for students to be able to conceive of what is happening than to manipulate mindlessly the numbers involved. Even the simplest calculation, arithmetic operation, formula, or equation, if used before understanding the problem, can be dangerous. Relationships need not be symbolically represented by algebraic formulas for students to understand the problem, plan a strategy, work on the information, and derive a reasonable answer. In fact, if thoughtful experiences with relationships are not done in the elementary school with concrete situations and meaningful problem-solving contexts, it is highly unlikely that students will be able to understand the abstractions of algebra, equations, or functions later.

We include graphing here as a special way of representing relationships. It is unusually powerful, deceptively simple, yet abstract and intimidating if the proper conceptual foundation has not been laid. A bar graph records the quantities of several different entities (e.g., the number of students who prefer each flavor of ice cream). Graphing relationships means comparing two measures to each other (e.g., the amount of solid waste disposed in various cities versus their populations).

Examine the curriculum you are to teach. What portions are devoted to these three different areas and the various topics and concepts? Does computation predominate? Are some excluded entirely? For which concepts will you have to seek good resource materials in order to supplement the curriculum?

Next consider the "problems" that are provided in the curriculum. Do they fit the definition of good problems? What problems might be used to initiate understanding of some key concepts? Can any be used to develop further a deep understanding of concepts? For which concepts will you have to seek good problems or develop problem-solving activities?

In your search for good resources and problems, you should have a firm idea not only of the concepts that you want students to address, but also of the kinds of thinking that they need to experience in order to develop conceptual understanding. Let us now consider how students come to grasp concepts.

Mathematical Thinking

Psychologists and mathematicians have somewhat different labels for and conceptions of what constitutes mathematical thinking and problem solving. Generally speaking, mathematical thinking is the broader term, and it involves four key areas:

- Reasoning.
- Communication.
- Metacognition.
- Problem solving.

Reasoning

When we encounter a situation, problem, or task of some kind, we do not merely sit back and passively "receive" information. Instead, we mentally attack the situation to try to make sense of it, constructing meaning in relation to our existing schemata. In some way, we relate the new information to our old ideas (even if ultimately we have to change some earlier ideas).

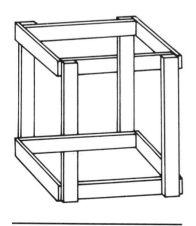

Figure 2.2

But how do we even "perceive" the new? What do we look at? What do we see? What do we focus on when thrust into a situation or when hearing a message? Consider figure 2.2.

What was the *first* part of the figure on which you focused your attention? What did you do next? How did you reconcile the inconsistencies in what you saw? If you have seen the same figure previously, what did you first think? Have you seen any similar figures before? How did that affect what you focused on first? These questions are essentially *metacognitive*—asking you to reflect on your own thinking.

One remarkable attribute of human thinking is that when we attack a task and attempt to make it meaningful, we *almost simultaneously* focus on particular aspects as well as construct patterns. A pattern is our way of making sense out of a very complex world or a complicated mass of information. We all continually *create* patterns from everything around us, synthesizing what we selectively focus on or perceive. Pulling ideas, data, or information together is crucial to our daily lives. If we didn't do this, we would be swamped with scattered and random information in such volume and complexity that we would be intellectually paralyzed.

These dual processes of focusing on various pieces and creating meaningful patterns are intimately related to two important forms of reasoning —deduction and induction. You probably memorized at some time in school that deduction is going from the general to the particular; induction is going from the particular to the general. But what does this mean? If you don't understand this sentence, our essentially deductive explanation of the two concepts was insufficient!

Try the following task. It is a game of pure induction, called Eleusis.

I magine a *series* of cards from a standard fifty-two card deck. What card or cards could come next in the series?

3 of hearts, 6 of clubs, 9 of diamonds, queen of spades

Any essentially inductive task requires sufficient information through a variety of examples. Yet, even with four items, you have probably noticed some aspects of this series. Previous experiences, formed into a schema, have probably suggested numbers, pictures, letters (A, K, Q, J), and four suits. We take the term *suits* for granted, whereas a child without such schemata for playing cards might be puzzled by this term.

Did you focus on the suits and notice that each of the four are represented in the series? Did you focus on the value of the cards and note that the numbers progressed, 3, 6, 9? If so, your substantial experience with our number system might have seen a potential pattern of counting by threes. But what schema could account for the queen? A rich schemata for card games might have suggested that within the 13 cards in each suit the ace often counts as 1, the numbered cards 2 through 10 as their stated value, the jack as 11, the queen as 12, and the king as 13. Therefore, you might have formed the conjecture that the cards represent a numerical sequence.

If your hypothesis is correct, what card or cards might occur next in the series? Can the series "wrap around"? If so, then the next card would be three higher than the queen and the sequence would go queen, king, ace, 2. But which 2? Does the suit matter? Is the sequence of hearts, clubs, diamonds, spades part of the rule?

In Eleusis, one person decides on a pattern and writes a rule for the pattern on a slip of paper. Players are dealt cards and then must create the initial series of permissible examples through trial and error. Players take turns holding up a card from their hands that they think might go next in the series. The "rule maker" who chose the pattern indicates whether the guess is permissible at this time by simply saying yes or no. If the answer is yes, the card is added to the series.

Thus, in the sequence above, what card should you try next? Suppose you try the 2 of hearts and it is correct. What have you learned? Are you certain of the rule? No, because even though the numerical sequence seems to be counting by threes with a wrap-around, perhaps the suit is irrelevant. What might come next? If the suits matter, then the 5 of clubs will come next. If not, then any of the 5s will fit. Here is a longer version of the series.

3 of hearts,	6 of clubs,	9 of diamonds,	queen of spades,
2 of hearts,	5 of spades,	8 of hearts,	jack of clubs,
ace of hearts,	4 of clubs,	7 of diamonds,	10 of clubs,
king of diamonds, and so on.			

What is the rule?

There are several ways to state the rule or pattern for this series. For instance, "After any initial card, alternate red and black suits, increasing the numerical value by three with wrapping around the numbers."

Acceptable rules for the patterns in Eleusis prohibit certain cards at a given point in a sequence, but allow them later. For instance, "play cards in the sequence club, diamond, spade, heart, and repeat" is allowed in Eleusis.

The ways in which we *represent* information are quite crucial to our understanding. They can dramatically facilitate or hinder how we decide what is relevant or irrelevant. In this case, we gave the examples by name instead of pictorial representation. The ways we represent information can be quite varied and some are more readily analyzed than others. Consider the incredible differences between words and pictures, language labels and visual images, horizontal and vertical lists, words and abbreviations. Certain representations are quite adequate for some people, but may be hopelessly inadequate for others less familiar with the particular context or representation.

The way information is *organized* can also facilitate discerning patterns. In the above example, we organized the list of cards so that every fourth card in the sequence was aligned vertically. This arrangement revealed a pattern in the choice of suit.

Students can play Eleusis as teams in groups of three or four. Start with a rule you devise to illustrate the game. Then the winning team can make up the next rule. We prefer using a giant deck of playing cards, available in most magic shops and some catalogs, so that the sequence can be placed in order on the chalkboard tray. In the simple version of Eleusis, a winner is declared when someone (or a team) has placed all of his or her cards into the sequence and correctly writes the rule for the pattern on paper.

A detailed description of Eleusis and a truly ingenious scoring system can be found in Martin Gardner's *Second Scientific American Book of Mathematical Puzzles & Diversions* (1961, 165–73). ●

Induction involves analyzing information and organizing it into a meaningful pattern. In a purely or highly inductive situation, the person has been given no explicit rule, concept, idea, or pattern to help make sense of the particular bits of information but must instead draw upon existing schemata.

The opposite would be pure deduction, when a person has (or is given) a general rule, concept, or principle to be applied to a mass of information or to a situation in order to create meaning order. For instance, the concept of *pi* (π) organizes for us the relationship between the circumference and the diameter of circles.

The power of understanding *pi* is undeniable. This relationship holds for all circles, regardless of size. It provides a means for exploring many other ideas such as area of circles and the volume of spheres and cones. The general applicability of the concept gives it great power. And herein lies a dilemma for the teacher.

There is a great danger in pushing *explanations* of concepts upon students. They may be powerful and general, but they cannot be deductively applied to new situations unless they are truly understood. And understanding comes (at least in part) from inductively deriving patterns of meaning through examples. Students need both examples and explanations. The examples are needed for them to wrestle inductively with the particular instances of the concept. The explanation may help give meaning to the particular examples being examined. However, an explanation by itself, with few if any examples, is essentially a deductive form of teaching. It requires the students to "take this rule, just as I (or the text) have stated it and go out and use it."

Students generally do not learn very well if the teaching is largely deductive. Lectures, explanations, definitions, general descriptions, and overviews rarely give people the raw material to construct meaning. Perhaps a few children who are gifted in mathematics can learn without examples. On the other hand, perhaps their interests lead to experiences outside of school that provide relevant examples. Most of us need examples and experiences, and lots of them. These are the particulars from which we build our understandings of concepts through an inductive thinking process.

Highly inductive teaching also has drawbacks. Science educators have learned through careful research on students' conceptions and misconceptions that inductive hands-on inquiry will not always culminate in understanding of scientific conceptions. A good explanation at the right moment may crystalize understanding of an experience. Explanations help most when there has been sufficient experience with the raw materials.

Students in school rarely encounter situations that are either purely deductive or purely inductive. Most teachers provide a balance of explanations of concepts and clarifying examples. However, most mathematics textbooks do not provide a sufficient number of examples for students to build up their understanding of concepts. Teachers must therefore supplement the texts with relevant activities.

When students are given data, information, examples, and particulars with which to grapple, their minds will struggle to derive meaning through induction. They will use existing schemata to pose potential patterns of meaning upon what they perceive. At some point in this process, individuals will derive a hunch, a possible pattern, a hypothesis. This awareness may lead to a comparing of the idea against the information, a form of systematic and formal testing. This hypothesis testing is a form of deduction, signaling a shift in thinking from inductive to deductive.

Consider what happened when you thought that you knew what the rule or pattern for the Eleusis series was. You could compare the next example in the series to the hypothesis you had in mind. The shift from inductively deriving a possible rule or explanation to deductive hypothesis testing is often a very satisfying one for students. Sometimes it is like swimming in a mass of seaweed and then suddenly finding yourself in clear water. If the hypothesis continues to work out for continued examples, the student can become exhilarated.

The process of formulating hypotheses and then testing them against the information gets cut off when the teacher steps in too soon with the authoritative explanation. The intellectual stimulation and exhilaration are thwarted when premature, teacher-fed deduction occurs. Students are denied the struggle for meaning and the satisfaction of finding it; they need not think for themselves.

To enable students to use mathematics, we must free them from overdependence on authority. We must give them the freedom to explore, to conjecture, to seek ways to validate, to convince others that their thinking is correct. We must give children opportunities to observe regularities and patterns and encourage them to describe what they observe in words, in mathematical statements, in pictures, or in models. . . . [We must] give them the time to puzzle through a situation, to go down wrong alleys, in an environment where asking questions, making conjectures, listening to others' arguments, and helping to evaluate their reasoning is a part of doing mathematics. This is, in fact, how mathematicians do mathematics. (Lappan and Schram 1989, 18, 20)

As this quotation implies, a major aspect of thinking in mathematics is sharing your thinking with others.

Communication

Communication is vital to doing mathematics for several reasons. First, there is a strong link between language and the way we conceive ideas.

We enrich our understanding of mathematical concepts by talking about them in our own language. Often when children attempt to explain their ideas, they realize in midstream a distinction that they had not made, gain a new insight, notice a new piece of information, or spot a flaw in their own logic.

In addition, talking aloud reveals students' schemata to the teacher. Observing students' actions or assessing their work may allow us to infer some aspects of their schemata. Listening to them explain a mathematical idea is similarly revealing. In fact, many researchers on mathematics learning have now shifted away from using tests to infer student conceptions and instead have students talk aloud while working on mathematical problems.

Three or four students discussing their ideas in a small group frequently end up rethinking them, even without teacher intervention. Of course, the teacher must set the stage properly for effective and productive student discussion. But a key idea here is quite contrary to popular ways of thinking about thinking—thinking as a internal, solitary, individual activity. Instead, we may now see as equally valid *social thinking*—people in groups collaboratively refining their ideas.

When a small group of students attacks a good mathematics problem, they share with one another the meanings they derive; they must clarify their thinking. Their ideas can be deductively applied by the group. If the teacher is moving among groups, listening to their interaction, she or he can intervene if they are not working productively or can offer advice for moving their thinking along, if necessary.

The *Standards* urges teachers to encourage students not only to discuss mathematical ideas but also to read and write about them. There are many ways that students can use writing as a tool for thinking in mathematics classes. Students should write down descriptions of how they attacked a problem, how various members of the group thought about aspects of the problem, what assumptions they chose to make, what conclusions they drew, and so on.

Many educators have referred to mathematics as a language, yet it is only recently that any have used what we know about language development in children to look at children's development of the language of mathematics. This discrepancy may result from the misguided attempt by some educators to reduce story problems and mathematics activities to their "mathematical essence," purged of extraneous language. Although mathematical language includes symbols and notations, mathematics educators and textbooks have been guilty of pushing children far too hastily into symbolic abstraction and memorization of dimly understood rules and procedures.

For instance, consider the following question from a textbook, "what is the result of dividing $\frac{5}{2}$ by $\frac{5}{12}$?" Can you imagine a teacher's voice barking "Invert and multiply!"?

Rarely, if ever, in life do we encounter disembodied numbers that we are supposed to do something with. We usually have concrete referents and a purpose in mind. Instead of focusing on the symbols, let's think about situations. What could be going on in the case of $\frac{5}{2} \div \frac{5}{12}$?

Imagine that you had some leftovers: $2\frac{1}{2}$ pizzas. From experience you know that each hungry teenager can eat 5 slices; each slice is $\frac{1}{12}$ of a pizza. Therefore, each teenager can eat $\frac{5}{12}$ of a pizza. How many teenagers can you feed with these leftovers?

Notice how talking about a real situation with natural language dramatically clarifies the essence of the mathematics involved; even in the very difficult case of dividing a fraction by a fraction, you can "get your mind around" what is going on. Pushing with the numbers without specific references in life or jumping into abstractions about operations in general does not promote understanding, unless a tremendous amount of conceptual development has already occurred.

Barring some kind of physical or psychological impairment, all children learn to speak. They develop oral language early and quite well prior to school. Oral language proficiency develops especially well when certain factors are present. Many educators have suggested that these same factors greatly facilitate reading and writing (see Cambourne and Turbill 1987). These factors can be applied to mathematical thinking:

- Immersion
- Demonstration
- Expectation
- Purpose
- Approximation
- Choice
- A climate for creativity

Immersion Children should be continually involved in hearing, seeing, and doing mathematics. Like the spoken word, mathematics is all around us. Noise and cacophony are also present; thus, the spoken word must be perceived. Likewise, teachers should help children attend to the presence of mathematics all around them: in art, in nature, in newspapers, in their environment. Teachers and students should be engaged in doing mathematics for real purposes continually, discussing ideas and creating displays of these ideas.

Demonstration Children should see knowledgeable people using mathematics well and enjoying it. Speaking can be useful, uplifting, elegant, poetic, and so on. For the power and beauty of mathematics to be realized, children should see others (especially teachers) who are excited by solving problems, using measurement equipment, finding aesthetically pleasing patterns, or engaging in a host of other mathematical activities. Like good speaking, adults can *model* good "mathing."

Expectation Children should be expected to understand mathematical ideas; teachers should convey a belief that all students can become mathematically powerful. Students should come to believe that mathematics is useful, enjoyable, valuable, accessible, and possible for them. Can you imagine someone believing that only the talented few could learn to speak? There are some who believe (erroneously) that many students are incapable of learning to read. Is mathematical thinking so arcane that only the illuminati can master it? Our society continually tells students in various ways that most people cannot do mathematics.

Some educators have suggested that one important reason that Asian children do better on the whole than American students in mathematics is that their societies believe that all students are capable of learning mathematics. Entire populations act on that belief, expecting students to learn, telling them that they can, and holding them responsible for doing so. If students believe that they can learn, then they meet obstacles as a challenge to be overcome with perseverance. If they believe that they are one of the many who are not good in mathematics, they will shrink away from difficulties, mistakes, and obstacles, safe with the excuse that they are not one of the fortunate few.

Purpose   When we speak, we usually have a desire to communicate, to be understood by the listener. Teachers of writing have realized the importance of students writing for "authentic purposes," for audiences that make sense and about ideas that matter to them. How often have you heard a student ask why a certain topic in mathematics was worth learning? If mathematics is so useful, why are its purposes unclear to students? The answer may be in the particular aspects of mathematics included in the curriculum.

A major reason for considering authentic situations that can be addressed mathematically is to encourage students to use mathematics for their own purposes. One likely purpose is to understand what is going on; another is to communicate this understanding to others. These purposes give students power.

Approximation   In learning to speak, children are rewarded when they come close, when they almost get it. We do not expect perfection because they are in the process of learning. Our daughter, at age four, once explained, "I misunderheard you." She conveyed her meaning well. Learning inevitably involves making mistakes.

With excessive drill exercises and worksheets, the traditional mathematics curriculum sends a clear message: you are either right or wrong. The demand for flawless computation works directly against clear thinking to get a sense of what is reasonable, an estimate, an approximation. In the situation of teenagers and pizzas, if someone has a good "feel" for what is going on, she could reason that $5/12$ is about a half pizza. Therefore, $5/2$ (five halves) would serve at least five people. Such reasoning is much more valuable than memorizing without understanding the "invert and multiply" procedure and calculating the exact answer (6).

Approximations do not apply just to calculations; approximations are central to reasoning, conjecturing, hypothesis testing, drawing inferences, and mathematical thinking. We want students to refine their thinking about mathematical ideas and become increasingly proficient in their use. Teachers can encourage this development by arranging activities that avoid narrow, right-or-wrong answers, by allowing successive approximations and refinements, and by rewarding students for various aspects of their work and progress.

Choice In learning to speak, children produce their own words; they choose what to say and how to say it. Educators are now realizing the value of encouraging students to write as soon as they can make scribblings on paper. Creating their own words, sounds, and spellings is an important part of creating meaning. Invented spelling allows a child to focus on meaning and ideas, not on merely memorizing the exact forms of the adult world. It is part of the process of successive approximation.

In mathematics we can encourage students to create their own meaningful interpretations, representations, and methods of recording information. Although we do not want them to learn incorrect facts or suffer from misconceptions, we can allow much more latitude in how they create their own understandings and the processes of mathematical inquiry.

A Climate for Creativity In each subject area there should be opportunities for students to think and explore new (and perhaps unusual) conceptions, metaphors, analogies, perspectives, ideas, problems, and situations. Students should be encouraged to create their own representations or models and express their ideas and understandings in a variety of ways. Since cognition itself is largely a process of constructing meaning and understanding in personal ways, students should be encouraged to formulate their own questions, design their own inquiries, and create their own criteria for decisions.

This all may sound like a tall order for younger children and potentially chaotic even for older ones. However, if this kind of thinking is valuable, then we should be working toward it continually. Teachers at each grade level should be discussing with one another how to help students become more able to think independently of the teacher and assume more responsibility for their learning.

Students need time to work on problem-solving activities, to formulate ideas, to think carefully. Realizations and understandings come after processing, thinking through, going over, refining, playing with ideas, discussing, sharing, elaborating, and so forth.

The time pressures on teachers to cover content topics are serious. Where will a teacher find the time for students to think, plan, solve problems, engage in creative problem-solving activities? The *Standards* shows how an emphasis on understanding can replace the time spent on drill and memorization. The *Standards* identifies topics and aspects of the curriculum in grades K–4 and 5–8 that should be deemphasized in order to provide time for problem solving, reasoning, communication, and conceptual understanding.

Students have to believe that their ideas are going to be appreciated and respected. This includes the child who asks a bizarre question at the wrong time or the classroom genius who has a better way to describe what we are trying to show the class. These wild ideas and crazy questions can be extremely valuable to the child who utters them as well as to the entire class. Occasionally (or frequently) the wild idea is a truly marvelous way to help the other students think about the topic under discussion; it makes a connection with their schemata that you had been searching for. ("Oh yeah! Infinity is like when you are holding a picture of yourself holding a picture of yourself holding a . . .")

All the forms of creativity we have mentioned flourish in a friendly, open, and supportive atmosphere. Intensive pressure, criticism, and competition definitely inhibit the flow of ideas, tunneling them into narrow and rigid thoughts. Obviously, the teacher must balance openness and order, joviality and seriousness. The noise level may increase, but that may be a good indication of active intellectual involvement in the task: organized noise, playful concentration, attentive excitement.

Creative play, imagination, inventiveness—whatever it may be called, it is not a frill. It is a vital part of thinking in mathematics and in life. Its exclusion from mathematics texts and curricula has contributed mightily to the tedium of the mathematics classroom.

Metacognition

Thinking about our own thinking and purposely making changes in how we think is the essence of metacognition (literally, over- or overseeing cognition). Some mathematicians refer to it as executive control or decision making. In metacognitive processes, individuals engage in

- self-planning or -strategizing,
- self-monitoring, or -checking,
- self-questioning,
- self-reflecting,
- self-reviewing.

We want each student to become increasingly able to engage in these processes willingly, capably, and consciously. When a teacher helps students use metacognitive processes, they become more successful learners and more able to take responsibility for their own intellectual processes. A teacher helps by providing examples, explanations, assistance, support, and suggestions. With practice and experience, the children are able to do more with less guidance from the teacher. The same basic process happens in thinking and in metacognition.

Metacognitive strategies should be built into the lessons or activities. The teacher can model these strategies for the students. In mathematical problem solving, students should learn to think through what is going on in a problem before trying to solve it. This self-checking for initial understanding—a metacognitive process—is crucial. Consider the following problem:

> Imagine a farmer who ties his dog with a 20-foot rope to one of the hooks on the walls of his barn (a 20-foot-by-30-foot rectangle). One hook is on the corner of the barn, the other in the middle of the long side. Which hook should he use to give the dog more running room?

How do you conceive of the actions being described? Can you visualize what is asked? Can you answer the question without drawing a picture of what is going on? With an accurate picture, it is fairly obvious which hook should be used. Drawing a picture is not merely a trick to get an answer; it is a strategy to help you think about what is happening. Figure 2.3 gives one possible picture for this problem.

Psychologists believe that metacognition develops primarily through social interaction with adults and other children who mediate a child's experience, giving feedback and suggestions. Awareness of the need for self-regulation (and other aspects of metacognition) comes through these interpersonal transactions. Obviously, one-on-one interaction (e.g., parent to child or tutoring) is most beneficial.

Therefore, educators have found that the kinds of collaborative interchanges among students working in small groups (e.g., vocalizing plans

· ·

Figure 2.3

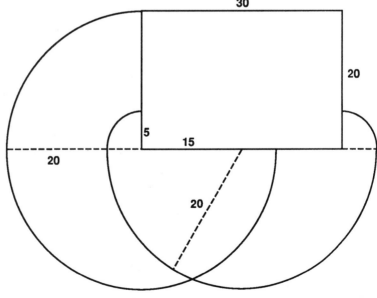

and strategies or asking task-based questions) promotes metacognition. What the teacher has modeled for the class, the students can do for themselves in small groups (with some help and practice). Perhaps, the modeling by the teacher is best translated to the individual child through some kind of small-group modeling by peers.

Another aspect of metacognition that makes it so important is its relation to the affective dimension. Children develop strong beliefs about their own competence. In the extreme, there are children who have decided that they will never succeed in any aspect of school; others believe that they cannot do mathematics. When such a child makes a mistake, he or she will attribute the error to inability, will see it as a confirmation of incompetence, and will tend to give up. In contrast, a child who believes in his or her own competence will deal with a mistake as a temporary obstacle, a challenge to be overcome by changing strategies: this child will slow down, rethink assumptions, and so forth.

How do we help all children to acquire confidence in their thinking in mathematical problem solving? How do we get them to believe they can succeed so that they persevere? First, we know that continual critical evaluation and negative feedback can be more demoralizing than enlightening. Formal testing could be dramatically curtailed. Setting up larger activities, with multiple facets and opportunities for feedback is much more helpful. And not all assignments need to be graded. Constructive feedback can occur without grades; the work can be called ''practice.''

Second, the teacher can provide opportunities for many small-group problem-solving activities. If properly developed, peer assistance within a small group can be more helpful than teacher feedback. This means you will have to spend some time helping students develop ways of giving positive yet honest and helpful feedback to one another.

Third, helping elementary school students to develop metacognitively can instill the willingness to think through, switch tactics, find erroneous assumptions, and so forth. These processes will go a long way to facilitate an attitude that obstacles can be overcome.

Our general concern for metacognition in mathematical thinking goes to the very heart of what it means to do mathematics. Our culture has a very misguided notion that doing mathematics means quickly coming up with the one right answer.

A student who is competent in mathematics is one who, when encountering a problem for which there is no obvious solution, will use whatever resources are available to attack the problem. Such a student will persist in trying to understand the problem, in conceiving of ways to represent it, in seeking ways to solve it. Persistence in using all resources—schemata, solution strategies, whatever—*and* to consider carefully and discard ineffective approaches is crucial. These processes are primarily metacognitive in nature.

If students spent more school time working with peers on meaningful problems, if they were encouraged to take the time to think carefully about all aspects of each problem, if they were consistently told that they were capable of doing these problems, if they discussed their ideas and became more aware of their own thinking as they worked on these problems, how would students feel about themselves as "mathematicians" after six years?

. . . .

The Phases of Problem Solving

About forty years ago, the famous mathematician George Polya described the way experts worked on mathematical problems. He saw four phases in the process of problem solving. Many textbooks suggest some version of Polya's model, in which students engage in

1. understanding the problem,
2. devising a plan of attack,
3. carrying out the plan,
4. reviewing.

The first phase, *understanding*, is critically important; it cannot be overemphasized. It is a very complex task involving

*   understanding the conditions of the situation,
*   understanding the language and terms used,
*   understanding the desired goal and constraints,
*   forming a representation of all of the above,
*   examining assumptions about all of the above.

Meaningful understanding depends in large measure upon the context of the problem. What experience and knowledge can aid understanding? For each student, understanding is a *process* of constructing representations of various aspects of the problem. Try the following process problem:

I have 30 students in my classroom. They have each promised to keep a secret for one full day. On Monday at 9:00 A.M. I tell a secret to 2 students. They must keep the secret until Tuesday at 9:00 A.M., when they may each tell 2 other students (who must keep the secret until 9:00 A.M. the next day, when they each may tell 2 more students). If these students do keep the secret for one day, on what day will the entire class know the secret?

How did you conceive of the problem: the initial conditions, the constraints, the goal? What assumptions did you make?

The second phase of problem solving involves *planning* how to attack the problem. It relies upon the understanding and representation of the problem. Students determine what problem-solving strategies might be used to attack the problem—a form of metacognitive thinking. In the preceding problem, should we draw a picture, find thirty people to act it out, make a list of the numbers of people? Students can be helped to think through: Is this strategy likely to help me get what I want?

The third phase of problem solving is *carrying out* the plan by working on the problem. During this phase, students should engage in self-monitoring. "Am I using the strategy the right way? Am I following the right progression?" "Am I getting closer to the solution?" "Where am I now? Is this where I thought I would be? Have I chosen the right strategy?" If their strategy is not effective, then students should specifically ask themselves: "What did I get out of this approach? Did I learn anything new that can be used in my next attempt?" Then they can rethink their assumptions, representations, and understandings.

An answer to the "secret" problem would be: If the 2 students who are initially told the secret keep it for a day and tell a total of 4 more on Tuesday, and these 4 tell 8 more on Wednesday, then these 8 will tell the other 16 members of the class on Thursday $(2 + 4 + 8 + 16 = 30)$.

In the final phase of *reviewing* a solution that has been obtained, students should reconsider the initial conditions, constraints, and goals to make sure that the solution fits. Invalid assumptions, misunderstandings, or erroneous steps along the way can produce an "answer" that violates something inherent in the problem. The teacher can make this reviewing very meaningful by encouraging broad reflection on the assumptions and strategies they used. Once again, metacognition is intimately involved.

In many problems, a clear initial understanding will allow students to judge the reasonableness of their answers. For most problems, there are basic upper and lower limits to reasonableness that can be derived from an initial understanding of the problem. The teacher can help students think about these limits *before* embarking on a solution. For instance, in our problem of arranging 26 students into groups of 3 or 4, we could help students think about upper limits by noting that 7 groups of 4 would be too many because that was the number that we used before 2 students were absent.

Students should engage in substantial metacognitive thought during each phase of problem solving. It clearly distinguishes problem solving from the automatic thinking based on rote memorization, associated with learning mathematics facts, or involved in making quick calculations on obvious questions. It involves a stepping back and looking at what you are doing, thinking about your own work.

For many teachers, motivating students to think logically or metacognitively is no small task. Inhibiting attitudes toward mathematics may have formed already. Problem-solving activities that link the world of the students to mathematical ideas are the best means of helping students overcome these obstacles.

3

. . . .

. . . .

. . . .

. . . .

. . . .

Teaching
Problem Solving

· ·

Experiencing and Conceiving Mathematical Ideas

How does a child build up an understanding of a mathematical concept? Ideas, images, memories, and words are bound up together in children's minds. The kinds of activities and experiences the teacher provides and the way she asks children to think about them can vary greatly in the degree of abstraction. Imagine a continuum of experiences from the very concrete to the very abstract. It might look like the continuum in figure 3.1, which shows various ways of representing mathematical ideas. Teachers can arrange for students to have experiences with each of them. In this sense, they are vehicles for potential understanding. They provide the basis for the major problem-solving strategies because of their potential to link mathematical thinking with mathematical concepts.

The three most concrete vehicles for understanding, as given in figure 3.1, are part of children's daily lives for years before formal schooling. Children are aware of their own bodies, encounter objects, move, act, and speak quite early in life. In fact, they have been exposed to many basic concepts of mathematics informally and formally at home.

The power of natural language can be seen in many Asian languages, which have a base-ten system built into their terminology. In English, separate words (concept labels) must be learned for each unit of ten (e.g., twenty, thirty, forty). Contrast these terms to the labels ''two-tens,'' ''three-tens,'' and so forth, used in many Asian languages. Once the concept ''ten'' has been understood, the language itself greatly facilitates conceptual understanding of the successive tens-units, which undoubtedly promotes understanding of the base-ten system.

Pictures and diagrams can vary enormously in their degree of abstraction—just compare a Rembrandt to a Picasso. Textbooks abound with pictures; we all recognize the value of images. However, pictorial representations require experience with the real things that they represent.

· ·

Figure 3.1

Concrete ⟵——————————————————————————⟶ **Abstract**

Physical Objects
Bodily Actions & Movements
Spoken Language   Written Language
Picture and Diagrams
Mathematical Symbols
Mathematical Formulas

Even the most faithful of pictures—color photographs—cannot always capture the essence of what is being represented. If you have never seen a *torus*, a photograph may help, but is it sufficient? Will it mislead? How much or what kind of meaning does it convey? Will a drawing mute the key features that are apparent in a photograph? How would you describe figure 3.2 in words? What do you see? To a child who has not yet learned to interpret the shading with depth, would this figure simply be two ovals and a smudge? Would an adult see an aerial view of a racetrack with a puddle?

Can language help? A *torus* is a *toroid* generated by a circle. Fine. But what is a toroid? It is a surface generated by a closed curve rotating about an axis in its own plane. Fairly abstract, you say? How about using an object that we have experienced? A torus is essentially a doughnut— referring to either its surface or its shape.

Written language is clearly more abstract than the spoken word. It relies on the connection of written symbols to the concepts experienced and labeled in our minds. Although we adults may enjoy reading, many children do not. Story problems in mathematics texts are a special form of torture to many students; unfortunately, so are most cogent and cleverly worded explanations of mathematical concepts. Will students likely read the textbook in order to understand the important concepts of the chapter? What schemata would be activated? What connotations would appear? What meanings inferred?

For abstractness, it is hard to beat the written symbols of mathematics. In their hunger for symbolic abstraction and powerful generalization, mathematicians have bequeathed to civilization some truly remarkable symbols, expressions, and formulas. Each has its referent in reality. Yet each has a sublime, ethereal quality that transcends specific referents. Notice how the equation $2 + 1 = 3$ may refer to two apples and one orange, or to any collection of things, or to no *particular* things at all.

Figure 3.2

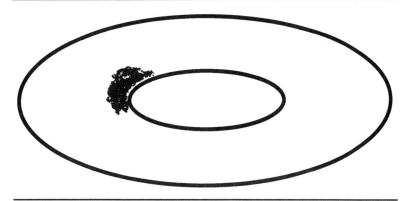

In like fashion, the formula $A = 2\pi r^2 + 2\pi rh$ shows that the surface area of a cylinder (A) can be expressed in terms of the radius (r) of its circular top and bottom and its height (h). Of course, it also uses a rather abstract little idea—*pi* (π). The symbols are also related abstractly through an equation (note the equals sign, $=$), the addition of two expressions, and multiplication of "variables" (r and h) and "constants" (2 and π). Also, in one instance r is raised to the second power (r times r).

As before, this formula can apply to a particular cylinder or generally to cylinders of any size. Such is the power and beauty of the abstract generalization. Is its meaning filled with ambiguity and arbitrariness? For most who encounter the symbols of this formula, absolutely yes. What is going on here? Why do these symbols arranged into this formula work? By eighth or ninth grade, when it is seen, most students are well beyond caring. For nearly a decade, they have been pummeled to insensibility with symbols they did not really understand.

Textbook and workbook pages are composed of the most abstract of the representations of our continuum: written words, symbols, and formulas. It is left to the teacher to ensure that students manipulate real objects and materials, that they discuss what they are seeing and doing in natural language, and that they see and draw pictures and diagrams that make sense to them. With concrete experiences, even abstract formula can come to life and be understood.

Even though this is a book with written words, symbols, and potentially incomprehensible pictures, we ask you to use your imagination and consider the following activity:

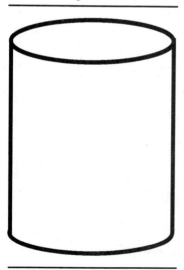

Figure 3.3

Bring in a large can from the supermarket, such as one that contained powdered drink mix. It should have a plastic lid that fits snugly on the top since its original metal top has been removed. Its glued-on label has been soaked off with hot water. Its metal bottom remains. Ask each student to bring cans of various sizes to school (see figure 3.3). The problem is to cover the outside of each in wrapping paper by using the least amount of paper.

Have each student cut two circles (for the top and bottom) from the paper. If we assume that the lip of the lid will not be covered, then the circles are equal. Students could place the can upright on the paper and trace the edge of the circle. A third piece of paper is needed for the outside surface of the can. With sufficient exploration, looking at it, rolling it, experimenting with scrap paper, students may be able to realize that the third piece should be a rectangle, wrapped around the can. How long are the two sides of the rectangle? One side must be as tall as the can. The other side must go completely around. How long is "completely around?" This distance is the circumference of the circle forming the top. How long is that? There is a special relationship between the circumference of any circle and its diameter: the circumference is π times the diameter (somewhat bigger than three times).

Your students will conclude that the wrapping paper needed to cover the surface of this cylindrical can (surface area) must include two circles (the size of the top and bottom) and one rectangle (with length and width equal to the height of the can and the circumference of these circle) (see figure 3.4). The area of each circle would be π times the radius squared. If we call the radius r, then the area of the two circles would be expressed as $2\pi r^2$.

The area of the rectangle would be its height times the circumference of the circle. Let's call height h. The circumference of a circle is π times the diameter or π times twice the radius. Therefore the area of the rectangle would be expressed as h times π times 2 times r (or $2\pi rh$).

When you add together the areas of the two circles and the

Figure 3.4

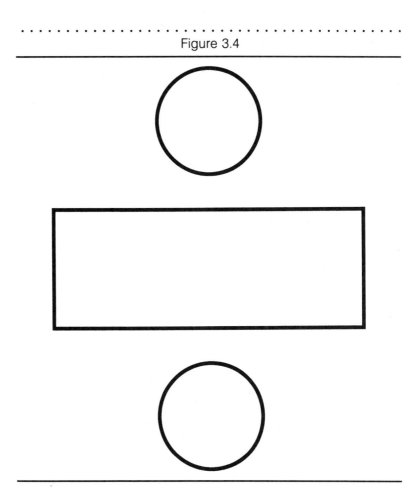

rectangle, you are back to the formula for the surface area of a cylinder: $A = 2\pi r^2 + 2\pi rh$.

Can students understand these concepts? Yes, if the understanding of each aspect of the problem has been properly *built up* through prior experience with concrete examples. The concept of area must be thoroughly grasped through many different situations and manipulatives. The concept of π must be equally clear through work with circles. The relationships and formulas must have conceptual meaning based on experience. Then, the reality of a task involving a can and paper would facilitate understanding of what was involved in determining the surface area of the cylinder. ●

Even though older students can think more abstractly than younger students, they still need to have meaningful situations, concrete models of what is going on, and opportunities to experience the mathematical ideas directly. Textbooks, curricula, and tests have set unrealistic expectations on teachers and students. Very few students can learn mathematical concepts from seeing only written symbols and abstract diagrams and from hearing brief explanations. High school students as well as first graders need concrete models or representations before moving to abstractions.

· ·

The Value of Problem-Solving Strategies

Since mathematical knowledge and thinking are intimately connected, we can help students use the kinds of mathematical thinking involved in different problem-solving strategies to enhance their conceptual understanding in several ways:

- By activating relevant schemata—what students already know that is needed to address a problem.
- By developing various ways to represent information.
- By provoking careful planning, monitoring, checking, and other metacognitive functions.

The metacognitive value of strategies should not be underestimated. Schoenfeld reminds us that

most of what we do is wrong. That is, most of our guesses—when we're working on real problems—turn out not to be right. That's natural; the problems wouldn't be problems, but exercises, if that weren't true. But the hallmark of good problem solvers is that they don't get lost forever in pursuing their wrong guesses. They manage to reject the ones that turn out not to be fruitful, and (eventually) to home in on directions that seem to help. . . . Research now indicates that a large part of what constitutes competent problem-solving behavior consists of the ability to "monitor and assess" what you're doing as you work problems and to make the most of the problem-solving resources at your disposal. (1987, 44)

Mathematical problems and real-life situations that can be examined mathematically can come in many different flavors. Some have a very specific focus and question to be answered. Others may be more open-ended and allow for substantial interpretation, modification, or exploration. Some may be based on everyday situations, others on more unusual or idealized circumstances. Some may require students to design an investigation, collect data over time, and analyze their findings.

Most resource books on problem solving focus on teaching students a set of strategies they can use on problems in the textbook. Also, many of the newer textbooks include some strategies. However, strategies are often presented merely as techniques unrelated to concepts in the curriculum:

When such techniques are taught in isolation, they hardly capture mathematical thinking; they hardly prepare students to use mathematics or to make sense of things by modeling or thinking mathematically. The artificial, narrowly prescribed problem-solving units in many texts have the flavor of painting by numbers. (Schoenfeld 1987, 40)

Instead of teaching strategies in isolation, teachers should relate them to the content of the curriculum. Lesh and Zawojewski state that a strategy such as drawing a picture

can be helpful in a wide range of problem-solving situations, but no one ever really masters this skill in a general sense (that is, in a way that is not restricted by context or content). The ability to recognize and generate relevant pictures and diagrams is linked to fundamental content understandings throughout every topic. . . . The kinds of pictures that are insightful, and not misleading, are closely tied to specific content understanding. (1988, 47)

Thoughtful use of strategies is an important part of problem solving, but not an end in itself.

Of the many problem-solving strategies seen in textbooks, five are particularly valuable in helping students to appreciate what is going on in a problem or situation. These five major strategies are representational in nature, corresponding to spoken language, concrete materials, physical actions, pictures, and written language and symbols, as shown in figure 3.1. They are as follows:

- Discuss the key aspects of the problem.
- Use objects to represent the problem.
- Act it out physically.

- Draw a picture or diagram.
- Make a table, or list.

When encountering a situation in life (as well as in a mathematics classroom), we have the ability to express our thoughts, understandings, and feelings through a variety of representational means. We can talk about our ideas, using words, terms, analogies, metaphors, and so forth. This expressive language can communicate our thoughts to others and can clarify them for ourselves. In conveying our ideas to others, we frequently demonstrate key actions with our hands or our whole bodies. Putting yourself in the middle of the action is a powerful way of imagining what is going on. Children's lives are filled with objects that they use to represent other objects or ideas. Much of their fantasy and play revolves around manipulative objects and toys.

Pictorial representations of objects and ideas, although somewhat more abstract than the others, are a frequent and enjoyable part of a child's world. Although students may differ in their feelings about how well they draw, all use pictorial representations as a regular part of their daily lives.

Representing information or ideas in a table, chart, or organized list is also more abstract than the first three processes, primarily because of the use of written symbols. We have urged great caution in the use of symbols. Since symbols are fundamental to mathematics, we must find sensible, meaningful ways to have students use them.

These five major problem-solving strategies are based on different ways of representing ideas. They can be powerful amplifiers of conceptual understanding for your students. Not only do students need extensive practice with each one, but they also need practice switching from one to another with the same ideas.

Five other strategies commonly seen in textbooks are more supplemental in nature. Some are rather general aspects of mathematical thinking; others are useful primarily with certain types of problems. They are as follows:

- Use logical reasoning.
- Look for a pattern.
- Simplify the problem and solve that version.
- Make a guess and check the result.
- Work backwards from the goal toward the start.

You should be aware that some mathematicians now believe that each general strategy (sometimes called heuristic) can be broken down into a collection of ten or twenty more specific strategies, each related to particular content and contexts. Thus, one could conceive of two or three hundred strategies. Therefore, we want students to become capable of using a few potentially powerful strategies in ways that illuminate mathematical ideas.

Building a Problem-Solving Program

There are several important considerations in planning a problem-solving program for students over the school year. If students have not encountered a problem-solving emphasis in prior years, we advise a careful plan for building up students' positive experiences and confidence. Allow them to have success with simplified process problems. Choose interesting and enjoyable activities and problems for them to work on. It is well worth the time and energy to teach students how to use the five representational strategies with relevant problems.

At this point, many teachers raise a serious concern: Where do I get the time to teach problem solving or these strategies? If the district has placed extraordinary pressures for coverage or requires certain facts and skills to be mastered on a specific schedule, it may be hard to imagine adopting a problem-solving emphasis. Several points should be considered.

Mathematical thinking and problem solving are valuable for your students and will allow them to progress faster with fewer mistakes in subsequent areas of the curriculum. Understanding pays great dividends. Even if it seems that ''additional'' time is being spent on problem solving, it will foster greater understanding and more rapid learning later.

Our approach to problem solving does not take time away from the curriculum; it becomes a means to teach the concepts of the curriculum. In this sense, it is a method of teaching as much as something for students to learn. This is the viewpoint of some of the newer (and, we think, better) mathematics textbooks. Teachers with textbooks that lack a problem-solving emphasis will have a more difficult time, but it is quite possible to reorient the use of the textbook. One simple way to start is to select one chapter or unit from the textbook that you can easily supplement with relevant problems. Use this chapter as a basis for introducing the problem-solving strategies.

A strong problem-solving emphasis in mathematics classes enhances student interest and motivation, improves attitudes and behavior, and ultimately *saves* time. After students catch on to the new game, they like it much better than the old one. The result is more time-on-task and less disruption. Less teaching time is spent on managing and correcting behavior.

Some school districts are not aware of what is happening nationwide in mathematics. You may have to tell them. If district guidelines and timetables for content coverage impede students' understanding, speak up. Get background material and publications from the National Council of Teachers of Mathematics and advocate a more thoughtful approach. Join the appropriate textbook selection or curriculum committee and fight to adopt a textbook series in which problem solving is thoroughly woven into every chapter.

Teachers with older texts that emphasize procedural computation often devote one day each week specifically to problem solving. Early in the school year, they focus on the strategy of "discussing the problem" for several weeks. The teachers then schedule two or three weeks of work with manipulatives to illustrate and practice this strategy. They often select a chapter from the book (e.g., geometry or measurement) that encourages the use of manipulatives.

The strategy of acting it out is often considered for a briefer period. Its use with relevant action problems is not so readily identified with a particular place in the curriculum. It is also introduced early in the year so that students can experience it and see its value. Drawing pictures and making lists are vital strategies for almost every area of the curriculum. Teachers usually spend a focused three or four weeks on each strategy separately. The versatility of these strategies allows them to be used with almost any curricular area.

By the middle of the school year, students should have a basis of experience with the five major strategies. They should understand their differences and their uses. They do not have to possess a high degree of proficiency: familiarity with them and positive attitudes are much more important during the first half of the school year. For many students, their initial experience with problem solving is the first time they express any positive feelings toward mathematics. In fact, many of them state that this kind of work is not mathematics: "It can't be math; it's fun."

. . . .

A Model for Helping Students with Problem Solving

How do these five major strategies relate to the four *phases* of problem solving that students should engage in? Discussing a problem is a valuable initial activity that promotes thoughtful analysis of the essential features of the problem or situation. It is probably the best method of helping students understand a problem. From this basis, students can then consider the potential value of the other four representational strategies and choose one to employ. With many problems, the use of one of these strategies will probably produce reasonable solutions. With more complex problems, the use of one will probably enhance students' understanding of the problem, even if it does not immediately yield a solution. Students should then circle back and try other strategies as they reconceptualize the problem or situation. Figure 3.5 gives an overview of what students should be doing in the problem-solving phases and the major ways the teacher supports them.

Figure 3.5

Teaching model for problem-solving activities

Teacher actions	Student problem-solving phases

---

1. Planning

    Select key concepts,
      activities, & questions
    Gather materials

2. Setting up the problem-solving activity

    Arrange small groups
    Present problem, question,
      situation, data, etc.

3. Monitoring each group's work

    Observe groups' processes
    Answer questions only after
      group has tried
    Intervene on group
      processes, if needed
    Suggest rethinking and
      extensions

Phase 1. Understanding

    Primary strategy: discuss the
      problem

Phase 2. Devising a plan

    Consider representational
      strategies

Phase 3. Carrying out the plan

    Try a representational strategy
    Try a different strategy, if
      needed
    Use other supplemental
      strategies, if needed

Phase 4. Reviewing work and conclusions

    Discuss for consensus
    Rethink the problem for different
      assumptions, representations,
      or perspectives
    Report conclusions

4. Debriefing the whole class

    Reconvene the whole class
    Help groups report
    Explain key concepts

Planning

The teacher must select appropriate concepts, activities, and questions. Some activities may involve translation or process problems that more obviously emerge from the domain of mathematics; some may be more like open-ended inquiries that obviously emanate from the lives of the students.

An important aspect of planning is gathering any materials that might be necessary to enhance the experience. The materials and other aspects of the "staging" can be directed toward a set of truly important concepts. An opportunity is then available for using a variety of representations and conceptions in order to deepen understanding.

Setting up the problem-solving activity

We assume that you will assist students to develop the skills for collaborating in small groups throughout the year. Some approach, model, or systematic training in listening, cooperating, making decisions by consensus, and so forth should be implemented with the students. Most students can learn how to work successfully in groups with sufficient guidelines and practice. The teacher must provide appropriate structure and teach the interpersonal skills of working together. Several excellent approaches to student collaboration and small group work have been extensively described (Slavin 1985; Johnson and Johnson 1987; Schmuck and Schmuck 1988).

For most problem-solving activities, the classroom of students should be arranged into small groups of three or four. Have the students get into their groups before beginning the problem-solving activity, so you won't be interrupted by students shuffling their feet or moving around desks.

The problem-solving activity begins when a situation is described, a question posed, data presented, materials distributed, and so forth. The structure of the activity can vary enormously. Sometimes we have simply handed out a slip of paper to every student in each group on which a process problem has been written. Sometimes we have demonstrated a scientific phenomenon with one set of materials that all could see. Initiating their thinking with a provocative problem or situation will greatly enhance motivation.

At the beginning of the year, you should lead the students through the four phases of problem solving with a few sample problems. You may find it valuable to emphasize the understanding phase, provoking a whole-class discussion of what the problem means. Students may question certain details and the class can discuss possibilities. You might tell them that they will not have to "solve" the problem at all, just think hard to understand what is going on. You may encourage many varied assumptions and interpretations of what the problem may mean.

Helping students to discuss and think during the understanding and planning phases is often quite difficult, especially when these students are encountering problem solving for the first time in upper grades. Many hastily want to begin computation. What's there to talk about? It is obvious what to do . . . or so they assume. Choosing excellent process problems (especially those with hidden assumptions) for work early in the school year will help convince impulsive students of the value of the first two phases. Another device is a strict procedure some teachers use: "pencils down" time. Students are strictly prohibited from picking up their pencils during the first two phases. With this rule in force, you can readily see when a student has begun to work on the problem.

Monitoring each group's work

When the students have developed some proficiency in the five representational strategies, the teacher's role is to monitor their work, like a roving consultant. In the next chapter, we will describe how to teach students to use the primary strategy for the initial understanding phase—discussing the problem—and we will illustrate the other representational strategies to be used in phases 2 and 3.

In monitoring the students, the teacher listens to each group, observes their collaboration, but does not directly intervene unless all the group members are truly stuck and desire help. Other approaches to small-group collaboration have somewhat different procedures and rules, yet all seem to suggest that each small group must learn to rely on its members. If a student has a question about the problem or activity, he or she should try to answer it within the group. If the members of a group cannot resolve the question, then they can ask for your help.

The more open-ended, realistic investigations in which students are designing their own data collection tend to require more intervention or support by the teacher. When students are learning how to measure and record observations or when each group is doing a somewhat different version of the activity, you may need to be somewhat more directive. In general, when planning an activity you should walk a fine line between sufficient structure so that students are able to learn, understand, and accomplish what you have in mind, yet enough openness and challenge so that they will have to think, plan, and create something that is truly their own. There is no magic formula or foolproof recipe for teaching through problem solving; teaching is uncertain, complex, artistic, and exciting.

When groups are finishing their work on a problem, they should develop consensus among the members on what they have concluded. Consensus is not always easy to attain. Obstacles to agreement often arise when members have not thoroughly investigated a problem or have not actually resolved different assumptions about what the problem involves. Some students may need substantial practice in communication skills to learn how to collaborate. Your intervention may be needed to assist group members in listening to one another, in sharing different viewpoints and assumptions, in carefully explaining what is being represented in a picture one has drawn, and so forth.

Conversely, some groups will assume that they have consensus when they have not. We have often seen groups that believe that they all agree on what was found, what can be concluded, or what the answers are . . . until one member has to report to the class the conclusions of the group.

A good way to help students reach consensus and develop an awareness of differing ideas is to require each group to formalize its conclusions in some way. Good devices are some kind of product or record, such as a written report, chart, graph, and the like. Of course, this product should be appropriate for the students' development and the nature of the activity. It doesn't have to be elaborate; it merely needs to communicate what the group *thinks*. It is advisable to require students to write their conclusions in complete sentences, not merely short phrases. Clarity of ideas is greater when whole thoughts are expressed.

Many teachers have concluded that a very valuable way of reporting conclusions is for students to write a description of what they did and what they found out—essentially a story. Putting their ideas into words and onto paper clarifies their conceptions. Teachers who use a whole-language or process-writing approach in their classrooms have found that students can readily write about their mathematical ideas simply because they are used to writing about their ideas.

It is inevitable that some groups will complete their work before others and that some groups take great amounts of time. The early completers may need your intervention to go back and more carefully think through assumptions and what they did, even when they have done good and reasonable work. Have they gotten all that they might have from the activity? Is there something that they haven't considered? Is there another way to look at the problem that would enrich their understanding? Is there more that they might do?

If all these questions are answered affirmatively, then you must decide if they should be given another related problem, sometimes called an extension. Our experience has been that the best extensions come from minor alterations of the initial problem. Therefore, changing the conditions, terms, constraints, or numbers of the initial problem may provoke good rethinking. Key questions start with "What if . . . ?" If students have already worked through a problem with good thinking, then the modified problem should not be quite as difficult. The time they take to develop some good ideas may allow other groups to complete their work on the original problem.

What about groups that seem to take forever? As the choreographer, you must make some important decisions—content, process, and managerial. From observing and listening to the group, do you know that the students are doing good thinking and truly wrestling with the important ideas? If so, it might be wise to let them go; give them time to reach their own conclusions. This may seem painful to you, but it is usually better to let them pull it together themselves. On the other hand they may be stuck and a well-worded hint, suggestion, or piece of advice may help them get unstuck. For instance, focusing their attention on something they overlooked may allow them to move ahead quickly. Doing the work for them, showing them how to finish, or giving them an explanation is *not* advisable. That kind of intervention sends a dangerous message: if we wait long enough, the teacher will do it for us.

Even though you may have to begin your review of the activity before every group of students has completed the problem-solving phases, several factors ameliorate this premature stopping. First, any problem-solving activity is one example of local concept development that will help students reach a richer and more complex understanding of a particular concept. Especially if groups have taken different tacts, you can use the divergence in assumptions, perspectives, representations, strategies, and so forth to develop various aspects of the concept. The next activity that addresses this concept can give another opportunity to work on conceptual understanding.

Second, a noncompetitive climate in the classroom means that a group does not "fail" if it does not complete all the phases. Encouraging diversity, creativity, and unusual yet reasonable interpretations fosters a climate of noncompetitiveness among the groups. If the tone has been set for clear and creative thinking (and not merely quick thinking), then when a group finishes becomes less important to students than the quality of their work. You must continually reinforce the values that truly matter in problem-solving activities:

- Respectful discussions within the group.
- Thoughtful ideas and careful plans.
- Imaginative perspectives.
- Awareness of what is being done and how.
- Rethinking and reviewing conclusions for reasonableness.
- Clearly communicating ideas and conclusions to others.

The way the teacher handles the groups during their problem-solving phases and after indicates what is truly valued.

Debriefing

When all the groups have finished their work or you are ready to begin the debriefing, you need to reconvene the class. This should be another "pencils down" time. Just as there are many different ways for students to pull together their conclusions, so are there various ways to present, report, or communicate their ideas to one another. There may be a spokesperson from a group to describe what they concluded. There may be drawings, charts, or graphs to be shown and described. There may be a written description to be read aloud. In fact, all may be done. Yet this sharing is only one aspect of debriefing.

In its essence, debriefing is your opportunity to get the thinking of each group into public awareness. You are drawing out the individual and collective ideas, conceptions, schemata, and so forth of the class. Different perspectives, assumptions, conceptions, strategies, and conclusions should be expressed, and debated in a whole-class discussion. We believe that ground rules for this sharing should include giving each group an opportunity to present their work uninterrupted. They should not be subjected to criticism or evaluation by others or by the teacher while sharing their work.

After all groups have presented, then you can lead the class in a discussion, in which you make sure that the major concepts and thinking at the heart of the activity are made explicit. You will have to juggle the students' explanations of their ideas with the conceptions that you want to establish. Your own explanations of the key concepts have been held back until this point. Your explanations of these can now build upon the raw experiences and ideas that they have just had; they can be related to, and rooted in, the students' immediate understandings; they can use their words, examples, meanings, and schemata to solidify and elaborate their conceptual understanding.

It is usually wise to let the whole class wrestle with the differences expressed by the groups before giving your own explanations. You should ask for comparisons and contrasts among the different groups. Of special interest should be different representations of the problem or situation. Did varying strategies lead to different understandings? Are there ways of integrating or synthesizing these differences? Are there other activities that we did on previous days that relate to what we just did?

In the debriefing, you are trying to broaden their schemata, deepen their understanding, and enrich their web of connections among conceptions. You seek to get the most mileage out of the particular example of a concept (local concept development) while building up rich, complex, general, and abstract understandings.

Evaluating Students' Problem Solving

Since we believe that problem solving should be a vehicle for building a deep understanding and broad use of mathematics, evaluation must include more than merely giving tests to determine grades. The *Standards* defines the major purpose of evaluation as helping teachers better understand what is happening within the hearts and minds of their students so that meaningful decisions about teaching can be made.

A variety of assessment methods should be used, including oral, written, and demonstration formats that are directly related to the curriculum that is actually being taught. These assessment methods should be an integral part of teaching itself. An excellent booklet by Charles, Lester, and O'Daffer (1987) offers several alternatives to testing. We will summarize several of their ideas because they fit well with our concerns.

We desire students to develop the following:

- Positive attitudes and beliefs about themselves and mathematics.
- Their abilities to think mathematically, to use problem-solving strategies, and to monitor their own thinking.
- Their knowledge of mathematics and concepts in related areas.

Even the best of standardized tests cannot adequately assess these concerns. Therefore, a teacher must establish several different ways for students to express openly and honestly both *what* and *how* they are thinking and feeling. Over time, students will become comfortable with regular routines in which the teacher observes individual and small group problem solving and asks students questions about what they are doing, how they are conceiving of a problem, and why. Such procedures are a kind of diagnosis of students' thinking and ideas. Charles, Lester, and O'Daffer also suggest occasionally using an observation checklist for each student in which a teacher notes items such as:

1. Likes to solve problems.
2. Works cooperatively with others in the group.
3. Contributes ideas to group problem solving.
4. Perseveres—sticks with a problem.
5. Tries to understand what a problem is about.
6. Can deal with data in solving a problem.
7. Thinks about which strategies might help.
8. Is flexible—tries different strategies if needed.
9. Checks solutions.
10. Can describe or analyze a solution.

(1987, p 18)

These authors also suggest several techniques that students can use to assess their own progress, such as simple reports and inventories. Yet, the most direct method that we use is the simple journal entry. If students have become accustomed to writing in their own journals as an ongoing part of daily classroom life, it is only natural for the teacher to ask them to write about what they have just experienced in mathematics. Ideas and feelings, expressed in their own written words, can be a relatively painless way for the teacher to learn more about the students' thinking.

Another intriguing form of evaluation suggests that teachers assess students' work in problem solving more analytically than the traditional simplistic right or wrong. If the quality of students' thinking is as important as the "answer," then we must clearly communicate this belief to students through our evaluation process.

For instance, we can make it easy for students to display their thinking by giving one problem at the top of one sheet of paper and asking students to show their work on the rest of the sheet. This device works especially well when students are using strategies such as drawing pictures and making tables, charts, or lists. Also, students can write complete sentences that state their hypotheses, inferences, and conclusions.

If the teacher can see their thinking, then he or she can use one of several schemes for assessing and scoring students' problem solutions in terms of the first three phases of problem solving:

1. Understanding the problem.
2. Planning a solution.
3. Working out an answer.

For instance, students may receive either 0, 1, or 2 points in *each* of these three areas. Thus, if the work exhibits a clear understanding of the problem and a valid use of a strategy, significant points would be awarded, even if a correct answer was not obtained. The criteria for these points are discussed and explained as part of the ongoing work. Then, whenever a student or a group works on a problem, this kind of feedback can be given. Note that this simple procedure is more than just giving partial credit; it makes clear distinctions among these three phases. It places an emphasis on good thinking and planning, as well as execution.

. . . .

Can It Be Done?

If this all sounds like an enormous and time-consuming undertaking, you are probably correct. However, remember that you do not need to feel as if everything we described here must be done fully each time you teach a concept. Each problem-solving activity is an opportunity to develop conceptual understanding. Some oranges have more juice in them than others; some have thicker skins. And some require more squeezing.

Truly important concepts deserve many activities. They will be appreciated differently and better on other occasions. If they are important, then they deserve to be understood as thoroughly as possible. Sometimes multiple class periods over several days are worth investing in. If students have committed their attention to an activity, if they are deriving substantial cognitive and affective benefit, then it may be prudent to let them go for another day or week.

An alternative has been suggested by an excellent teacher of problem solving, Carole Greenes. Mindful of the value of such extensive inquiries in mathematics, she has suggested that schools formally change from daily periods of mathematics to three longer ones during the week (e.g., from five periods of forty-five minutes to three periods of seventy-five minutes).

When students spend time thinking about mathematics, it is not wasted time. We can help them think in more sophisticated and productive ways. But time spent memorizing rarely leads to meaningfulness. Time spent listening to deductive explanations without related experience rarely generates understanding.

4

Five Major Strategies
for Mathematical
Thinking
and Problem Solving

. . . .

Helping Students Get Started

Teachers need to help students develop their use of the five representational strategies for problem solving. Students should wrestle with the messy, nonobvious features of a real problem and play around with what is happening in order to begin to "see" some possibilities or the essence of the inherent mathematical concepts. Once they begin to draw some inferences, they need to think carefully and work toward confirming their hunches, hypotheses, or conjectures. A major part of this process is communicating their ideas to one another. The primary strategy for helping students truly understand a problem in phase 1 is discussing their conceptions. The other four strategies (using objects, acting, drawing a picture, and making tables or lists) should be considered in phase 2 (devising a plan) for use in phase 3 (carrying out the plan).

It is not always possible to predict which of the major representational strategies will most facilitate these processes. Students may have personal preferences; if given a choice, they might "overuse" one and ignore the value of another. Therefore, we urge you to provide guided practice with each of these strategies that will culminate in students' appreciating the value of each.

Guided practice involves the teacher demonstrating one strategy and then *requiring* students to use it with various problems. In these cases, phase 2 consists of thinking through how to use a particular strategy, rather than which strategy to use. This chapter illustrates how to teach students the most important features of each strategy through a process that builds their experiences and capabilities.

When students have had practice with several strategies, the teacher can help them see how different strategies can be used with the same problem. Students need a lot of practice seeing the relationships between different representations of the same situation (e.g., objects and pictures). The ability to switch between representations must be learned through practice.

When students are helped to become more aware of what they are doing and why, their problem-solving performance improves, often dramatically. You can teach students to use a variety of metacognitive "prompts" while using these strategies. For instance, when initially confronted with a problem, they can ask themselves, "Have I ever encountered any similar problems?" In planning what strategies might be helpful, they can ask, "What will each of the strategies I have learned get me? Which strategies seem more likely to work, given my assumptions?"

With coaching from the teacher as they practice strategies, students can internalize such questions as:

- What exactly am I doing?
- Why am I doing it?

- How does it fit with my plan for working on this problem?
- Am I on the right track?
- What would be useful to do right now?
- How will it help?
- What will I do next?

These questions illustrate some of the *self-monitoring* that we want to become habitual. Students should learn how to monitor their progress and understanding. When finished, students should look back on their work, review what was done, see if it was what they wanted, and so forth.

. . . .

Discussing the Problem

Spoken language is powerfully linked to schemata. When students have to describe in their own words what is going on in a problem, understanding is enhanced because they slow down, think carefully, and explain their ideas. Thus, discussing the problem not only helps clarify its essential aspects, but also provokes reflection.

Bear in mind that not all problems are story problems in the textbook. Students are not necessarily reading a problem and then discussing it. You may have described a problem orally or discussed a situation. You may have presented them with some information and asked them a question. You may have given them some materials or manipulatives and asked them to create something, as in the stacking of blocks. The strategy of discussing the problem is a broad-based method of getting students to use their own natural, spoken language.

When you first illustrate problem solving to your students you can model this strategy yourself by leading the entire class in a discussion of what the problem means. Have a large chart on the wall as well as handouts of an age-appropriate version of these key questions to ask about a problem:

- What factual information is given?
  (What do we know for certain?)
- What has to be determined?
  (What do we want to find out?)
- What special conditions or restrictions exist?
  (What limitations do we have to think about?)
- What assumptions might be made?
  (Have we missed something?)

The emphasis should be on generating ideas and possible ways of thinking about the problem or situation. In many respects, the discussion should be like brainstorming, where full disclosure of possibilities is more important than premature decisions.

While working in their small groups, students should discuss the questions you have modeled with the class. With practice, students will become proficient at helping one another carefully consider what is stated or being asked. One serious caution—beware of students who want to leap into a solving mode. If a student grabs a pencil to show the others what is going on or what to do, it usually means he or she has made some assumptions about the problem and hastily chosen a strategy to use. Therefore, this strategy must be done in ''pencils down'' time.

Getting students to slow down and think about a problem is not always easy, especially if they are used to calculating answers quickly to one-step translation problems. We have found that students can be encouraged to think through their assumptions with an intriguing type of problem called ''Fermi questions.'' They get their name from the famous physicist Enrico Fermi, who was known for his uncanny ability to generate reasonable approximations for seemingly impossible mathematical problems or questions. In these problems, there is no right answer. Practice with Fermi questions will greatly help students learn to attack problems from real-life situations. For instance, how many drops of water are there in Lake Michigan? It may seem that insufficient information is available. However, when reasonable assumptions are combined with simple calculations, one can narrow the range of values within which the answer must lie.

The teaching emphasis is on the process of problem solving, the decisions made along the way that lead to reasonable answers. Students should be helped initially to think through ways of attacking the problem and discussing the kinds of assumptions that they would have to make. The actual calculations become secondary in importance. For instance, consider this question: How many tennis balls can you carry across the room at one time without using any devices such as bags, baskets, and so on?

First, have the class examine a tennis ball. Then the class should discuss what it means not to use any devices. When a clear *conception* of the question has been established, you could have the entire class or small groups brainstorm places on the body that could be used for carrying tennis balls or ways to carry them. This process of conceiving of possibilities is crucial. Will some students assume that you cannot use your clothing (e.g., stuff tennis balls inside your shirt, pockets, etc.)? Will some assume that the balls must be carried in your hands? When assumptions have been clarified, either through consensus of the class or your suggestions, the students can generate reasonable answers. For a finale, you could provide tennis balls to allow experimentation under different assumptions.

Let's take a somewhat more difficult question: How many golf balls will fit in a suitcase? If you use the same general tactic, the students might first discuss how big a golf ball is. If they assume that it is about an inch in diameter, then they can envision that one golf ball will fit into a cube space, 1 inch by 1 inch by 1 inch, or 1 cubic inch. They could look at a golf ball but should not actually measure it. Next, the class might be broken down into small groups to decide on how big the suitcase would be. You should let each group decide on the dimensions of their suitcase. These dimensions might vary from those of a briefcase to those of a steamer trunk. If one assumed that the suitcase were 30 inches by 24 inches by 8 inches, a good approximation would be 6,000 cubic inches. (An estimation might use 30 × 10 × 20.) Thus, about 6,000 golf balls would likely fit into this suitcase. The 30-by-20-inch base would hold 600 balls; the height of 10 inches would yield 10 layers. Even if more tightly packed than in the 1 cubic-inch spaces, the number will not likely exceed 8,000. ●

Here are some Fermi questions you could use with students. You can modify them to fit different age groups. They are progressively more difficult.

1. How many balls can you keep in the air at one time (simultaneously), if you throw them up one at a time?
2. How many jelly beans could you hold in both your hands cupped together?
3. How many steps will it take to walk across the classroom?
4. How many pieces of popcorn do you get in a large container at the movies?
5. How many students would fit in this room if we took out all the furniture?
6. How many fully inflated basketballs would it take to fill the gymnasium?
7. How many breaths do you take in a year?
8. How many sheets of tissue paper would it take to make a stack up to the ceiling of this room?
9. How many meals will you eat in your lifetime?
10. How many raindrops will it take to fill a cup?
11. How many gallons of gasoline will it take to drive from Fairbanks, Alaska, to Miami, Florida?
12. If the total amount you earned in your life were given you at a rate of so much per hour for every hour of your life, how much would your time be worth?
13. How many words are there in the *World Book Encyclopedia*?
14. What is the surface area of the skin on an adult human's body?

As you can see, the assumptions you make are important. Problems 10 and 14 have been considered by experts; their guesses are 4.6×10^5 and 1.7×10^4 square centimeter. Discussing assumptions forces students to consider carefully what is involved in the problem.

Here are some suggestions for teaching this strategy to students:

1. Model the use of the four key questions with the entire class on several problems. Choose problems that are inherently interesting

and that may contain unusual assumptions. Ask students the questions and give them plenty of time to think and answer. You should keep the thinking going by asking, ''Are there more ideas?'' It is better to allow some dead air than to stifle creative ideas.

2. If the students are having some difficulty or seem to be stuck, you should think out loud yourself, showing the students that it is good to take time to think carefully.

3. After working with the entire class and modeling yourself, have a group of three or four students volunteer to discuss (but not try to solve) a problem out loud as a group for the class. Choose a fairly easy problem that still illustrates what you want them to do. Ask one student to be a recorder, writing down any decisions or answers of the group. Suggest to the group that they make sure that every member gets a chance to discuss ideas about the problem.

4. Assign all the students to small groups to discuss a problem but not work through to a solution. Again, have one student in each group volunteer to be the recorder and urge each group to give sufficient air time to each member.

5. When first helping students with these discussions, you may want to give all groups a specific time period for discussion (e.g., three minutes). When this discussion period is over, have the recorder from each group tell the class what they discussed and decided about the problem. You should help the entire class briefly discuss any major differences in thinking among the groups. Any clearly erroneous ideas or assumptions should be clarified. Then groups should proceed ahead to the other problem-solving phases based on their assumptions.

Using Objects

There are two major ways of using objects, materials, or manipulatives in problem solving. First, objects can be used to represent various aspects of a problem or situation. Thus, stacking blocks facilitated conceptual understanding of multiplication, division, and prime numbers.

A second method of using manipulatives is particularly related to geometry, which requires physical models for real understanding. Whether studying computational concepts such as angular measure or area or considering perceptual ideas such as symmetry, students must experience tangible realities.

Objects, materials, and manipulatives are not just for young children; they are also necessary for older students who are struggling with intellectually challenging concepts. Premature jumps to pictorial, let alone symbolic, representations can be devastating to comprehension. We will show here several examples of both these ways of using manipulatives for problem solving: using objects to represent aspects of a problem and using objects within geometric problems.

Consider a die, a simple cube usually seen with six different numbers of spots on it. Figure 4.1 shows three views of a die, revealing its six faces. This die has a different color on each face, indicated by different letters. Your task is to determine which colors are opposite each other.

As an adult, you can probably use logic to figure out which sides (colors) are opposite which. The three drawings only provide information about which sides are not opposite others. One strategy would be to focus on one particular color and determine which colors could not possibly be opposite it. You might need to jot down some notes.

However, having an actual cube to write the letters on or to color dramatically changes the task. There is no pressure to remember what cannot be opposite what. The task becomes perceptual and manipulative, recreating what appears in the three drawings. Often, the use of objects not only makes a problem real and tangible, it relieves the memory strain.

We have given pairs of students a wooden cube and six blank square stickers (address labels, cut into squares). They must carefully look at the three diagrams and write the six letters or put large colored dots onto the labels. Then they can affix the labels onto the cube in an appropriate manner. Working with these objects and materials, most third and fourth graders can readily solve the problem and appreciate the value of the manipulatives. ●

Here is another example of a problem that can be solved by using objects. Do rectangular yards with the same perimeter have the same area? This question assumes that students have been introduced to both these concepts through manipulatives. However, we do not have to pose the question in such an abstract form.

Figure 4.1

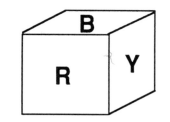
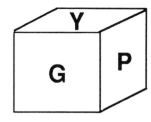
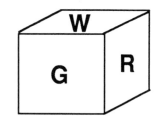

A rrange students in pairs or threes and give each group 36 toothpicks. Ask them to imagine that these are pieces of fence, 1 yard long, and you want to enclose part of the backyard for your dog. One of the toothpicks can be a gate. Arrange the pieces in a rectangle that will give the biggest area for the dog. Show the example of a 1-by-17 rectangle yielding an area of 17 square yards. Ask them to keep a record of the rectangles they find and their area. You may find some students work somewhat randomly and others more systematically. A pattern does form in which the area increase as the rectangle gets shorter and fatter, more like a square.

$$
\begin{aligned}
1 \text{ by } 17 &= 17 \text{ square yards} \\
2 \text{ by } 16 &= 32 \quad '' \qquad '' \\
3 \text{ by } 15 &= 45 \quad '' \qquad '' \\
4 \text{ by } 14 &= 56 \quad '' \qquad '' \\
5 \text{ by } 13 &= 65 \quad '' \qquad '' \\
6 \text{ by } 12 &= 72 \quad '' \qquad '' \\
7 \text{ by } 11 &= 77 \quad '' \qquad '' \\
8 \text{ by } 10 &= 80 \quad '' \qquad '' \\
9 \text{ by } 9 &= 81 \quad '' \qquad ''
\end{aligned}
$$

The pattern flips at this point; a 10 by 8 is the same as the 8 by 10 rectangle. Eighty-one square yards is the largest area. Quite a remarkable difference between 17 and 81 square yards!

When working with problems that have numerical patterns, students should be asked to write down a sentence or two that describes the pattern they see. Of course, collecting one's thoughts and summarizing them requires practice. You should be very encouraging and not overly critical as they develop this ability. In this problem some students noted that "the longer and skinnier a rectangle, the less its area." Strictly speaking, this statement could begin with a clause such as "For rectangles with a perimeter of 36 yards . . ."

In addition to provoking clear thinking and reflection, asking students to write down their conclusions may help them see things they did not at first glance. For instance, in this problem an insightful sixth grader noticed that "when you change the perimeter by adding one to the width and subtracting one from the length, the area goes up by an odd number. Each time you get the next smaller odd number." Look carefully at the numbers and you will see that pattern. Going from the skinniest rectangle (width of 1) to the next with width of 2, increases the area by 15 square yards. The next change (increasing the width from 2 to 3), gets an additional 13 squares yards. And so on until increasing the width from 8 to 9 adds only 1 square yard to the area.

There are many geometric concepts and relationships that require the use of manipulatives for understanding. This problem can form the basis for exploration of the relationship between perimeter and area. It starts with a specific, imaginable situation that is represented concretely with manipulatives. Possible patterns can be investigated with other perimeters (e.g., 32 toothpicks). Repeat with 28. They should discover that the largest area is always formed by a square. The smaller they make one side of the rectangle, the smaller the area. Will this relationship hold for perimeters where a square is not possible? Have them try 26 toothpicks. The rectangle most like a square has the largest area. ●

The following suggestions may help you teach the strategy of using objects to your students:

1. It is usually best to assign students to groups of two or three with one person at a time working with the objects or manipulatives. Other group members can record what they find on a handout sheet that you have prepared. Students should switch roles either between shorter problems or during longer problems. All should discuss the problem as well as actions while working with the manipulatives, but they take turns actually working with the objects.

2. To ensure a smooth operation, prepare objects, materials, and manipulatives the night before class. Have everything precounted, prewrapped, presorted, and so forth. Trying to set up or count out materials with thirty students clamoring for them is a nightmare to be avoided. Rubber bands, envelopes, zip-lock baggies, paper bags, boxes, plastic food containers, and other devices can be used as packets to be handed out to each group at the beginning of an activity.

3. When students are given a packet of materials at the start of an activity, we suggest that you have them count them or check to see that they have what you think they do. The essential point of a problem-solving activity can go haywire if students get in the middle and don't have what they should. Even when you have done careful preparation of materials into packets, you can still make a mistake. Students should always repackage the materials for you when they are finished. They should make sure that all objects have been recombined, but don't assume that they have been accurate.

4. If at all possible, do not use packets that students have put back together with a second class or for a second activity without checking them yourself. If you are doing the same activity with two classes on the same day, give yourselves a few minutes sometime in between to check the packets, or prepare enough the night before for both classes.

5. In discussing the problem activity with the class after they have had a chance to work with the manipulatives, it is sometimes helpful to have a very large version of the same manipulatives yourself for demonstration of the key ideas. Especially if the idea or concept

depends on students' actually seeing a relationship or position, then for you to have a large and easy-to-see object can greatly enhance their understanding. We have often made extra large versions of manipulatives from heavy construction paper or oak tag and then fastened them to the corkboard or stuck them on the wall. Using small manipulatives on an overhead projector, even if transparent, is usually not as effective a large scale models.

. . . .

Acting Out Problems

Many problems are based on actions. Accurate modeling of the problem requires students to carry out these actions to discover a solution. Unfortunately, textbooks often suggest pictorial representations when concrete actions would be more appropriate for students' level of thinking. In fact, life often contains situations in which only some kind of reenactment will help adults see what is going on. Let's examine a number of problems to demonstrate the value of this strategy.

Here is a problem for younger children:

A rabbit, a kangaroo, an iguana, and a pig decided to have a race. The iguana was the slowest. The rabbit was faster than the pig but slower than the kangaroo. Who won the race? Who came in second, third, and fourth?

Have the students act out this race, working in groups of four (or five, if an observer is used). One of the first things you and they will notice is that they need a means for telling who is playing each animal. Students could hold pictures or name tags.

Although an older student may be able to hold the logical relationships among these four animals in mind to solve the problem, younger students cannot. Acting out the problem will help clarify the fundamental ideas involved. Although it is not stated and must be inferred, the kangaroo is faster than the pig. Why? It is stated that the rabbit is faster than the pig. The kangaroo is faster than the rabbit (which must be inferred from the converse statement that the rabbit is slower than the kangaroo). Therefore, the inference can be drawn that the kangaroo is faster than the pig.

After the students have reenacted this race, they will be ready for a discussion of these relationships. They will have had a concrete example upon which to build understanding. Of course, other examples of such relationships should be invoked, such as the heights of three different children in the class. Bobby is taller than Mary. Andy is shorter than Mary. When the three children stand up next to each other, the relationships of "greater than" and "less than" can take on concrete meaning as well as the inference that Bobby must be taller than Andy. ●

If you review resource books for mathematics problems, you will undoubtedly encounter one or more variations of some classic action problems. Here are two.

A farmer is going to market with his hungry dog, two fat geese, and three bags of corn. Unless the farmer is present to stop them, the geese will eat the corn, and the dog will eat the geese. The farmer has managed to avoid any trouble until he comes to a river that must be crossed in a small rowboat which only has enough room for him and two of the six things he has to bring with him. How can he get all his possessions across the river without one of the animals eating something?

A man and two boys want to cross a river and only one small canoe is available that can hold either the two boys or the man. What must they do in order for all three of them to get across the river?

There are several similarities between these problems besides crossing rivers. Perhaps your students can make up their own more realistic stories that have the same essential mathematical features after they have worked on some of these. How about astronauts and cosmonauts in space capsules?

These two problems are often shown in pictorial form to record the different states or positions of those involved. For instance, the initial state of the first problem might be represented as

Although you can interpret this drawing as the farmer and his six possessions on one side of the river and nothing on the other, students do not always find such drawings compelling. On the other hand, with proper labels for students to play the parts, these problems can be enacted readily. Acting these problems out can make for an animated and engaging activity.

Although the problems differ, they both require a significant shift in thinking by students. The path to a solution is not direct. Careful attention must be paid to the specific constraints of the problem. We suggest that you try these problems yourself. Instead of acting it out, use some objects to represent those involved. Obviously, students could use objects to solve these problems also, but the action is particularly suited for role playing. We will show you pictorial solutions to these problems in the next section.

Somewhat more difficult problems describe true-to-life situations that appear illogical. Consider the following problem:

> Three friends arrive at a hotel together to find that there is only one room left for the night. They agree to share it, paying the clerk $90, $30 dollars apiece. The next morning, the manager realizes that they have been overcharged and sends the bellhop up to their room with a $15 refund. The bellhop ensures himself of a tip by keeping $6 for himself and gives only $9 to the men. Therefore, each guest has paid $27 dollars for his room and the bellhop has kept $6. Three guests at $27 apiece is $81 plus the bellhop's $6 makes a total of $87. What happened to the other $3?

This problem involves keeping track of what pot of money you are thinking about. In life, there are many situations in which arguments develop over who owes how much to whom. As before, using manipulatives (e.g., play money) would work well, but acting it out with the play money would be even more clear. Try working on the problem.

The stated question mixes two perspectives, as people often do. It does not make sense to add the bellhop's tip to what the men paid for the room because it is already included in their cost. Once the bellhop returns $9 to them, their cost is $81, not $90. Where is the $81? The bellhop has $6 and the hotel manager has $75.

Another type of problem commonly found in resource books lends itself well to acting out. These problems can be used to help students switch from acting out to pictorial representation.

> The five starting players for the school basketball team came out onto the floor at the start of the game as their names were called. As they did, each one slapped a high-five to the other members on the floor. How many high-fives were there?

With five players, the first one out slaps no one. The second slaps only the first (that is 1 slap); the third slaps the first two players (2 more slaps); the fourth slaps the first three players (3 more slaps); finally the fifth player out slaps the other four (4 more for a total of 10). The basketball players offer a good illustration of focusing on one player's action at a time.

There are many variations of this problem. The nine Supreme Court justices shake hands with one another at the start of the session. Eight tennis players were engaged in a tournament in which each one played all of the others once. Their essential similarity is trying to determine the number of happenings among pairs. Thinking about eight tennis players or nine judges can be very confusing without a systematic method of doing the actions and recording the results. If students enact the problem, they can see what is going on. For instance:

H ave nine students portraying the judges stand in a circle. If they started shaking hands with one another, it could be very confusing to note how many handshakes occurred. However, one student could start shaking the hands of each of the others, calling out the number of handshakes. After he has shaken each person's hand (8 shakes), he would be finished. The next judge would shake seven judges' hands (7 more shakes). Why wouldn't the second judge also shake eight judges' hands? He does, but one of these shakes was already counted when he shook the first judge's hand.

These problems are often represented in pictures. We have found that the pictures make sense to students only *after* the acting out. The pictures are then representing something concrete that they have experienced. Figure 4.2 is one way of picturing the

. . . .
Figure 4.2

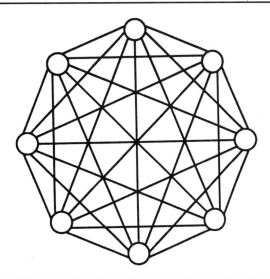

tennis tournament, discussed above. In this figure, the circles represent players and lines between them, the matches. If you count the lines, you'll find the total number of matches. This is a bit tricky for students to conceive until after they have acted out several of these problems. Notice that 7 lines come out from each tennis player (circle). That is because each player plays 7 matches, one with each of the other 7 players. Students are often tempted to say that there must be a total of 56 matches: 8 players, each playing 7 matches, is 8 times 7 or 56. Actually, each match involves two players, therefore the 56 must be divided by 2. There are 28 matches. Considering each person individually (as we did with the handshakes) avoids this pitfall. The first player plays 7 others (7 matches), then the second player plays 6 additional players (6 matches), because we already counted his match with the first player. And so on. ●

Here are suggestions about teaching this strategy to students. Several of these ideas have been mentioned already.

1. This strategy has some limitations: it requires space, time, a certain number of people, and so on, depending on the problem. Students should realize that it is useful for certain problems and may be inappropriate for others. It is especially valuable when a textbook problem would be very difficult to solve logically or with other strategies.

2. We suggest starting with relatively simple problems with action that can be readily modeled. Have a small group of students reenact the problem for the whole class after they have discussed what is going on among themselves.

3. You can let the first group of students who try this approach realize for themselves the need to have name tags or labels of some kind. Thereafter, students should decide who will act the part of each entity and how they might be labeled.

4. If a problem includes somewhat complicated actions (such as the detour problems), you should have the group of students who work together include a recorder who has no part to act out. Actually, several recorders in a group are possible. This fact allows you to partition the students into groups for problems even if the number of people in groups is unequal. For instance, a class of 28 students, working on the basketball players problem could have 2 groups of 5 (no recorder, all have to keep track) and 3 groups of 6 (5 actors and 1 recorder). You could also have 4 groups of 7, each with 5 actors and 2 recorders.

One very helpful aspect of acting out a problem comes in the discussion afterward. As we saw in the handshake and tennis tournament examples, once students have acted out a problem, they have a better feel for what went on, a better understanding of the action, than they might have from logic or calculations. Therefore, after discussing the actions and the mathematical aspects of the problem, you can then translate these ideas to other representations, especially pictures and diagrams.

Drawing Pictures and Diagrams

Pictures and diagrams must be compatible with the schemata that students have in their minds. Pictorial representations are abstractions, simplifying reality in some way. They streamline the action to its essential features, allowing the analysis that you want to occur. However, the way that the textbook author or the teacher depicts or simplifies real objects or situations may not connect with children's schemata.

When encountering a problem, stated in words, we tend to recreate the words into visual images. Whether through experience and training (such as an artist might have) or genetics (such as the inheritance of spatial perception ability), some of us are more adept at visualization and pictorial representation than others. Many students need help and practice in learning how to depict words and ideas.

In early grades, students should have experiences in drawing pictures to represent life and should also begin to see examples of how others in our society have chosen to represent reality through pictures. For instance, figure 4.3 may be perceived in a number of ways. Is it a box or a cube; solid or hollow? To one young child perhaps it would be merely nine straight lines; to another, a square connected to a diamond and a parallelogram. By what perceptual device does it invoke a conception of a three-dimensional object? Only experience with this convention of representation would do so. Students need such experiences along with explanations of what we have chosen to do.

For difficult problems, asking students to draw a picture of how they are thinking about the problem can be helpful and insightful. For instance, let's look again at the problem of the farmer and his possessions:

Figure 4.3

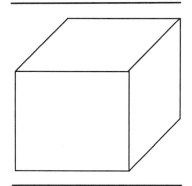

A farmer is going to market with his hungry dog, two fat geese, and three bags of corn. Unless the farmer is present to stop them, the geese will eat the corn and the dog will eat the geese. The farmer has managed to avoid any trouble until he comes to a river that must be crossed in a small rowboat which only has enough room for him and two of the six things he has to bring with him. How can he get all his possessions across the river without one of the animals eating something?

In this problem, a major error in thinking among students is focusing on the far side of the river while forgetting about the other. A picture that contains the three places of concern (the near side, the far side, and the boat in the river), can help students maintain the essential constraints of the problem: (1) the dog can't be in a place with a goose unless the farmer is present, (2) a goose can't be in a place with a bag of corn unless the farmer is present, and (3) the farmer must row the boat with only two of his possessions at a time. Therefore any of the following moves or states violates a constraint:

D GG		D C		D CC	
		F		F GG C	
F CCC		GG CC			

By drawing each move or state as they are done, the student can systematically check to see that all conditions are being met. Here is a solution to the problem with each step numbered.

(1)	(2)	(3)	(4)
F D GG CCC	D CCC	D C	D C
	F GG	F CC	
		GG	F GG CC

(5)	(6)	(7)	(8)
D C	GG		
F GG	F D C	F GG	
CC	CC	D CCC	F D GG CCC

This problem is sometimes called a "detour" problem because there comes a moment when the solver must make a move that seems to be going in the wrong direction. In state 4 the two geese and two bags of corn have been crossed, but state 5 shows the farmer bringing the geese back to the initial side of the river. The key idea here is the unique position occupied by the geese. They are in the middle, able to be eaten by the dog and able to eat the corn. The inference must be drawn that they cannot be with anyone or anything else but the farmer (or alone).

The other detour problem was as follows:

> A man and two boys want to cross a river and only one small canoe is available that can hold either the two boys or the man. What must they do in order for all three of them to get across the river?

Here one way to represent what they must do:

Start	Move 1	Move 2	Move 3	Move 4	Move 5
B B M	M	B M	B	B B	
─────	─────	─────	─────	─────	─────
	B B	B	B M	M	B B M

In order to transport one man across the river, four moves are required. The fifth move allows the two boys to come across. Resource books often have a version of the problem with five or more men and two boys. Regardless of the number of men, it will take the two boys four moves to get each man across and one more for themselves.

Here is an example of a problem that younger students could solve by drawing pictures. It illustrates the kind of early experiences that must occur if students are to develop abilities at using this problem-solving strategy effectively.

> Mrs. Jones's class decided to decorate the classroom for a party. Twelve balloons were tied in a row along one wall. Every fourth balloon was blue. How many blue balloons were there?

Younger students could readily draw a picture of twelve balloons in a row and then shade or color in every fourth one. Even if their pictures were inaccurate, you would get a good idea about who was misconceiving the problem and in what way.

Here is a problem that students in third or fourth grade could readily use pictures to help them solve:

> You have been asked to arrange 30 chairs in the library into rows with the same number of chairs in each row. What are all the possible ways to arrange the chairs?

Some students could readily conceive of the mathematical essence of the problem. Other students would not necessarily make the connection to multiplication and division. In fact, we have repeatedly seen that third or fourth graders need many, many varied experiences with what seems obvious to adults as identical situations (mathematically speaking) before they can conceive the relationships. If students have had experiences with manipulatives and problems such as this one, drawing a picture to solve it may be very beneficial. A group of third-grade students drew the picture below to help them find the solutions.

```
XXXXX    XXXXX    XXXXXXXXXX    XXX    XXXXXXXXXXXXXXXXXXXXXXXXXXXXXXX
XXXXX    XXXXX    XXXXXXXXXX    XXX
XXXXX    XXXXX    XXXXXXXXXX    XXX
XXXXX    XXXXX                  XXX    XXXXXXXXXXXXXX
XXXXX    XXXXX                  XXX    XXXXXXXXXXXXXX
XXXXX                           XXX
                                XXX
                                XXX
                                XXX
                                XXX
```

The front of the room

Some students will draw these 6 arrangements and leave out the other two possibilities: 15 rows with 2 each and 30 rows with 1 each. The power of their schemata for chairs in rows seems to prohibit these two "illogical" arrangements. Such students may need manipulatives to help them see the other two possibilities. Pictorial representations are more abstract than using objects to represent the key features of a problem.

When problems are posed appropriately for the conceptual level of the students, drawing pictures will assist in understanding what is going on in the problem. For instance, consider the following problem:

There are 12 small, square tables in the media center. Each table can seat only 1 person on each side. If the tables are pushed together to form one big rectangle, what arrangement will allow the most people to be seated? How many people would that be?

Figure 4.4 shows two possible arrangements of the 12 tables, one seating 16 people, the other 14. Note this drawing denotes the table tops by squares and a person (or chair) by an *X*. Of course, students could manipulate small squares to solve this problem. However, most third graders can conceive of the problem and represent the conditions pictorially. The key mathematics concepts involved are perimeter and area. Since they

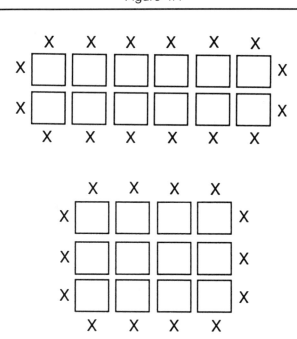

are not necessarily obvious, the teacher should make sure they get discussed after students have worked on the problem. In this problem the area (i.e., the surface of the tables) is always the same (held constant) while we vary the perimeter (i.e., the seating room around the table). Interestingly, this problem asks us to consider the area in square table tops (not in square feet) and the perimeter in seat widths (not inches).

Twenty-six seats are possible, if one makes one very long rectangle from the 12 tables: one table across and twelve long as in figure 4.5.

Earlier, we used toothpicks to find the largest area while holding the perimeter constant. This problem is essentially the converse: the largest

. . . .
Figure 4.5

perimeter of rectangles with the same area will occur in the longest, thinnest rectangle.

The next problem is an example of how drawing a picture can be quite necessary in some cases. Please draw a picture to help you solve it.

The ten volumes of a set of encyclopedias is sitting side-by-side in order on a shelf. A bookworm has crawled into the first volume. It starts on page 1 of volume 1 and begins to chew a hole through the 10 volumes before it dies of over indulgence at the final page of volume 10. How many inches has it traveled if each cover is ⅛ of an inch thick and the pages of each volume are 2 inches thick?

Drawing pictures is absolutely essential to solving this problem. Even with an appropriate picture, the task still presents some challenges. How far does the bookworm chew? Without any picture at all, one might be tempted to simply calculate that each book is 2¼ inches wide (the 2 covers and the inner pages). Since there are 10 volumes, the bookworm must eat through 22½ inches. This reasoning would be wrong because it does not eat through both covers of volume 1 or volume 10. But also wrong would be the reasoning that merely subtracting ⅛ inch for each cover not eaten through from 22½ inches would suffice. Examine figure 4.6 very carefully.

Where is page 1 of volume 1 and the last page of volume 10? Assuming that the 10 volumes are placed in numerical sequence as in this figure, page 1 of volume 1 is at the far *right* side of that book. Similarly, the last

Figure 4.6

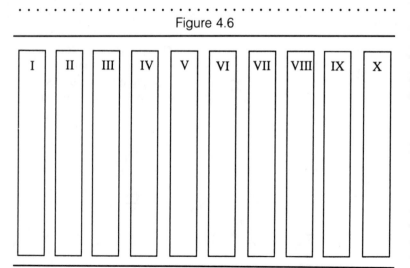

page of Volume 10 is at the far *left*. A fair inference from the exact wording of the problem would mean that the bookworm ate only through the front cover of volume 1 and the back cover of volume 10; it did not eat any pages in either of these books. Therefore, it ate through 18¼ inches.

This is not a trick problem. It is a difficult one that requires an accurate picture and careful thought, as do many problems in mathematics and real life.

Pictures and diagrams have the power to translate complexities into manageable realities. Consider the following problem:

A small plane carrying 3 men makes a forced landing in the desert. The men decide to strike out in three different directions in search of oases and civilization. They agree to divide equally the existing food and water. They have 15 canteens, 5 full of water, 5 half-full of water, and 5 empty. All canteens are the same size. Since they may reach an oasis, they will need to carry extra canteens, even if empty. How can they divide both the water and the canteens equally among themselves?

In either discussing or trying to solve this problem, most students assume that you have to pour water from one canteen to another to get equal amounts of water for the 3 men. From simple arithmetic, they can determine that the goal of the problem is to provide each man with 5 canteens and 2½ canteens of water. They assume that the next step involves some clever way of pouring the water to get 5 half-filled canteens for each man. Working with a good drawing offers an almost obvious alternative. Examine figure 4.7.

Can you see how to give each man 5 canteens that collectively contain 2½ full amounts? It could be done by one man taking 2 full, 1 half-full, and 2 empty canteens; another man doing the same; and the third would be left with 1 full, 3 half-full, and 1 empty canteen. No pouring, just logical thinking suggested by a drawing.

One final example may illustrate how problems that are quite difficult logically can become simple with good pictures.

Figure 4.7

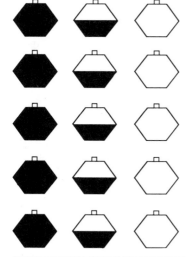

A penny gum-ball machine contains 5 different flavors. It holds 30 gum balls, 6 of each flavor. You want to get 3 of the same flavor (it doesn't matter which flavor). What is the maximum number of pennies you might have to put in to be certain to get 3 of the same flavor?

Of course, you could provide bags of gum balls to students for them to try the first problem. However, letting them draw pictures of what could happen can be an excellent experience for them. Figure 4.8 shows how one group of students reasoned with the help of a drawing (actually several drawings). They imagined gum balls dropping out in various ways and drew pictures in which the gum balls were sorted into 5 piles according to their flavors (designated by the letters R, B, Y, G, and P). Since the problem asks for the worst possible happening (that is, the maximum number of pennies needed), they drew gum balls coming out that did not give 3 of the same flavor. They found that 10 could come out—2 of each flavor—but the eleventh would have to be the third gum ball of one of the flavors. So 11 pennies is the most you would need to get 3 of a kind.

Certainly, someone familiar with these kinds of problems could reason logically without the need of a picture. Students rarely can do this. Even students who solved this problem used several different pictures first to grasp what might occur. For instance, the first 3 *might* be the same flavor. Three of the same *might* occur in the first 4 or 5 gum balls. But drawing what might happen revealed what the problem really required—what it means to consider the most you could possibly need (i.e., the worst-case scenario). To children engaged in habitual wishful thinking, careful consideration of possibilities is a valuable experience.

We have discussed several ways to help students learn to use this strategy effectively. Here are some additional considerations.

. . . .

Figure 4.8

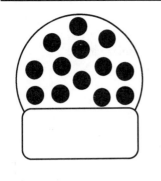

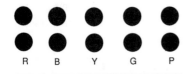

R   B   Y   G   P

1. It is valuable for students to see one another's pictures and diagrams. Such sharing helps develop understanding of the medium itself. Many problems can be solved by pictures that students can draw on the chalkboard. We would not suggest this for long, involved drawings.
2. Since pictures are often very personal and idiosyncratic, this strategy is tricky to use in groups. Even pairs can get into arguments about whether this stick figure is good enough, and the like. Having two or three students discuss the problem and then each make their own drawings (which they can also describe and discuss with one another) can be very effective.
3. You may want to assign a problem to be solved by drawing a picture for homework. Students can discuss in groups the basic features of a problem in class, but work on it at home. If they give you their pictures early enough in the day, you may be able to photocopy one or two very different pictures before mathematics class. You can use these when reviewing the problem to help all students see different ways of representing the problem.

Once again, beware of the highly abstract diagrams and pictures of the textbook. Allow adequate time to discuss what is being represented by each aspect of a diagram. You may even suggest that students modify or recreate diagrams from the book so that they make more sense to them. Sometimes their creations will be better representations for their schemata. Other times, their pictures will reveal misconceptions about what is going on. Representing, like problem solving, is an active process. Students need many opportunities to express their ideas and understandings.

You may find it odd that we did not mention bar graphs as pictorial representations in this strategy. There are many kinds of graphs that present information in a remarkably useful form. We will discuss them in chapter 6 in regard to handling statistical information.

Making Tables and Lists

Teachers should be careful in using tables and lists with students because what is perfectly obvious to the adult may appear overwhelmingly abstract to the students. These devices are frequently idiosyncratic, making good sense to the one who made it but not necessarily to another. Consider the differences between the following two tables, one made by students, the other by an adult. Both address the problem: What are all the different ways to give someone change for a quarter?

Both tables accurately provide the twelve possibilities. Both use words and numbers. However, there are some major differences between them. Table 1 is a recording device that a group of three students used to list the possibilities as they worked them out. They conceived of possibilities through mental arithmetic and wrote them down. This list makes sense to

Table 1

5 pennies and 2 dimes
5 pennies, 1 dime and 2 nickels
5 pennies and 4 nickels
10 pennies, 1 dime, and 1 nickel
10 pennies and 3 nickels
5 nickels
2 dimes and 1 nickel
1 dime and 3 nickels
15 pennies and 1 dime
15 pennies and 2 nickels
20 pennies and 1 nickel
25 pennies

the students who made it. Depending on their conceptual level, they may or may not be able to grasp what table 2 is doing.

Table 2 is organized logically. It was created by someone who imagined the ways to use the most of the largest coin first, then the next largest, and so on. It has a major virtue in being able to illustrate several pertinent mathematical patterns. For instance, as the number of large coins decrease, the number of smaller coins must increase. Also, the pennies can only combine in groups of five. This highly organized table also shows that we have systematically considered all the possibilities; there can be no others. With table 1 we cannot be this certain.

Despite these virtues of the highly organized table 2, it is unrealistic to expect students to be able to create such tables without the necessary experience and practice. To force a high degree of organization or abstraction can be self-defeating. Instead, they can be helped to see what it means to be organized, systematic, or logical in their use of lists. Students begin by making their own sensible, natural tables and recording lists.

For instance, consider the following problem that younger students can readily imagine:

> For breakfast in the morning you may choose among three different cereals: corn flakes, oatmeal, or wheat chunks. You must also choose a juice: either apple juice or orange juice. What are all the different breakfast combinations that you could have?

As in the change for a quarter problem, students must generate all the possible combinations. Obviously, they could just rattle off some possibilities that occur to them and then write them down. For younger students

. . . .

Table 2

Dimes	Nickels	Pennies
2	1	0
2	0	5
1	3	0
1	2	5
1	1	10
1	0	15
0	5	0
0	4	5
0	3	10
0	2	15
0	1	20
0	0	25

and even older students encountering these problems and the list-making strategy for the first time, using a list simply as a recording device is quite appropriate and natural.

When students have generated several possibilities, you should ask, "Can you think of some others?" If they cannot, you can ask, "Do you have all the possibilities?" If they believe so, you should then ask, "How do you know you do? How can you be certain?" These question are designed to help the students begin to think more logically and systematically about the problem and how to attack it. This shift in thinking can begin to produce lists that are more organized, such as the following combinations:

1. Apple juice and corn flakes.
2. Apple juice and oatmeal.
3. Apple juice and wheatchunks.
4. Orange juice and cornflakes.
5. Orange juice and oatmeal.
6. Orange juice and wheatchunks.

Of course, there are several different ways to generate the possibilities through systematic thinking. In the above list, thinking about what cereals would be possible with apple juice generates three breakfasts. Then thinking about what cereals would be possible with the other juice produces the other three. A student could begin by considering what juices you could have with corn flakes and then systematically go through the other cereals. There are many excellent process problems involving finding combinations that students can readily grasp because they relate to their lives.

The use of tables and lists is more complex and potentially more abstract than the others we have discussed. This complexity comes from the use of written language and symbols and from the possibilities for formatting (organizing, arraying, etc.), describing, and labeling the information. The two tables of possible ways to change a quarter and the list of six breakfasts are straightforward in comparison to the following table.

	Cereals		
	C	O	W
A	A&C	A&O	A&W
Juices			
O	O&C	O&O	O&W

This matrix table contains the relevant information in a highly symbolized format. It has all the virtues of organization that we discussed. However, it is much too abstract for younger students. On the other hand, older students, who have had substantial experience with generating combinations, can be shown how a two-dimensional matrix can help to organize information. Its structure can greatly facilitate logical thinking in certain kinds of problems. For instance, try to solve the following problem that might actually occur:

Four families are planning their monthly cookout together. One family will bring the main dish, one the dessert, one the beverages, and the other the paper products (napkins, plates, cups, etc.). They usually try to alternate who brings what. This month, the Browns cannot cook and offered to stop at the store for either the beverages or the paper products. The Smiths bought expensive steaks for everyone last month and do not want to bring the main dish again. Everyone wants Mrs. Fratelli to make her delicious homemade ice cream this month; she agrees. The Grobniks are willing to bring whatever will be helpful.

This is one of several different kinds of "logic" problems. Those most commonly found in resource books are solved using a particular kind of table, sometimes called a logic chart. The four families and four items can be used as two sides or dimensions of a *matrix*.

	Main dish	Dessert	Beverage	Paper products
Brown	N	N		
Smith	N			
Fratelli		Y		
Grobnik				

We can enter information into sixteen cells of this 4 by 4 matrix when we are certain what they must contain. We can only be sure of three definite No conditions and one Yes. Notice that we should not enter Yes for the two possible items that Brown *might* bring (beverages and paper products) because we are not sure which will eventually be the one. However, we know that Fratelli will definitely bring the dessert, and a Yes can be entered in that cell.

The matrix provides a way of organizing our thinking in order to draw inferences about possibilities. From this table we can conclude that since the Fratellis are bringing the dessert, they will not bring any of the other three items; nor will anyone else bring the dessert. This is a critical inference that leads to the most valuable feature of a logic table. Whenever one determines a definite Yes, one can enter a definite No in certain other cells on both dimensions of the matrix.

	Main dish	Dessert	Beverage	Paper products
Brown	N	N		
Smith	N	N		
Fratelli	N	Y	N	N
Grobnik		N		

An inference that the table now reveals rather well is that the Grobniks are the only family that can bring the main dish. Therefore a Yes must occur in that cell.

	Main dish	Dessert	Beverage	Paper products
Brown	N	N		
Smith	N	N		
Fratelli	N	Y	N	N
Grobnik	Y	N		

Filling in a Yes for the Grobnik's bringing the main dish means that No can be entired in two more Grobnik cells.

	Main dish	Dessert	Beverage	Paper products
Brown	N	N		
Smith	N	N		
Fratelli	N	Y	N	N
Grobnik	Y	N	N	N

Many of the logic problems that are available in handbooks present a rather direct sequence of inferences that lead, one at a time, to checking off Ys and Ns to find the only possible solution. However, this problem is more open. Notice that at this point, the two remaining families, Brown and Smith, each have two possible items that they could bring. This fact means that there is more than one possible solution to this problem. The table shows this quite nicely. While the two solutions could be found by other approaches, the table is especially suited to show the multiple answers to this problem.

There are many books in which each logic problem solved is by using a different matrix. This logic problem was relatively simple and could be represented by a two-dimensional matrix. More complicated problems require adding more dimensions.

Please try each problem yourself to make sure what is required before assigning it, even as "just for fun." We also urge you to review any problems you assign, thoroughly discussing the reasoning involved. It is frustrating for students to work on problems that are much too difficult for their present capabilities, but working out a problem that the teacher does not discuss also sends a negative signal.

Tables and lists can be powerful devices for solving problems involving computation, numerical relationships, and patterns. By providing the initial structure of a table, the teacher can facilitate students' thinking and help them learn how to create their own tables. The following problem would be very difficult for fourth graders without the structure of a table.

Frank and Joe began reading an adventure novel on the same day. If Frank reads 8 pages each day and Joe reads 5 pages each day, what page will Joe be reading when Frank is on page 56?

There are several ways of conceiving this problem, each with related mathematical concepts. However, computational approaches may be beyond your students. For instance, focusing on Frank, we know that he reads 8 pages each day and has reached page 56. Therefore, he read for 7 days (56 divided by 8). If Joe read for 7 days at 5 pages per day, he would reach page 35. Alternatively, the problem might be seen as a ratio problem: 8 is to 56 as 5 is to what number ($\frac{8}{56} = 5/x$). Textbooks often force students to solve such problems through these computational procedures before they are developmentally or conceptually ready. However, using a table not only can solve the problem, but can also build a basis for understanding what is going on mathematically.

For students learning how to use tables in order eventually to construct their own, you should provide the structure and the headings of a table such as the following.

	Pages read	
	Frank	**Joe**
Start	0	0
End of Day 1		
2		
3		
4		

The table gets students started in their thinking. You might then ask the class what additional information the problem gives. Students could fill in 8 and 5 for the number of pages read at the end of Day 1 by Frank and Joe. Remind students of the four basic questions that they should consider in discussing a problem. Ask them what else they know and what they are trying to find out in the problem. Then they can consider particular conditions of the problem and their assumptions. Assuming that each day Frank reads 8 additional pages while Joe reads 5, students should try to determine on what day Frank has read 56 pages. Then they can follow Joe's progress to see how far he has read at the end of that day.

Filling in the table may seem like a simple task, too mechanical to be of value. However, if you want students to learn how to construct their own table to solve problems, they need structure in their initial experiences.

Problems such as this allow students to see number patterns very directly. Although less concrete than stacking blocks, the multiples of 8 and 5 have a clear referent in students' minds. Frank reads 8, then 16, then 24 *pages*. By the end of the fourth day, he will have read 32 pages. Many students become excited when they see that 4 times 8 is 32. The pattern of multiplication is meaningful, not just an arbitrary set of number names that was memorized. Seeing this pattern and realizing its significance provides a solid foundation for computational procedures. Experiences with these patterns is beneficial and probably essential to understanding such relationships.

A tricky aspect of making tables for problems such as this is the thought behind the headings. Compare the following tables for the same problem. Table 1 may solve the specific problem, but it will not necessarily build the mathematical knowledge we just described.

	Table 1 Pages read			Table 2 Pages read	
	Frank	Joe		Frank	Joe
Day 1	0	0	Start	0	0
2	8	5	End of Day 1	8	5
3	16	10	2	16	10
4	24	15	3	24	15
5	32	20	4	32	20
	and so on			and so on	

Although the students who created table 1 used it to solve the problem correctly, they missed the relationship between the number of days and the number of pages (e.g., 4 times 8 is 32 and 4 times 5 is 20). Therefore, it is valuable for the teacher to discuss the category in table 2 of pages read by the *end* of the day. Table 1 implicitly refers to pages read at the beginning of the day. The difference is subtle, but very important. Students can be helped to think carefully about the headings of each table they see in books and create themselves.

Of the many other mathematical problems that can be addressed by making a table of some kind, we want you to consider this following set of five related problems. Try to solve them by making simple tables.

---

1. Cheeseburgers cost $2 and hot dogs cost $1. If there are 20 children in the class and 10 want cheeseburgers and 10 want hot dogs, how much money will we need?

Problem 1 starts with a familiar situation. We know how many of each item we want and we know their costs; we can do two multiplications and add them.

---

2. Soldier action figures cost $3 each. Wrestler action figures cost $1 each. If you had $10, how many of each could you get? Spend all your money; get at least one of each.

Problem 2 presents a situation that is essentially reversed. They have the amount to spend that must be juggled between two different items of different cost. Because the numbers themselves are not formidable and the situation is conceivable, most students from second grade up can conceive of what is going on. They can even handle the constraints of spending all $10 and getting at least one of each.

---

3. Some of the children at a family gathering are thinking about going to the movies. Adult tickets cost $4 and children's tickets cost $2. The people have only $20 among them. At least one adult must go to the movies. How many adults and how many children could go?

We have used this type of problem with third and fourth graders with great success. It is similar to the problem of arranging twenty-six students into groups of three or four. These problems involve the same mathematical idea. The quantities involved must be positive integers. With a little help getting started, especially after using manipulatives and drawings with very simple versions of these problems, students can learn how to create their own tables. Making a table is a more powerful method than using manipulatives or drawing a picture because it can record and organize possibilities and can facilitate using related concepts, such as multiplication.

For instance, after some instruction, a group of fourth graders used the following table for problem 3.

Adults ($4)	Children ($2)	Total ($20)	Solution
5	0	$20	
0	10	$20	
2	8	$24	
1	8	$20	X
4	2	$20	X

In this table, notice that students can see two ways of using up all the money for either all adults or all children. These two are usually seen first if a student has a good concept of multiplication and division. However, the first option (5 adults) would seem contrary to the assumption that it is children who want to go to the movies. The second violates the condition of the problem that at least one adult must go. The third option in the list does not fit with the total amount of money available.

Notice how setting up a column for the total helps the students to check each possibility carefully. Without this column, students may not catch erroneous answers. We also ask them to add a fourth column that requires checking to see if a possible answer fits the conditions of the problem (as the last two do). Therefore, the table facilitates calculation, recording, thinking, and solving. There are other possible answers to this problem; the table can help students find them all.

With help and practice, students can learn to make their tables more systematic. This process should not be rushed. Here is another example:

---

4. Orville was lying in the grass watching a parade of unicycles and bicycles go by. Unfortunately, because of the crowd, he could only see the wheels. He knew that his brother and two friends were in the parade riding their unicycles. Also, his sister and two of her friends were in the parade riding their bicycles. He saw fifteen wheels go by. How many of each kind of cycle might there have been?

A group of third graders solved the problem with the following table.

Unicycles (1 wheel)	Bicycles (2 wheels)	Total wheels	Solution
15	0	15	
14	1	16	
5	5	15	X
0	8	16	
4	6	16	
3	6	15	X
7	4	15	X
9	3	15	X
11	2	15	
13	1	15	

The table helps students work with the numbers involved to discover some patterns such as when one goes up, the other must go down; and you can't have an even number of unicycles because the total (15) is an odd number. Having students discuss or write down these insights is valuable. Notice that the students continued to increase the number of unicycles by consecutive odd numbers. They did mark the last two as solutions until one member of the group pointed out that they had decided that the problem required at least three of each type of cycle. They erased the two Xs.

The following problem is similar to these others, but adds a twist often seen in textbooks.

---

5. Nine children from the baseball team and their coach go for Sloshees after the game. The convenience store only has two sizes of cups left: the small Sloshee for 50¢ and the large for $1. The coach is dieting and doesn't want anything. He only has $6 to spend on the team. How many Sloshees of each size can the team members get?

Problem 5 adds a type of constraint not found in the other problems. If the task were only to juggle the quantities of 50¢ and $1 to get a total of $6, this problem would be like the others: there could be several different ways to satisfy the conditions of the problem. But the added constraint of 9 children on the team limits us to one answer (or perhaps, no answers that will work out evenly). Ironically, this narrowing of possibilities seems to make the problem more difficult.

Many problems of this type in resource books do add this constraint on the solution in order to force one right answer. Obviously, this is not necessary. Multiple solutions to some problems in your curriculum are well advised. Life is rarely so neat and simple.

The following table for problem 5 shows some fourth graders' sophisticated use of a table as a strategy. They started with all 9 children getting a large Sloshee and systematically decreased the number in that column while keeping the total children at 9.

Small Sloshee ($.50)	Large Sloshee ($1)	Total	Solution
0	9	$9.00	
1	8	$8.50	
2	7	$8.00	
3	6	$7.50	
4	5	$7.00	
5	4	$6.50	
6	3	$6.00	X
7	2	$5.50	
8	1	$5.00	
9	0	$4.50	

There are several definite numerical patterns to this table. Because they generated the numbers themselves, the students were able to get a strong grasp on what happens when decreasing the larger amount while increasing the smaller. For instance, one noted that the answer will not have an odd number of small Sloshees because that would produce a total with 50¢ in it.

Did you want to set up an algebraic equation for some of these problems? Did your mind immediately see such a representation? For instance, problem 5 would have two equations:

$$.50x + 1.00y = 6.00 \qquad x + y = 9$$

These are the famous two equations and two unknowns, the simultaneous linear equations of algebra. If you want your students when they're adolescents to be able to understand simultaneous linear equations (as opposed to just crunching out the algorithmic solutions to them), then when they are younger they need the conceptual foundations in meaningful contexts with strategies they understand.

Laying this foundation means more than giving students one or two process problems of this type. It means having them wrestle with a dozen problems that vary in ways like these above, with different meaningful contexts and different kinds of numbers. At first, the students will not realize that the problems have the same essential structure. You will have to illustrate the basic conceptualization of varying two quantities under different conditions.

Let us summarize some of the key aspects of helping students learn how to solve problems with tables and lists.

1. Learning how to make their own tables requires substantial practice. Tables are much more abstract than the other major strategies. However, patient work with tables can yield powerful dividends in understanding.

2. Initially, you must carefully choose problems that are not overly complicated. You may have to provide more structure to students' tables, giving them handouts with the headings and the first few entries. The goal is to help them understand a problem sufficiently to see how its information can be represented in list, or table form and then to be able to create their own. This developmental process comes from working with many examples. Because this strategy is the most complex and abstract of the five major strategies, more examples and more time should be devoted to students' development than with the others.

3. The teacher must help the students learn to create their own formats, structures, and headings. You must give them increasingly more leeway in creating the structure of the table, or list. Students should be allowed to use lists as recording devices and then to see how to reorganize their own lists. Do not be afraid to let students

progress slowly as they increase the degree of structure of their tables.

4. In order to generate many examples of problems to work on, encourage students to create their own problems or modify existing ones. Of course, this kind of creativity is valuable with any kind of problem; yet, the problems that lend themselves to lists and tables (such as the examples in this section) are easy for students to create or modify. They usually enjoy making up their own for others to solve.

5. You should let students share their tables with one another. It is generally better for you to select two or three different tables made by students for the class to consider than to use one from the book that appears excellent, but may be too sophisticated.

5

Five Supplemental
Strategies for
Mathematical Thinking
and Problem Solving

. . . .

Developing Problem-solving Sense

In this chapter we will illustrate the five strategies mentioned earlier that may be used in conjunction with the major problem-solving strategies. Ultimately, we want students to develop what we might call "problem-solving sense," a good feel for various ways of attacking problems based on mathematical knowledge and thinking. With practice, students will readily and smoothly incorporate into their thinking reasoning logically, looking for a pattern, simplifying the problem, guessing and checking, and working backwards.

These supplemental strategies should be introduced after students have had substantial experience with the five major strategies. You as the teacher should arrange activities for students to practice these strategies, to see which are appropriate in various situations, and to become aware of what each are doing and why. Therefore, you may want to choose several problems that readily lend themselves to using these strategies and to model their use, just as we did in the previous chapter with the major strategies. An important difference here is that you can be explicit with students that these are companion strategies. It is really quite difficult for students to use them by themselves.

. . . .

Using Logical Reasoning

In chapter 2 we discussed the centrality of reasoning to mathematical thinking. Here we will illustrate several ways to use deductive reasoning to attack problems. In the next section on looking for patterns, we will be more concerned with using inductive reasoning.

Most problems in previous chapters have relied upon deductive reasoning in some way, carefully and systematically applying an idea to a problem or situation, determining what could be assumed from a set of facts or initial conditions, checking to see that each constraint was honored, and so forth. Some problems quite specifically required that we reason "if this is true, then that must also be true." The following problem uses a familiar structure (the days of the week) to help students understand how a matrix can facilitate logical thinking.

> Five families are going to carpool to and from school next year. From looking at the calendar, it is clear that each of the 5 days in the week is equally represented over the 185 days of school. For various reasons, some days are good and some are bad for each family. But each family wants to have the same day all year long (so they won't get confused or forget). The Jones family cannot do it on Monday, Wednesday, or Friday. The Schnapps can drive Wednesday or Thursday. Monday or Tuesday are possible for the Rambinos. Mr. Grouch can do it on either Thursday or Friday. Wednesday or Friday is fine with the Dawson family. Figure out a schedule for these families.

Figure 5.1 shows how this initial information would be entered into a matrix. Notice that the days of the week should be on the horizontal axis because of our familiar schema for a calendar. Although the days could logically be placed on the other axis, such an arrangement is contrary to students' experience. Tables should facilitate thinking, not interfere with it. The cell entries are the noes (N) not the yeses, because these noes are definite but we have not settled on any definite yeses yet.

The matrix can help one to reason that Rambino must drive on Monday, which requires Jones to be Tuesday. Thereafter, two solutions are possible. If Schnapps drives on Wednesday, then Dawson must drive on Friday and Grouch on Thursday. If Schnapps drives on Thursday, then Grouch must drive on Friday and Dawson on Wednesday.

One marvelous extension of such a problem is for students to create their own scenarios using this problem as a model. They can write a story in which five people must perform some kinds of tasks on five days of the week. Creating possible constraints is the heart of the problem.

You might find it interesting to note how several strategies can be related even when it is not obvious. A matrix can be used to analyze a problem from chapter 4 concerning the faces of a cube. Consider three views of the same cube shown in figure 5.2. Each face has a different

. . . .
Figure 5.1

	Mon	Tues	Wed	Thur	Fri
Jones	N		N		N
Schnapps	N	N			N
Rambino			N	N	N
Grouch	N	N	N		
Dawson	N	N		N	

· ·
Figure 5.2

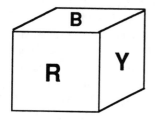 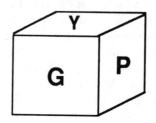 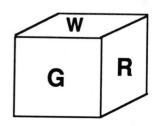

color, denoted by a letter. The problem is to determine what colors are opposite each other. One can record the basic information shown in these three views of the cube in the matrix shown in figure 5.3.

This matrix records if one color can be opposite another. From the three views one can reason that (1) no color can be opposite itself and (2) each view shows three colors which cannot be opposite each other. Therefore no (N) can be entered into appropriate cells in the matrix.

An intriguing feature of the matrix is that the pairing of potentially opposite sides produces a redundancy. That is, if R cannot be opposite B, then B cannot be opposite R. Also, note the diagonal that shows how colors cannot be opposite themselves (the Ns are in parenthesis).

We strongly suggest that you teach this type of matrix to upper-grade students by having them work with all the cells, even though that means double entries. When they are older and highly skilled in such a chart, then they can use only one side, if they choose. See figure 5.4, in which the dashes indicate cells that we can ignore. This matrix requires careful attention to both a row and a column each time one analyzes a particular item.

A careful examination of figures 5.3 or 5.4 reveals the only possible solution. Look down the R column in either figure (or across the R row in figure 5.3). R is not opposite B, Y, G, or W and therefore must be

· ·
Figure 5.3

	R	B	Y	G	P	W
R	(N)	N	N	N		N
B	N	(N)	N			
Y	N	N	(N)	N	N	
G	N		N	(N)	N	N
P			N	N	(N)	
W	N			N		(N)

opposite P. With similar logic, one can determine that Y must be opposite W and G opposite B.

It is important to help students realize that any organized list has its own inherent logical structure that is often like a two-dimensional matrix. For instance, the organized list for finding all the ways to make change for a quarter (in chapter 4) began by conceiving of the greatest number of the largest coin possible: two dimes. The logic used was to start at one end of an imagined continuum (the most of the largest) and hold that constant while checking all possibilities before working down. One could just as readily begin with the most of the smallest (all pennies) and work up.

Venn diagrams can greatly assist students in sorting out muddled or incomplete information. There are many examples of problems in texts and resource books that require the use of Venn diagrams, yet most are remarkably artificial to students. This powerful logic device should be initially taught in conceivable contexts, so that students can get their minds around the facts of the situation and see what is actually going on.

Some curricula give younger students a start on this kind of logic through the use of attribute blocks. If your students have never been exposed to sorting blocks, you may find it profitable to introduce attribute blocks. The usual set of attribute blocks varies in shape (square, triangle, and circle), size (large and small), and color (red, blue, and yellow). Younger children can be asked to sort all the blocks into areas designated by overlapping hoops. For instance, we can pose a specific sorting problem by labeling the areas as shown in figure 5.5. We strongly urge helping students to understand and use the two-circle Venn diagram before presenting them with three circles. Unfortunately, some resource books jump ahead too quickly to three-circle diagrams such as the one shown in figure 5.6.

The language used to describe each of these areas is worth emphasizing. It can help students grasp the logical relationships. Students can be given the problem of sorting the blocks into the appropriate eight areas of the three-circle diagram, after they have clearly shown an understanding of the two-circle diagram.

. . . .

Figure 5.4

	R	B	Y	G	P	W
R	—	—	—	—	—	—
B	N	—	—	—	—	—
Y	N	N	—	—	—	—
G	N		N	—	—	—
P			N	N	—	—
W	N			N		—

Figure 5.5

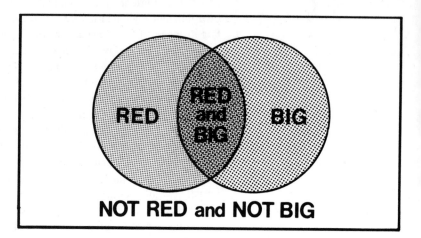

NOT RED and NOT BIG

Figure 5.6

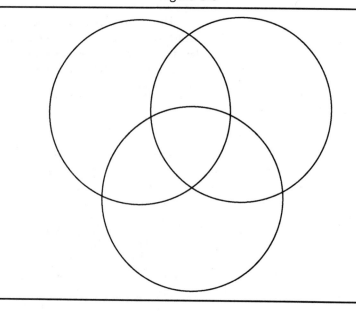

A helpful step in building understanding of the two-circle diagram is for students to make up their own categories for others to use in sorting the blocks. The teacher can quickly tell that a student has not fully grasped the key relationship if he or she concocts inappropriate categories. For instance, if the student suggests that the two circles would be for red and green blocks, the teacher can gently ask, "What blocks would go in the overlap?" Developing the habit of identifying and labeling each area of the diagram helps build understanding.

After students have had experiences with applying the rules others have devised for sorting blocks into the four areas of a two-circle diagram, the teacher can shift from this deductive mode into an inductive one. We have made attribute "blocks" out of brightly colored posterboard and drawn a large, two-circle Venn diagram on a chalkboard. The teacher announces that there is a set of secret rules for sorting the attribute figures that the students can discover by trying out various pieces. In turn, students (or groups) can decide to try a particular figure in one of the four areas by walking to the board and showing where it might go. The teacher answers yes or no. If yes, the teacher puts tape on the back of the figure and places it in that area of the diagram. With students who are just learning the kind of thinking involved in this activity (and with younger students), the teacher should tape the figure into its proper place, even if the answer was no.

When a number of examples have been taped into place, some students will be able to derive the categorical rules inductively. Students who think they have discerned the categories can write the labels for the two circles on a slip of paper. Older students will be able to test hypotheses by selecting specific pieces to try.

S ometimes logical reasoning can be developed within an enjoyable game. Careful reasoning is hard work, yet children will often engage in sustained and rigorous thinking in order to play an enjoyable game. The game of Train Station can start very simply but become as complex as you and your students desire. Train Station always starts with several train cars connected. There is always a beginning and an end of the train. Going from left to right is usually helpful for students. We recommend that students use Unifix cubes to represent the train cars. For instance, a simple train might have two cars (one Red and the other Green):

First Car   Last Car
[R]   [G]

On paper, we could show this initial situation simply as [R][G].

At the train station, a person can change the configuration of cars according to a set of rules, which can be simple or complex. For instance, the following rules are fairly simple (and good ones for students to try as they are learning the game):

1. If a green car is first, you may add a blue car to the end.
2. If a red car is first, you may remove the last car.
3. You may interchange the first and last cars at any time.

Rules 1 and 2 allow you to add (or remove) a particular car to the train only when the cars meet a certain condition. Appropriate cubes should be stuck onto (or taken off) the current train's cubes. Rule 3 allows you to switch the first and the last.

The purpose of the game is for students to learn to make logical, rule-governed transformations, valid and systematic applications of rules, that can change the state of the objects before them. This kind of thinking is a valuable part of many branches of mathematics. The game situation makes the abstractness of this purpose much more concrete and interesting.

The question for the problem-solving activity is: Can this train [R][G] be changed into a different particular train (for instance, [B][R][G]) with these particular rules? The rules should be displayed prominently in the classroom where all can see them. The teacher should provide some examples for each rule so that its meaning is clear to students.

With careful reasoning using objects or charts, students can solve the problem. In this example, they might reason as follows: [R][G]; using rule 3 gives [G][R]; using rule 1 gives [G][R][B]; using rule 3 gives [B][R][G]. ●

A careful record of the rule that was used to transform the train cars at each step allows another person to quickly check to see if this solution is accurate.

In helping students understand the game fully, they should be asked to take this initial train ([R][G]) and determine what other trains are possible with the three rules. After each transformation, have students apply the rules again. Several principles about Train Station emerge: for a given train, some rules cannot be used; sometimes applying a series of rules merely returns one to a previous state; finally, it is possible to eliminate all of the cars.

We are aiming for students to be able to create their own trains and, eventually, their own rules. Obviously, this capability is easier to develop in older rather than younger students. The next step would be for students to select a different starting train (e.g., three cars) and use the same rules. By applying each rule, students can create other trains. Students should choose one to challenge the rest of the class to determine how it could be done. Of course, they should have a written record of the rules applied to each transformation that will lead to the proper train.

When you feel that the students understand how to apply such rules deductively and keep track of the states of trains as they change, then they can experiment with their own rules. Creating rules that can be readily understood by others and unambiguously applied is challenging; it is usually best done in pairs or groups of three students. They will catch one another's illogical creations early enough to avoid time-consuming, wasted effort.

Here are some complex and intriguing rules that older students have created:

- If two cars of the same color are next to each other (adjacent), they may be removed.
- Two red cars at the beginning or end may be replaced by one Blue car.
- A green car that is in between two Blue cars may be removed.
- If a red car is at the beginning, duplicate the remaining cars and add them to the end. Thus [R][G][G][B] becomes [R][G][G][B][G][G][B].
- A certain sequence (e.g., [R][G][B]) anywhere in the train can be replaced by another sequence (e.g., [B][R][G]).

Perhaps the most pertinent features of Train Station for teachers to help students with are the careful attention to details and the specific application of individual ideas. These are important aspects of reasoning, especially of deductive logic. In each of these examples of activities that use logic in mathematical thinking and problem solving, the teacher must be sensitive to differences among students in cognitive development and intellectual habits. Some students may have great difficulty focusing on individual pieces of information and applying them to the situation at hand. What is obvious to the teacher and some students may not be obvious to others. They will need gentle guidance that points out what should be done. Other students may be caustic, rather than gentle, in pointing out the logic behind their thinking unless good norms of cooperation and mutual respect have been established in the classroom.

Many texts and resource books jump too quickly to complex and general forms of problems requiring logic. We have found that students need "staging," a careful building up of specific, narrow examples that lead to the more complicated forms of problems. For instance, in the Train Station game, we start with a limited form of the problem (initial and goal states) and three simple rules (constraints). Although the best thinking comes when students compose their own situations and rules, to start at such a complicated stage would leave most students in the dust. However, working through several stages of complexity to get to the optimal format can be done with all students. Some require more time and more examples than others.

Looking for a Pattern

Mathematical patterns emerge in life and nature in surprising and unusual ways. Geometrical and numerical patterns abound. Students must play with information and materials in order to get the feel for what is going on. Patterns are most evident to students after they have wrestled with examples and carefully contemplated what is before them.

When scientists and mathematicians encounter phenomena in the world how do they conclude what rule or mathematical principle is involved? With induction, tentative hypotheses are considered possible until further notice. On the other hand, if there is an established concept, principle, rule, or theorem that can be applied to the phenomenon, then we can use deductive logic to demonstrate the validity of a conclusion. We should teach students how to use inductive and deductive reasoning to discern patterns in phenomena and problems.

Consider the following problem from a current textbook:

> A miner had struck it rich in his gold mine. In the first week he took 1 wheelbarrow of gold from the mine. The next week he mined 2 wheelbarrows full of gold and the following week, 4. If he continues this way, how many wheelbarrows of gold will he bring out of the mine during the tenth week?

You probably inferred the series 1, 2, 4 . . . What term comes next in the series? Would you say 8? Some students would say 7. Given the actual information in the problem, there is really no way to know with certainty which series is correct. Both are equally likely.

The answer that the textbook provided was 512 wheelbarrows of gold. Students who answered 45 would be disappointed. They reasoned differently from the textbook writer. The principle that underlies the miner's work cannot be determined with certainty. Do the terms double, increasing geometrically (1, 2, 4, 8, 16, 32, 64, 128, 256, 512) or do they add an additional unit each time, increasing arithmetically (1, 2, 4, 7, 11, 16, 22, 29, 37, 45)?

If the problem appeared at the end of a chapter on geometric progressions, most students would calculate 512, without considering other possibilities. They would simply apply deductive reasoning *without really thinking* about the problem. It is more important for students to be thinking, conjecturing, and defending their reasoning, rather than jumping for the most salient explanation.

Consider the situation of a supermarket clerk stacking boxes in a special display. He wants to stack boxes in a triangular tower: 1 on top of 2, 2 on top of 3, as in figure 5.7.

In a real-life situation, we might simply ask, if he has room enough to put 9 boxes along the bottom row, how many boxes will he need altogether? Younger students may need to make the tower, stacking blocks to represent the boxes and then counting them. Others could imagine a simple pattern: 9 + 8 + 7 + 6 + 5

· ·
Figure 5.7

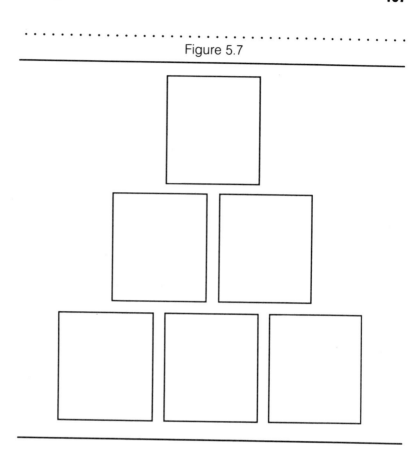

+ 4 + 3 + 2 + 1 = 45. This simple situation can be used to show how an organized list or table could be constructed.

		Total Blocks
Top row	1	1
Second row	2	3
Third row	3	6
Fourth row	4	10
Fifth row	5	15
Sixth row	6	21
Seventh row	7	28
Eighth row	8	36
Bottom row	9	45

What patterns do you see? A tower of blocks would show a concrete representation of the series 1, 3, 6, 10, 15, 21 . . . 45. Many textbooks simply give a series and ask students to give the next number or determine the rule. Often these abstractions are barely meaningful to students. The organized list of what happens with *real objects* allows students to see how the pattern actually works.

If you encourage students to work with objects and phenomena, they will encounter numerical patterns such as this one. There are about a dozen common patterns that pop up frequently. ●

	Total blocks	Difference between rows
Top row 1	1	
		2
Second row 2	3	
		3
Third row 3	6	
		4
Fourth row 4	10	
		5
Fifth row 5	15	
		6
Sixth row 6	21	
		7
Seventh row 7	28	
		8
Eighth row 8	36	
		9
Bottom row 9	45	

Several words of caution are in order. Many resource books have examples of numerical patterns. However, they often require students to fill in tables by calculating without working with objects—a big mistake. Jumping prematurely to symbolic forms without the experiential wherewithal is usually disastrous, because students crank out calculations without really thinking about what they mean. Students are usually willing to look for patterns, and this search becomes most meaningful when they know what the numbers refer to.

Furthermore, some books want students to find the algebraic formula that represents the rule—a great idea when students are ready, but not before. It makes no sense to students when the teacher talks about the "n^{th}" row, some imaginary row in the distance somewhere. Going to the general case with abstract symbols can only make sense after extensive experience with the raw data and developmentally appropriate work with abstract symbols. All these prerequisites take time that is well worth taking.

While we are in the supermarket, let's consider the pattern that emerges when the clerk stacks spherical objects such as oranges. There are several ways he might pile them into pyramidlike stacks. Imagine 3 oranges fitting snuggly together into a triangle. One orange could be placed on top. Another way to support 1 orange would be to fit 4 oranges together into a square (see figure 5.8).

The first question for students to contemplate is, if we created large pyramid stacks in these two ways, how many oranges must be placed underneath these two rows in order to properly support those above? This situation is hard to visualize; physical models are needed.

. . . .
Figure 5.8

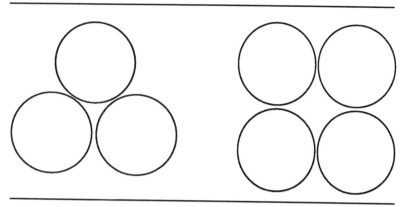

Bring to class a large collection of spherical objects (e.g., tennis balls, golf balls, ping-pong balls, marbles, or actual oranges). To ensure that these piles would stay together and not merely roll away, you will need a "lip" of some kind to hold the bottom row in place (e.g., from books or blocks of wood).

Understanding the numerical patterns of such piles were critically important to the nineteenth-century armies that had to stack cannon balls. They needed to know how many cannon balls could be arranged in these ways for particular heights. When dealing with thousands of such heavy spheres, they did not want to move around any more than were necessary. They could not make the piles too high for a man to lift off the top ball.

When students record their findings from stacking spheres, they may begin to see some patterns, often referred to as the triangular and square numbers.

	Pyramids	
	Triangle	**Square**
Top row	1	1
Second row	3	4
Third row	6	9
Fourth row	10	16
Fifth row	15	25

Each pattern can be readily created in a two-dimensional representation with circular disks (such as pennies). For instance, students can see how 6 pennies form a triangular shape in the same way that 6 oranges in the third row of a stack would. The circles can *represent* the spheres in terms of the key aspect of fitting together a number of them into a triangular or squarelike arrangement.

You can help older students move to yet another representation of these patterns with graph paper, placing circles into adjacent squares to create the square patterns. Isometric paper with equilateral triangles can be used for the triangular patterns.

Ask students to determine how many oranges would be on the bottom of a ten-row pyramid of each shape; the answers are 55 versus 100. Why is there such an incredible difference? How big must the "display table" be to accommodate these piles? Many intriguing questions spin off from the situation. ●

. . . .

Simplifying the Problem

By simplifying a problem, students can sometimes get an essential understanding of the conditions or necessary actions. For instance, sometimes the size or nature of the numbers in a problem intimidate students, thereby obscuring what is going on. Simplifying the numbers by rounding or just making them smaller may help students see the essence of what might be done. Consider the following problem:

> Farmer Brown has 4,656 hogs on his farm. If he sells 97 each day, how many days will it take to sell them all?

Will these numbers distract or deter students from thinking clearly about what is happening in the problem? If so, then they could use comparable but simpler numbers such as 4,700 hogs and 100 sold each day.

You should carefully evaluate potential problems for students and "prune" the numbers to those that won't get in the way of their thinking. There will be ample time to use additional problems later in the month or year that have messy, large numbers that can be best handled by a calculator, *if* the students understand what is going on in the problem.

A major concern for mathematics educators is helping students develop number sense—a feel for numbers, their properties, and relationships. Number sense comes from extensive *positive* experience: familiarity, use, and comfortableness. When students have to work with numbers that are intimidating and inconceivable to them, they cannot develop the conceptual understanding, feeling, and sense that is needed.

Another form of simplification involves examining the simplest case of a situation. When we looked for patterns in stacking oranges, we started with the top of the stack, the initial case with just one item. Then we systematically increased the stack by examining one row at a time. Trying to find out how many are in the tenth row is impossible without seeing the patterns inherent in previous rows. Going back to the beginning, or the simplest case often brings insight. For instance:

> How many handshakes occur between two little league teams of 25 players at the end to the game?

Would students be able to leap to a solution process? Should they act it out with two classrooms? Should they draw a picture with two columns of 25 circles, with one moving up and the other down, lines representing handshakes occurring among these 50 circles?

Instead, encourage them to examine the simplest case. One player per team shakes hands with the opponent (e.g., after a tennis match): 1 shake. Two opposing players (e.g., a double match): 4 shakes. Three opposing players: 9 shakes. Has the essence of what is going on emerged? Four opposing players: 16 shakes. There is a pattern. Focus on one of the teams: each player shakes the hand of every opposing player. Figure 5.9 has one kind of diagram of this situation. Four players per team means there are 4 opponents for each of the 4 players on the team to shake hands with (4 times 4). If the two teams have the same number of players, we would get the square numbers. Now we can go to the particular problem of 25 players per team and confidently state that 25 times 25 or 625 handshakes must occur.

The diagram helps students see that this situation is *not* the same as the handshakes between judges (seen in the previous chapter), wherein

. . . .

Figure 5.9

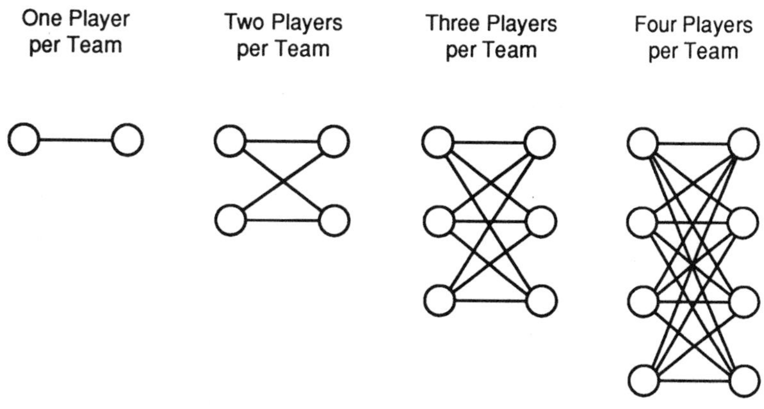

| One Player per Team | Two Players per Team | Three Players per Team | Four Players per Team |

every person shakes the hand of every other person. If all 50 baseball players shook every players' hand, they would be shaking hands with their teammates. In this problem, they are only shaking hands with their opponents. The essence of the problem is different because the relationships among people are different. Consequently, the mathematics is different. Students often zoom in on an apparent similarity (handshakes) without realizing the crucial aspects of the situation at hand.

By returning to the simplest form of the problem, they can see what is actually transpiring more readily than if they tried to go right after the full-blown version of the problem. Granted, some students can see the essence of the situation from a good diagram of the problem as stated. They could make two columns of 25 circles and begin drawing lines to represent handshakes. But would they grasp the multiplicative relationship between the number of players on each side? You can tell if students did truly understand this problem by asking them to determine how many handshakes would occur between two teams, one with 25 players and the other with 30.

Geometrical problems often require simplification in order to realize what is going on and what may be required. In chapter 7 we will illustrate how to work with simple cases and gradually increase the complexity to develop relationships and patterns.

Making a Guess and Checking the Result

If guesses are educated and not wild, they can be very profitable. Educated guesses depend on a good initial understanding of the circumstances of the situation or problem. In the previous chapter, we described the value of discussion to provoke understanding. We illustrated these ideas via Fermi problems that required initial understanding, sound assumptions, and reasonable approximations. Thus, one aspect of making a guess involves mathematical reasoning based on specific assumptions.

For instance, students could consider how much pizza should be ordered for a class party. What assumptions should be made? There will be 2 adults (the teacher and a parent) and 25 students. Will all 27 eat the same amount? Should they assume that some people are heavy pizza eaters and some light? Should we think of the amount that people will eat in terms of slices?

After a brief discussion of such general questions, small groups of students should attack the problem. The most common assumptions and conclusions we've seen are as follows:

- We assume that all people eat about the same amount.
- We assume that we will order large, 16-inch pizzas, to get the best price.

- We assume that each person will eat 4 slices, which is a high estimate to make sure we do not run out of pizza.
- We assume that there are 12 slices in each pizza.

Therefore, 27 people will each eat $\frac{4}{12}$ or $\frac{1}{3}$ of a pizza and we will need 9 large pizzas for the class.

Obviously, altering assumptions will result in a different answer: e.g., 3 slices per person gives $\frac{1}{4}$ pizza apiece, requiring us to buy 7 whole pizzas—no one sells $6\frac{3}{4}$ pizzas.

Another important form of guessing and checking allows students to try to derive an answer and then see how well it fits the conditions of the situation or problem.

A sk students to imagine that before going off to camp in the summer, they take $10 in birthday money to the candy store. They want to buy 14 candy bars, 1 per day for the two weeks at camp. The store has only two kinds of candy bars that they really like: Bone-crushers at 75¢ apiece and Finger-lickers at 50¢ apiece. Assuming there is no tax, how can they spend *all the money*, the full $10, and get 14 candy bars?

If students have done other problems of this general type, they will probably make a table, perhaps even an organized one as we described in the previous chapter. Building upon their experiences, you can help students see that there are two kinds of guesses that are effective in finding a good answer to this problem: trying the extremes and trying the middle. Both have the flavor of saying; what if . . . or what would happen if?

Ask students to see what would happen if they were to try to buy all Bone-crushers for the 14 days? They will find that 14 Bone-crushers at 75¢ apiece would go over their budget ($10.50). Astute students will realize that this total is very close to the amount they have and reason that they can probably get Bone-crushers for nearly every day—maybe 13 of them.

Another good initial guess would be to try the middle (7 of each kind) and check the result. Seven of each would cost $8.75. Students usually do not realize that, because this total is less than what they can spend, they can buy more of the expensive kind (still adhering to the requirement of only 14 candy bars). The teacher needs to help students recognize these key aspects of problems of this kind either in discussion afterward or when introducing the guessing strategy. Of course, in problems in which guessing the middle quantities yields too great a total, then less of the expensive kind must be bought. The next table shows what students find when trying the two extremes and the middle guesses to this problem.

Finger-lickers at 50¢	Bone-crushers at 75¢	Total ($10)	Solution
0	14	$10.50	
7	7	8.75	
14	0	7.00	

Any one of these as an initial guess would help clarify the location of the solution. However, the two top entries do give better clues of the solution than the bottom guess. In any problem, some guesses are closer and more revealing than others. As students develop number sense, they will make better guesses and estimates. In fact, students with fledging number sense, especially for such quantities as 50¢ and 75¢, may need to use all three of these guesses. Getting a fix on what happens at both extremes as well as the middle point is a good approach for most of us when confronting unfamiliar territory. With these three guesses arrayed in the table and space left for subsequent guesses, students might get closer to the solution by guessing 4 and 10, then 3 and 11, then the solution. ●

Finger-lickers at 50¢	Bone-crushers at 75¢	Total ($10)	Solution
0	14	$10.50	
2	12	10.00	XX
3	11	9.75	
4	10	9.50	
7	7	8.75	
14	0	7.00	

The value of guessing in the middle is a good strategy to illustrate with a game called "Number Guesser":

Have a student think of a number between 1 and 100, write it secretly on paper, and have the class try to guess the number. The student merely responds with "too high," "too low," or "that's it" to the guesses. We suggest using this game with small groups of students in a tournament in which each group plays against each other group. The object is not only to guess the number, but to use the fewest guesses to do so.

Some students discover on their own that a good strategy is always guessing the middle. For instance, an initial guess of "50" will tell you which half of the distribution contains the correct number. Guessing the middle again narrows it to either 25 numbers; the next middle guess to either 12 or 13 numbers, and so on. The following table shows a typical game with this strategy being used.

	Guess	Response	Inference (the number is between . . .)
First	50	too low	51 and 100
Second	75	too low	76 and 100
Third	87	too high	76 and 86
Fourth	81	too low	82 and 86
Fifth	84	too low	(it must be 85)
Sixth	85	that's it	

Even when the guess goes a little bit on the "longer" side of the middle, students using a middle guessing strategy should get the number in seven guesses. In a discussion afterwards, the teacher can illustrate why this guessing strategy always works so well by using a table of the first 100 numbers or a centimeter stick and showing the effect of taking successive halves of a distribution. ●

Let's try the middle guess strategy with one more problem for older students.

The toy company has to mail boxes mixed with glass marbles and rubber balls to customers. The marbles and balls are the same size. Each box can hold 50 of these spheres. The glass marbles weigh 2 ounces apiece and the rubber balls weigh 1 ounce apiece. To get the best rate from the post office, each box should hold a total weight of 80 ounces. How should each box be filled with 50 spheres to get the full 80 ounces?

Note the following table that students used with a middle strategy to determine the answer.

	Glass marbles (2 ounces)	Rubber balls (1 ounce)	Total weight (80 ounces)	Solution
First guess	25	25	75	
Second guess	40	10	90	
Third guess	30	20	80	XX

The first guess showed that more of the heavier spheres might be used. The second guess increased the number of the heavier spheres too much. In fact, students often guess the correct answer on the second try because they increase the heavier spheres by five rather than ten. Are these lucky guesses? No, educated guesses, based on a clear sense of what is going on.

. . . .

Working Backwards

In our lives, we encounter a number of situations or problems in which we know what the end result is and want to figure out how to get there. Similarly, in dealing with mathematical problems, students may know what happens and want to reconstruct the antecedents because they did not keep track along the way. Carefully reasoning from the end to what probably occurred at prior steps is not always easy. However, in conjunction with other strategies, students can be helped to appreciate what is required in working backwards.

Students can readily imagine that they want to purchase a toy or some commodity and must earn the money to do so. If a student's weekly allowance is $3 and an additional $5 can be earned about once a month for doing a special chore, how long will it take to save the $68 cost of the toy?

This problem is like the preceding ones in some ways. Some combination of $3 amounts and $5 amounts will be needed. But the $5 can be obtained only once every four weeks. Therefore, for each four week period four $3 and one $5 amount ($17) can be collected. Four of these $17 increments would add up to $68, so 16 weeks would be needed.

If you are familiar with problems in textbooks that ask students to work backwards, you may think that this problem does not sound like working backwards. After all, didn't the students have to add up increments of $17? Consider if the problem had not given the total, but instead had asked: If a child gets $3 per week for an allowance and can also earn $5 each month for doing special chore, how much money can be earned in 16 weeks? Then a multistep translation could simply have reasoned that 16 times $3 is $48 from the allowance. Then 16 weeks divided by 4 gives 4 months; 4 times $5 gives an additional $20, for a total of $68.

Knowing the total that must be worked up to calls for somewhat different reasoning than the multistep translation. We will grant that a sophisticated student could figure out that $17 every 4 weeks could be divided into 68 and the multiplied back times 4. But the logical flow of these two problems is quite different.

Most of the current textbook problems that allegedly teach working backwards are incredibly artificial. They describe situations that students cannot imagine, refer to circumstances that would not happen, or contain information that no one would reasonably know. They are so divorced from life that students do not seriously think about them. For instance, many are of this ilk:

> A sailor is marooned on a desert island with a batch of coconuts. During the first week he ate half of them. In the second week, he ate half of what was left. In the third week, he ate a fourth of what was left. In the fourth week, he ate a third of what was left. In the fifth week, he ate half of what was left. In the sixth week he ate the remaining coconut and was shortly thereafter rescued. How many coconuts did he start with?

The mathematics is quite interesting and the story could be jazzed up a bit to be more interesting: Ben Gunn, Long John Silver, and so on. Nonetheless, students frequently see the illogic here. The sailor must have known how many coconuts he started with. Who would ask such a question? Why all these fractions? The problem becomes a silly riddle, not a meaningful use of mathematics in their lives. Problems such as this should be considered puzzle problems. They are not valueless, but the curriculum must contain many, many good process and authentic problems before one salts in a few puzzle problems. If the curriculum consists primarily of marooned sailors and coconuts, students will dismiss mathematics as insubstantial fodder. (If you are still interested, he started with 16 coconuts.)

A more true-to-life situation for students is trying to determine what score must be obtained on the last test or assignment of a marking period to receive a particular grade in the course. For instance, if you had scores of 72, 85, and 88 on the first three tests, what will you need on the fourth test to get an A in the course? To be assured of a B? Assume that the tests all count the same amount toward the grade and the cutoffs for A and B are 90 and 80, respectively.

Working backwards would mean that an A would require 360 total points (because 360 divided by 4 yields 90). The sum of the first three tests is 245, therfore 115 points would be needed on the fourth test. Unless bonus points are given, you are out of luck. OK, let's go for the B. A minimum of 320 total points would be needed. If 245 have been garnered so far, only 75 more points are necessary to squeak through with a B. You can make this into a very real problem by asking students to take their own scores in some subject and determine what they will need to get the next highest grade (or maintain their current grade).

A final problem for older students requires working backwards with careful attention to antecedent conditions (i.e., What must have occurred earlier in order to produce the consequences)?

Consider a gambler who played blackjack at the casino for three hours and won $125. Upon leaving, he wondered about how many hands he won and lost (or his winning percentage). This situation is quite conceivable. To reconstruct what must have happened, we need one other piece of information and must make an assumption. The gambler placed $5 bets on each hand that night. (For those who know something about blackjack, he never split or doubled-down.) All of his winning hands paid $5 and all losing hands cost him $5. If we assume that each hand took 4 minutes to play, what was his record of wins and losses (or his winning percentage)?

Working backwards, we would reason that if he won a total of $125, then he must have won 25 more hands than he lost. This is a critical and subtle point. If he played for three hours (180 minutes) with each hand taking 4 minutes, he must have played 45 hands. Students could make a table to examine how 45 hands could be split up between winning and losing in order to find the only case where there were 25 more winning hands than losing: 35 wins and 10 losses or 77 percent winning hands (35 of 45)— an incredible run of luck.

Notice two tricky places where students can get stuck by reasoning badly. At the very beginning, some may quickly jump to the conclusion that he played 25 hands and won them all. Yet winning $125 at $5 per hand would only tell them the difference between winning and losing. This is the key "looking backwards" from the end result to antecedent conditions. The other difficulty often comes when they determine that 45 hands had been played. Some rush to conclude that there were 25 wins and 20 losses. They focus on the 25 wins, forgetting that there were 25 more wins than the losses.

Once they grasp what is going on in this problem through a careful breakdown of the steps in reasoning, students can consider what other outcomes might have occurred to the gambler. How might those 45 hands come out? What would the high and low ends have been? All losses would have been $225 gone and the reverse for all wins. Could he have broken even? Not with an odd number of hands. If the hands went 23 to 22, he would have lost or won only $5. ●

Integrating Strategies into the Curriculum

These supplemental strategies can be blended together with the five major representational strategies in powerful ways. We suggest that you give students specific help to learn what is entailed in each strategy, what kinds of thinking are involved, what actions might be taken. Then students should have ample practice with problems that can help them develop a good feel for each. After such initial assistance, they should be encouraged to use combinations of strategies in solving problems.

The crucial aspect of helping students learn to use these strategies is providing experiences that relate mathematical thinking and concepts. In the following three chapters, we will examine various areas of the curriculum through a problem-solving orientation. As we pose problems that you might use with your students, please notice how these various strategies can be used to bring out the important concepts and ideas as well as to generate rich mathematical thinking.

6

Numbers and Measurement

· ·

Problem Solving and Computation

The purpose of this chapter is to illustrate how a problem-solving approach can teach mathematical concepts and thinking in the curricular areas of numbers, measurement, computation, estimation, computational geometry, statistics, and the like. For many students, problem solving is synonymous with reading a story problem, figuring out what arithmetic operation(s) to perform, and doing the appropriate paper-and-pencil calculations to get the exact answer.

In contrast, mathematics educators now are calling for a dramatic broadening of how we view computation. When confronting a problem or situation, we want the student to make some intelligent, strategic decisions concerning computation. The first step is understanding the nature of the problem or situation. The problem may not require computation at all. Students should ask themselves: If the problem does call for working with numbers, is an exact answer required? Will an estimate or approximation suffice? Should one estimate high to ensure that enough material is obtained (as in wallpaper or pizza)? Is there a range of acceptable possibilities? The Fermi questions posed in chapter 4 emphasized formulating assumptions that help students slow down and truly understand what is going on in a problem.

If a student decides that the problem or situation calls for an exact answer, then he or she must make further decisions. Can I work with these numbers in my head? Will I need to use a paper-and-pencil algorithm to calculate the exact answer? Are the numbers so large or cumbersome that I should use a calculator to find the exact answer? What students conclude about these questions will depend on their facility at calculating, their number sense, their operation sense, and their knowledge of appropriate procedures and algorithms.

For instance, consider a translation problem of how much money would be required to buy 11 students each a dessert costing $1.30. For some students, this is not even a good problem because obvious computation is involved. Others, after some thought, might determine an appropriate strategy would be to add 11 $1.30s. Those who realize that their knowledge of multiplication could be used may still vary considerably in their ability to do the computation. Some might use the standard paper-and-pencil algorithm to calculate the exact answer. Others with a shaky grasp of this algorithm (but knowing that multiplying 11 times $1.30 is appropriate) would get the exact answer by using a calculator. Still others (a few) might be able to do the exact calculation in their heads via mental arithmetic (e.g., 11 times $1.30 is the same as 10 times $1.30 plus another $1.30, or $13.00 plus $1.30, which equals $14.30).

Therefore, we can distinguish among these various forms of computation: estimation, mental arithmetic, paper-and-pencil algorithms, and use of calculators (or computers). Learning *how* to do each well is very important; learning *when* to do each is equally important.

Problem-solving activities can be the vehicles for students to build proficiency in *each* of these forms of computation. At the same time, the teacher must also give serious attention to developing a strong sense of numbers and operations, and of a host of vital concepts. Problem-solving activities can also be the major vehicle for building number and operation sense and for understanding concepts.

. . . .

Computational Estimation

In computational estimation, rather than calculating the exact answer, students must grasp the basic idea of the quantities and actions involved and make some judgments. For instance, if we wanted to buy 3 skirts that each cost $28, how much money would we need (excluding tax)? We might make the following estimate: 28 times 3 is about 30 times 3, which is 90. A strong grasp would be that since we used 30 instead of 28 (and 30 is a little bigger than 28), the estimate of 90 is on the high side (28 times 3 is a little less than 90).

In many situations in life, such approximations are more useful than actual calculations. Of course, these estimates must be done well. In our example, using 20 instead of 28 is a bad choice; it is too far away. Why did we pick 30? First, it is close to 28. Second, it is an *easy* number to work with in this situation. There is a set of excellent handbooks for grades 6 through 8 on computational estimation (Reys et al. 1986). These books illustrate several quite different strategies for estimation appropriate for various situations.

In problem solving, estimation can be an excellent way for students to determine the reasonableness of an answer they obtain. For example, consider the following translation problem:

Sally sees a dress in the store that she wants to buy. Its price is $86.99, which she cannot afford. One week later she sees a sign on the store window stating that all merchandise is 25% off. What is the new price of the dress?

To obtain the exact answer requires some rather tedious multiplication or a calculator. Textbooks are filled with such translation problems. We suggest that if you want the students to calculate the exact answer, that you first require them to estimate an approximate answer. In this problem, the estimation strategy of using compatible numbers could be used in the following manner. The original price is about $88. A reduction of 25% is the same as one-fourth. One-fourth of $88 is $22, which is subtracted from $88 to give a sale price of about $66.

Why choose 88, why not 80 or 90? In thinking about what is going on, realizing that you'll be dividing by 4 suggests that you should choose an approximation for the original price that is an obvious multiple of 4 (a compatible number) so that the division can be done easily. Although 90 is an even number and a multiple of ten, it does not readily lend itself to being divided by four. On the other hand 80 does, as does 84 and 88. Since 88 is the closest to the original price of $86.99, that is the best value to use.

Estimation is a process of *thinking* that helps students conceive of what is going on. It asks students to suspend exact calculation until they understand the conditions and the goals of the problem. Making the numbers easier to work with allows them to conceive of the problem. In some respects, it is like the strategy of simplifying the problem.

Unfortunately, after three or four years exposure to traditional mathematics curricula, students believe that the real goal of the math game is to get the correct, exact answer. This estimation business is only for those pages in the text titled "Estimation." The rest of the time, it is the exact answer that counts.

Our experience with children has been that it usually takes several years of teachers who value estimation and really emphasize it before students will habitually use estimation strategies in their own problem solving. Estimation can be a key metacognitive process for understanding and problem solving; we must develop its use in our students.

There are four major ways to build estimation into a problem-solving program that will establish a strong conceptual understanding of what it is for students and how it helps them:

1. Help them see the difference between mental arithmetic and estimation by doing both with them.
2. Illustrate various strategies for estimation and have them practice them with real problems, not merely drill exercises.
3. Require that every translation problem in the textbook be attacked via estimation before formal calculations. Have students write down the thinking they did in order to estimate. They can then do the calculations and find the exact answers. Using calculators for intricate computations is just fine.
4. Absolve students of calculating the exact answers. Just because the textbook page states that students should find the exact answer to a problem, doesn't mean that you have to require them to do so.

With extensive practice at estimating, students will develop the mental habits of trying to understand what is going on in any type of problem and estimating answers before calculating.

Number Sense

Children experience quantities in their lives well before school. Yet continual school experiences with quantities are essential to build the conceptual basis of understanding needed for computational mathematics. Manipulatives are fun, but not just for fun; they are truly building blocks for concepts. The early grades must provide experiences with physically counting concrete objects, sorting, classifying, and so forth. Arranging real entities into groups of ten is essential for developing a true understanding of base ten and place value. Grouping and regrouping quantities of sticks, counters, or cubes can help students see fundamental aspects of number. Excellent problem-solving activities with manipulatives that introduce concepts of quantity and enhance initial understanding can be found in the *Mathematics Their Way* materials (Baratta-Lorton 1985).

Working with objects can also help build a sense of the relative magnitudes of numbers. With pegboards and a large quantity of "pegs" (e.g., golf tees or Lite Brites) teachers can demonstrate some key concepts with fairly large numbers. A pegboard sheet of 4 feet by 8 feet can accommodate over 4,700 pegs of some kind. We have also had children work with a "penny-board." We glued horizontal strips of plastic molding for panelling on to a pegboard. The molding had slots into which one could slide pennies. We posed the question: How many pennies can be slid into the molding strips? A bizarre yet compelling question for children. After estimating, they get to slide them in and count. Children rarely get to play with and see thousands of pennies arrayed before their eyes. They usually estimate far too low.

Students need such experiences to get a feel for how much a hundred or a thousand is, or that 52 is about half of 100, or that 97 may seem large compared to 3 but small when compared to 1,000.

There is at least one tricky aspect for the teacher to consider in arranging problems that deal with quantity. "Pure quantity" refers to the number of actual objects, but numbers can also refer to measuring units. Children are exposed to some measures prior to school, most commonly to linear measures like inches and feet. To what extent have they developed deep conceptual understanding of linear measurement? Carefully selected problem-solving activities can help students develop conceptual understanding of particular kinds of measurement and standard units.

If your students have had some initial experiences with various units of measure, there are sets of unusual "problems" called "ThinkerMath," which Greenes, Schulman, and Spungin (1989) have put together for Grades 3–4, 5–6, and 7–8. The format is always the same: a paragraph of three or more sentences describes a situation in which numbers are used. However, blanks have been inserted where the numbers should be and the numbers are jumbled off to the side of the page. The problem is to fit the numbers where they belong. Here is an example that we made up by adapting a real newspaper article.

The Second Edition of the *Oxford English Dictionary* has been published recently. If you have $_____ , you can pick up the dictionary's _____ volumes, numbering _____ pages, and defining _____ words. The set weighs _____ pounds and occupies _____ feet of shelf space.

Insert the following numbers in their proper places:

4   20   137   2,500   21,728   616,500

Note how determining where the six numbers fit requires a good sense of relative magnitude of these numbers as well as "measurement sense" for weight and length. The increase of volumes, pages, and words can be logically inferred. The correct order for inserting the numbers is: 2500; 20; 21,728; 616,500; 137; 4.

Enjoyable, experiential, problem-solving activities for children can really involve food and candy (two important schemata in their lives). Many resource books suggest counting, graphing, and estimating activities involving candies such as M&Ms, Skittles, Reese's Pieces, and Lifesavers. The essence of these problems involve the variations in quantities of the different colors that can occur in packaging. Small bags (or rolls) can be bought for each student to use. Students can make tables to represent the data from their own bag in a variety of ways. For instance:

Have each student make a simple bar graph with squares cut from construction paper of comparable colors to the candies or with sticky square-shaped labels. One colored square represents one piece of candy.

To help younger students make the transition from the concrete candies to the graphical representation, you can ask students to line up their candies on their desks by color in vertical arrays. Then students should make their own bar graphs that copy this array by gluing the individual squares into columns on paper. For younger students, this one-to-one correspondence between the concrete objects and the squares of the bar graph is very necessary. It is a transitional step to the more abstract bar graph in which graph paper is used. ●

Charting and graphing a variety of phenomena are fascinating to children of all ages. Younger students love to see giant bar graphs that show almost anything they know about: how many of them were born in each month; how many of them like which flavor of ice cream the best; the list is almost endless.

Using color coding on bar graphs is a very powerful device to focus attention and facilitate analysis. In chapter 4, we mentioned a class collecting data on their own beverage consumption (especially soda pop). These data could be charted and color coded in many different ways. After the students have had some guided experience with making tables, charts, and graphs, you should let them take raw data and work in small groups to create their own graphic representation of the data. This is a marvelous opportunity to allow for the creative extension of what they know.

A somewhat different kind of graph involves two different quantities, one on each axis. Consider the following activity for younger students that can build their understanding of such a representation of information:

Provide each student with a small box or bag of some food or candy that are all the same color (e.g., red hots, raisins). Students remove the candy from the box and carefully separate them. This time they need only count how many pieces were in the box. Because pieces vary in size, there will be some variation in the totals in each box.

First, record how many pieces each student has. Ask the students what they might conclude from this information. Then ask them to discuss in pairs or small groups how they might *organize* this information to help them see more clearly what might be concluded. Students will probably come up with some kind of list that groups the students who found the same number of pieces, perhaps even ordering these groups by the number of pieces, as in the table in figure 6.1.

Ask the students to work in pairs to create a bar graph of this information. Provide graph paper, but allow them to try to discover a representation that they think makes sense. When they have finished, ask them to show their graphs to other students and explain why they did it that way. Finally, have each group describe their graph and what they learned from sharing it with others. Both

. . . .

Figure 6.1

Number of pieces in the box	Number of students with that many
36	1
35	0
34	2
33	4
32	8
31	9
30	3
29	1

Numbers and Measurement

Figure 6.2

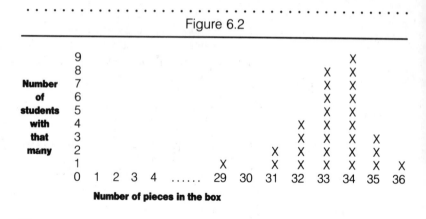

Number of students with that many

Number of pieces in the box

axes on the graph must be carefully labelled. The scales must be clear to others.

Figure 6.2 is the traditional way to array this information in bar graph form. Once students fully understand the conventional format of the bar graph in figure 6.2, they can be led directly into the type of graph in figure 6.3. The issue is to change from bars or squares on the horizontal axis to lines. Large graph paper is helpful to show the basic "number line" that is used for the number of pieces, just as a vertical number line has been used for the number of students. Then a point on the chart means the intersection of two lines, each representing a quantity from one of the scales.

This kind of frequency chart is very common in newspapers and magazines. It is well worth understanding. Because it requires plotting points that correspond to two numerical values on perpendicular axes, it can help build the foundation for upper-grade work with coordinate graphs and functions. ●

Figure 6.3

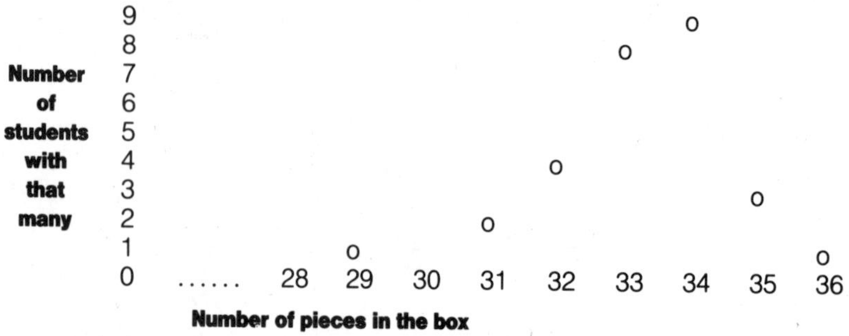

Number of students with that many

Number of pieces in the box

. . . .

Part/Whole Relations

Students cannot develop true understanding of part/whole relations and the varied conceptualizations of mathematics (fractions, decimals, and percentages) without extensive use of concrete manipulatives. Fortunately there is a vast reservoir of colorful and engaging manipulatives available through catalogs and suppliers. Many companies also publish handbooks with problem-solving activities for their manipulatives.

Most students have developed a rich schema for money. Most are strongly motivated to understand how coins and paper bills "work." They have many experiences out of school that build a sense of equivalence (e.g., two nickels equal a dime, and so forth). Their schemata offer fertile ground for building concepts in our base ten system and part/whole relations.

Every elementary school teacher should obtain a quantity of play money, coins and bills. Students should be required to exchange various denominations of coins and bills for equivalent amounts as well as make change for hypothetical purchases. Let's go several steps farther.

Our natural language tells us much about parts of a dollar. If one dollar is the "whole" quantity, then students should discuss why we use common labels like quarter and half dollar. Even dime and cent suggest what part of a dollar they constitute.

After dealing with equivalences and change, ask students to work only with bills of $100, $10, and $1. Every time they do an addition or subtraction problem with dollars, they can model it with these specific quantities of these bills. For instance, having $137 means having 1 one-hundred-dollar bill, 3 ten-dollar bills, and 7 one-dollar bills. Give groups of young students these bills. Have them write down how many of each they have in that order. Then have them actually take away $28. After several such experiences, have them write down the written symbols by which we record what is happening when 1 of the ten-dollar bills must be exchanged for 10 one-dollar bills.

In a similar fashion students should be introduced to decimal fractions though extensive hands-on activities with one-dollar bills, dimes, and pennies. Their money schemata provide a good opportunity for conceptual understanding of the base-ten decimal system. One hundred pennies is the same amount as one dollar. Ten pennies are the same amount as one dime. A teacher can weave descriptions among representations of physical money and the language of natural fractions ("This dime is one-tenth of a whole dollar because ten of them make a dollar"). Then these same manipulatives can be used in various transactions similar to those with bills. Take 28¢ away from $1.37 (1 dollar bill, 3 dimes, and 7 pennies). Finally, the symbols system for recording these transactions can be shown, complete with decimal point, which quite sensibly marks the place where bills are separated from coins.

A tragic mistake that many textbooks make is forcing students into dealing with three decimal places before they have grasped what one or two mean. We strongly suggest experiential activities with dimes and pennies to establish a clear reality of two places simultaneously and not dealing with three decimal places for a long time.

When two decimal places are well grounded in their experience and understanding, we introduce the third place through a problem such as the following:

I magine that two poor carpenters find a small sack with 7 dimes and 7 pennies on the ground on their way home from work. In desperate need for money, they want to divide the money equally between them. What can they do? Students can determine that six of the dimes can be divided, three apiece, six pennies, three apiece, and one dime can be somehow exchanged for ten pennies to be divided five apiece. But what about the remaining penny? All possible answers that involve waiting for another penny to appear or discarding the extra penny must be rejected. At long last, someone (or you, the teacher) will realize (or can suggest) that being carpenters, they would always need nails. Coincidently, you happen to have small nails (brads) that are sold ten for a penny.

Now we enter into another round of situations and problems wherein students must wrestle with the meaning of the brads. If ten brads are worth one penny, how many are worth one dime? How many brads constitute one whole dollar? You have introduced into their schemata a concrete representation for *one-thousandth* that is linked to their powerful base-ten, decimal, money schemata. ●

Thereafter, you can initiate activities in which they must make "change" for parts of a penny with brads. And brads become the concrete reality for the third decimal place in the written symbolization.

We have found that these activities complement other manipulatives that are well suited for fractions of tenths, hundredths, or thousandths such as cubes. However, the base-ten money manipulatives, including bills, dimes, pennies, and brads, provide a strong transfer to the written symbol system.

. . . .

Operation Sense

The *Standards* makes it quite clear that the arithmetic operations of addition, subtraction, multiplication, and division are *concepts*. It is dysfunctional for children to memorize "math facts" without developing elaborate schemata and conceptual understanding through experiences. Just as working with concrete objects facilitates the development of number sense, manipulating materials builds knowledge of relationships that is essential for operation sense—a real feel for what is happening when we add, subtract, multiply, or divide. Solid conceptual understanding of these operations with whole numbers is a prerequisite for being able to see what happens when the quantities are parts of the whole.

Consider the following problem-solving activity as one of many that will build up students' conceptions of multiplication and division. This activity uses pegboards (a 4-by-8-foot sheet, cut into three smaller sheets 4-by-2⅔feet), pegs, sets of Unifix cubes, and a large quantity of small objects (such as pennies or bingo chips).

Arrange the students into nine small groups of 3 or 4. Have nine tables or desks set up around the room (e.g., three in each of three corners). In one corner, each of the three tables should have piles of 40 pennies or chips. In another corner, three tables each have 48 Unifix cubes. The other three tables each have 36 pegs. Near these last three tables (perhaps on the tray of the chalkboard) are the three pegboard sheets.

Each group goes to one of the nine tables and is told that there are three tasks to perform: (1) finding all the ways they can arrange the pennies into piles that have the same amount, (2) finding all the ways to arrange the cubes into stacks of equal height, and (3) finding all the ways to arrange the pegs into rows and columns that make rectangles or squares. You should demonstrate each of the three tasks with a smaller amount of items such as 12. Distinguishing rows and columns may be new and tricky for students; therefore, explanations and examples are crucial.

Tell them that each group will get a chance to try all three tasks. At each table are recording sheets set up with two columns. These sheets are clearly labeled for pennies (Piles and Number in Each Pile), for cubes (Stacks and Number in Each Stack), and for pegs (Rows and Columns).

Allow anywhere from five to ten minutes per task. It is OK to have all groups move to the next task, even if the recording sheets are not fully completed. All nine groups should move in unison; probably clockwise around the room. Each group should tackle its second task and use the new, appropriately labeled recording sheet. When given enough time, they can all move to the third and final task. You will probably note that each task seems to take the groups a bit less time. ●

In the postactivity discussion, you can ask some open-ended initial questions to explore what they saw as differences among the tasks. For instance, Which task was the easiest? The hardest? Why? What were some similarities among them? Some differences? Many students will not immediately realize that the three tasks are essentially the same because the three contexts exert a powerful pull on their minds. Discussing the basis of similarity is important.

Then you can go into a more formal discussion of each task, asking each group to report in turn on one possibility they had found. You can go through the pattern for each task (36, 40, and 48) on the board. Usually some students will have noticed the patterns while doing the tasks and suggested to the group that they just write down the possibilities instead of doing them physically (or they could do a physical check). You should order answers to help students see the pattern of factors, flips, and so on. Also note that 36 pegs will form a square when using 6 rows and 6 columns.

In this discussion, you can emphasize how multiplication and division are related because the students have just had a powerful and very concrete experience with the operations in three somewhat different forms. These tasks can be repeated with different numbers.

· ·

Units and Measuring

Length (distance or linear measure) is encountered directly and frequently by students. Ask students to brainstorm with you all the terms we use to measure distance, length, height, width, and so on. Write their ideas on the board.

Students will likely suggest some of the ancient or poetic measures (such as cubit) or context-specific measures (such as hand, furlong, fathom, and parsec). It is amazing what students have read or watched. These units are worth discussing in their contexts. Who uses the unit furlong?

Instead of a single list of terms and equivalent units, ask students to sort these terms into three groups: traditional English units, metric units, the other more unusual units. Then ask them to try to order each list from smallest to largest without worrying about equivalences.

Using a standard measure can only be appreciated after exploring relative length. The need for establishing standards can be demonstrated readily by asking students to measure the length or width of the classroom in "baby steps." How many "feet" long is the room? Since shoe sizes or lengths of feet will vary, different numbers will occur. You will get a wonderful reaction if you next show them a baby's shoe and ask: How many of these will it take to measure the room? Ask each student to write down an estimate. Let them handle the baby shoe, hold it next to their own shoes, and so forth. Will all students immediately realize that there must be more of these baby shoes than their own? If some do not, you will know that you need to do more work with equivalences (e.g., one dollar in pennies is the same amount as one dollar in dimes, but there are more pennies because each one is a smaller amount than a dime). Discussing how to measure a room with shoes/feet can lead into an appreciation for the standardization of the length "foot." ●

The metric system requires experiential work, measuring a wide variety of distances (lengths, heights, and so forth). Students should work with centimeters and meters to build a strong feel for these distances. Although we do not believe that you should ask them to convert between metric and English, if they have established a clear sense of inches, feet, and yards, they can estimate that a yard is a little smaller than a meter and centimeter is a bit smaller than half an inch.

Why has this country so mightily resisted changing to the metric system? Perhaps there are many reasons. Nonetheless, there is one unit of metric measure that students have a very clear conception of—the liter (or more specifically, two liters). The popular, double-liter container of soda has established a strong experiential basis for this quantity. It will probably take an equivalent amount of sustained contact with other concrete objects in their lives before children grasp other units of metric measure.

The following activity reveals how students conceive metric distance.

P rovide a handout that asks students individually to estimate in *centimeters* the following features of their faces:

- Height of your face.
- Width of your face (roughly from ear to ear).
- Distance between your two eyes.
- Width of each eye.
- Length of your nose.
- Width of your nose.
- Width of your mouth.
- Distance from your nostrils to your lips.
- Length of your ears.

Estimates must be written in ink so they cannot be changed. When students have made these estimates, they each are given a sheet of drawing paper and a centimeter measure and must draw a face based on the measurements they listed. Reassure the students that the drawing need not be artistic but must accurately use the figures they estimated. Amusing drawings and lively discussions will result.

Finally with a partner's help, each student uses the centimeter measure to determine the actual measurements of these lengths and records them next to their estimates. In a follow-up discussion you can ask which lengths were most off, by how much, and why.

If you believe that your students would be overwhelmed by the complexity of drawing facial features for this activity, you can give them a handout with these features already drawn. They need only cut them out and glue them on paper after measuring the appropriate lengths. ●

Students also encounter the phenomena of weight fairly early. However, unlike linear measures, weight (or more technically, mass) cannot be directly seen; it must be felt. Accurate and sensitive measurement of weight or mass requires careful use of delicate instruments. However, more approximate measures can help build an experiential base.

A two-pan balance scale is a worthwhile and versatile device for the classroom. With it, students can measure various objects in terms of other objects or standard measures, if available. For instance, several excellent activities from the AIMS project (Activities Integrating Mathematics and Science) use plastic teddy bears as the standard unit of weight. Recall the activities that weighed peanuts and their shells. A teacher could ask: How many teddy bears do the shells weigh? For a catalog, write to AIMS, P.O. Box 8120, Fresno, CA 93747.

A good exploration is the interrelation of weight and sizes of a number of common objects. Television shows often have villains requesting money in "small, unmarked bills." How big would a million dollars be in one-dollar bills? Could you lift it? Ask your students to think up other similar situations. ●

When we ask about size of such objects, we address volume in some form. Ask students to consider a question like, How many showers would it take to fill your swimming pool? Liquid volume or capacity puts a slight twist on the relation of size and weight. Then students encounter the confusing notion of ounces that measure weight and ounces that measure liquid volume. How can we sort out these issues?

Let's start with a notion of volume that builds on the concept of area. If students have been helped to develop a solid, experiential basis for measuring linear distance and then area in square units, the next step is conceiving of space in cubes. Here is a sample activity.

G ive students 16 cubes of the same color. Ask them to describe what a cube is. What are its essential features? They could use Multi-link cubes as long as they realize that the connecting links are irrelevant; we are focusing only on the cube. Their task is to take the 16 cubes home and create a single building with all sixteen. Any architectural style is permissible; it can have towers and turrets. The only criterion is that it must be a single structure. One advantage to Multi-link cubes is that students can create a building that will stay together when they bring it in to school on the following day.

In the next class, ask students to determine the *surface area* of their own building. Make a table on the board of the different areas. Determining surface area by counting the visible squares is a bit more tricky than it sounds. It requires keeping careful track of which squares have been counted. In addition, should one count the squares on the bottom of the building? Is the bottom a surface? Many students will say no. Surface seems to imply exposed to the air. A good way to facilitate the discussion is to have ready a building that can be easily turned to sit on several different bases (e.g., a rectangular solid). Through this example, you can help students see that just as a single cube has six faces, we must look from all six directions at the surfaces of these buildings.

Which buildings have the smallest surface area? Which have the largest? The more tightly packed together the 16 cubes are, the smaller the surface area. Remind the students that the volume stays the same because we always are dealing with 16 cubes.

Next, ask students to pack the cubes together tightly into rectangular solids. Find as many as they can, recording their dimensions on the board. There are three possible solids: $16 \times 1 \times 1$, $8 \times 2 \times 1$, and $4 \times 2 \times 2$. What are their surface areas? What patterns do they see? Notice how the three dimensions always multiply to 16. Multiplication does not apply only to two numbers. Stand these solids up as towers and ask students to determine how many cubes are on the bottom *layer* of each? Note how multiplying the length times width can give the total, just as in area. How many cubes are in the next layer? And so on. How many layers are there? Therefore, multiplying the three dimensions together gives the total cubes involved. That is the power of multiplication.

Also notice that as the rectangular solids come closer to a large cube, the surface area decreases. To see this pattern and the multiplication effect even more clearly, give an additional 20 cubes to each group of students. Ask them to find all the rectangular solids with 36 cubes. There are seven: $36 \times 1 \times 1$, $18 \times 2 \times 1$, $12 \times 3 \times 1$, $9 \times 4 \times 1$, $6 \times 6 \times 1$, $9 \times 2 \times 2$, $6 \times 3 \times 2$, and $4 \times 3 \times 3$. Check their surface areas.

Using this activity as a base, you can ask students to determine how many of these cubes it would take to fill various rectangular solids. You could provide various small boxes. Students should use the cubes as a measuring unit and get approximate answers. Thus, the boxes do not have to have a perfect fit with the cubes. If students have understood the multiplication principle for three-dimensional measuring, they will not need to fill these boxes, merely measure about how many cubes would be needed for each dimension. It is helpful to show a clear plastic box that can be filled with cubes and then demonstrate measuring the outside dimensions as well.

Once again you and students arrive at the question of a standard measure for volume. Students can use a cube that is 1 unit in each dimension: a centimeter, inch, foot, meter, etc. It would be very advantageous to provide students with some of these standard cubes, especially a cubic centimeter and a cubic inch. It is also helpful as a follow-up activity to tape together six heavy cardboard sheets, one foot square, to make a cubic foot. How many of these will it take to fill the classroom? That is, what is the volume of the classroom in cubic feet? Having several of these unit measuring cubes will be instructive. Of course, students can take the linear measurements of the room also. Round off to the nearest foot to get the approximate volume.

Ask students if they would like to determine the volume of the room in cubic centimeters or cubic inches. Why not? A principle worth getting the feel for is that units of measure should fit the approximate size of what we are measuring. Why get into gigantic numbers when using a larger *standard unit* will keep the numbers manageable? Older students might want to do the actual computations on a calculator of the cubic centimeters in a room. ●

This sense of volume and working in three dimensions can help older students answer the question: How big is a ton of bricks? How big is one brick and how much does it weigh? Then figure out how many of these bricks would make a ton? With the number of bricks in mind, how might these be stacked in three dimensions to make a rectangular solid? Keep all the bricks positioned in the same direction, then consider the three different dimensions of a single brick.

For example, if you brought in a brick that weighed 5 pounds, then a ton of these bricks (2,000 pounds) must consist of 200 bricks. Ask students to imagine arranging 200 bricks in layers; how might this be done? One of many ways would be 5 layers, each with 40 bricks. A layer of 40 bricks might be placed in a rectangle 5 bricks long and 8 bricks wide. What would the dimensions of such a rectangular solid be? If each brick were $2 \times 4 \times 8$ inches, the rectangular solid made of bricks would measure $10 \times 32 \times 40$ inches. Therefore, a ton of bricks is roughly 1 foot high, 3 feet long, and 3 feet wide.

How would various strategies help here? Would a model of these bricks made with Legos help students see what must be done? Would a picture that showed the dimensions of the bricks on the bottom layer help? How about a chart of the three dimensions of the bottom layer?

Finally, let's consider the puzzling coincidence of "ounces." How many ounces in a pint? How many ounces in a pound? If fluid ounces refer to liquid volume, why aren't they cubic something, like other measures of volume? This is one of the many marvels of the English language and probably a good reason we should switch to the metric system. If we search various reference books we find that one ounce is equal to 1.804 cubic inches. This obscure fact would make one gallon about 230 cubic inches, or about $4 \times 6 \times 10$ inches. No wonder this fact has been kept a secret for years. In contrast to this English system, the metric system is remarkably sensible.

Bring to class some empty, clear double-liter containers. Obviously, one liter is half this amount. This is the standard measuring unit for liquid volume. You may recall that metric measures for units smaller than the standard decrease in powers of ten with the prefixes deci-, centi-, and milli-. That is, a deciliter is one-tenth of a liter, a centiliter would be one-hundredth of a liter, and a milliliter is one-thousandth of a liter. When measuring distance, we usually think of meters and centimeters, although millimeters are sometimes used for very small distances.

Here is the curious fact that relates these measures. One cubic centimeter *equals* one milliliter; they both measure volume. To drive this fact home to students, showing that mathematical measures do make sense, try the following. Through one of the various catalogs, buy a number of milliliter measures. Some larger ones (1 liter or 500 milliliters) come in the shape of a hollow cube; the students should measure the dimensions. Other smaller milliliter measures are shaped like spoons. Students should compare the 1-milliliter spoon to a one-centimeter cube. If the cube were hollow, it would exactly hold the contents of this 1-milliliter spoon.

Ask students to estimate how many of these 1-milliliter spoons it will take to fill the empty soda containers halfway (i.e., one liter). Mark one bottle at the halfway point. Have ten groups of students each pour 100 of these milliliters into 10 containers. When finished, pour these 10 into the marked container. They should come up to the half-filled mark—1,000 milliliters or 1 liter.

Ask students to pour this 1 liter of water from the cylinder bottle into the 1 liter cube to ensure that it is the same amount. Then ask students to estimate how many of the 1 centimeter cubes it will take to fill the 1 liter cube. One liter the size of a cube is 10 centimeters on each side (1,000 cubic centimeters). Have them try it. These actions will greatly facilitate the equivalences. ●

To round out this discussion of metric measurement units, you may be interested to know that mass is also related directly to length and volume. One cubic centimeter (1 milliliter) of water weighs 1 gram. We often think of metric weight in kilograms (1,000 grams). One liter of water weighs 1 kilogram. With a standard set of metric weights and a balance scale, you can have students weigh these empty and filled containers relating these measures.

How big is a metric ton of water? A metric ton is 1,000 kilograms (about 2,200 pounds). It is equivalent to a kiloliter (1,000 liters) in volume. How big is 1,000 liters? It is 1 cubic meter. If we had a cubelike bucket that was 1 meter on each edge, we could stand by a waterfall and catch a metric ton of water. Well, maybe Paul Bunyan could.

. . . .

Computational Geometry

Geometry is multifaceted; it can include the one-dimensional properties of lines, the two-dimensional properties of figures on a plane, or the three-dimensional properties of objects in real space. Students can manipulate, create, count, and measure.

In this section, we will illustrate several important concepts through activities relying on computational geometry, a term we first read in Seymour Papert's book *Mindstorms* (1980). He developed the Logo computer language as a medium for students to explore computational geometry by creating their own graphic designs and figures using mathematical concepts that are embedded in Logo. See the handbook by Hyde and Turner (1988) for a collection of mathematics activities using Logo. We want teachers to be very clear about the important geometrical concepts that involve computation and measurement and those that do not. Students need to see that many wonderful aspects of mathematics are qualitative and relational and not quantitative and numerical.

Making triangles

We begin with an activity to get third grade students thinking about some key properties of triangles. You need to obtain a large quantity of straws. You should premeasure and cut the straws in lengths of 3 to 16 centimeters, one of each length per student. Mark the centimeter units on one side of the straws. However, you may want students to mark these units themselves in order to practice working with linear measure. In either case, a short line must be accurately marked at each centimeter. Paper straws are easy to write on, but some permanent markers can be used with plastic straws. The task for small groups of students is as follows:

Bend each straw into a triangle by folding it at only two of the centimeter marks. Using each length of straw, students should try to find all the possible ways to make triangles with just two bends. Students should write down the possibilities at each length, as they find them.

As students manipulate longer straws, the possibilities increase. On the board, they can array their findings in a table, using several categories according to the number of equal sides (see figure 6.4).

At one of the lengths some students may depart from actually manipulating the straws and calculate triplets of numbers that add up to that amount (e.g., at 8 centimeters they might say: 2-2-4, 1-3-4, or 1-2-5). Ask them to make these triangles. Why won't they work?

As the table is being formed, ask students to predict what

. . . .

Figure 6.4

Total length	Three equal sides	Two equal sides				No equal sides		
3	1-1-1							
4								
5		1-2-2						
6	2-2-2							
7		1-3-3	2-2-3					
8			2-3-3					
9	3-3-3	1-4-4				2-3-4		
10		2-4-4	3-3-4					
11		1-5-5	3-3-5	3-4-4		2-4-5		
12	4-4-4	2-5-5					3-4-5	
13		1-6-6	3-5-5	4-4-5		2-5-6	3-4-6	
14		2-6-6	4-4-6		4-5-5		3-5-6	
15	5-5-5	1-7-7	3-6-6	4-4-7		2-6-7	3-5-7	4-5-6

patterns seem to be emerging. Ask them also to develop a way to ensure that they have found all the triangles for each length.

After completing the entire table, ask them to write down their conclusions about patterns contained in the chart. Can they predict what would happen at larger lengths? Then you can explain the patterns involved by having them present and discuss their written conclusions. For instance, equilateral triangles only occur when the total length is a multiple of three because three equal sides are needed. For odd numbered lengths (after 3), an isosceles triangle can be found by making a side of 1 and splitting the remaining length in half. At 7, making a side of 3 and halving also works. And so forth.

A major conclusion that students should reach is that triangles can be formed only when the sum of any two sides is greater than the third side. They may express this idea through its converse: you cannot make a triangle with one side equal to or longer than the other two sides. ●

Making quadrilaterals

To help students get a feel for quadrilaterals, try the following activity:

Bend straws of lengths of 10, 11, and 12 centimeters (measured and marked as before). Obviously, three bends are needed to make a quadrilateral. Give individual students three straws, one of each length, and ask them to create one quadrilateral from each straw, tape the ends together, and record the side lengths.

Arrange students in pairs and give each student three more

straws of these lengths. Ask students to report the side lengths of the quadrilaterals they have created to their partners, who must then recreate them.

Students will discover several interesting aspects of quadrilaterals from this simple activity. The measurements of side lengths are insufficient to determine the actual shape of the figure. Any quadrilateral can be "squeezed" by pushing two opposite corners toward one another until the figure has very little area.

Students also realize that these quadrilaterals may be turned around: that is, the figures may be rotated. Also, they discover that the order in which the numbers are taken often affects the drawing of the figure. Unlike a triangle, the sides of a quadrilateral may be seen as pairs of sides that are opposite each other. For instance, if one student said that he'd made a quadrilateral with measurements 2, 4, 2, and 4 inches as its sides, which of the drawings in figure 6.5 would his partner imagine?

The order of the numbers also may get mixed up in a related issue: mirror-image symmetry. Consider the two quadrilaterals in figure 6.6. Are they the same or different?

There is no way to *rotate* one of these quadrilaterals so that it looks like the other. If a student says he has found a quadrilateral with sides measuring 1, 3, 4, and 2 inches, which of these two might it be? In both cases, the side with length 3 is opposite the 1 and the 2 opposite the 4.

These quadrilaterals mirror one another. You can imagine a mirror between the two in which one produces the image of the other. Cut these quadrilaterals out of cardboard. If you flipped one over, exchanging front to back surfaces, then the two would be identical. Some quadrilaterals have a mirror image and some don't.

Ask students how they could measure and describe their quadrilaterals so that a person would be able to draw accurately

. . . .

Figure 6.5

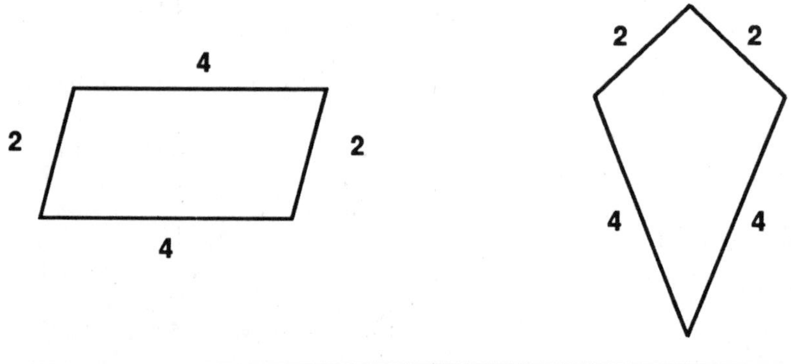

· ·
Figure 6.6

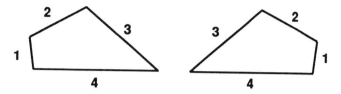

what had been seen. First, a quadrilateral becomes stable (the angles don't vary) when one or both diagonals is fixed. Why? Since a diagonal runs across the figure, connecting opposite corners, drawing even one diagonal creates two stable triangles, back to back. Two diagonals create four triangles. Therefore, if students were to measure the lengths of the sides and the two diagonals, they'd greatly help clear up the ambiguity of what their figure looked like.

Second, it would greatly help another person's understanding if the order of the quadrilateral's measurements were recorded in some standard fashion such as clockwise. That way others would know what sides were adjacent and opposite to each other. Such a number scheme would also show which one of the mirror-image pairs was being described. ●

We have a way of putting these two ideas into practice for older students that may seem a bit unusual at first, but students catch on quickly and enjoy this activity.

Draw figure 6.7 on the board or newsprint for the students. This is a device for constructing quadrilaterals. The "cross" is formed by the two intersecting diagonals of a quadrilateral, whose sides are not yet drawn. Notice that the "cross" has four parts to it: four line segments that each have three dots on them. It is a simple task to make a quadrilateral by connecting four dots, one from each adjacent line segment. For instance, if the four dots at the ends of each line segment were connected, a square would be formed. What are the different quadrilaterals that could be formed using this device? A reproducible handout with many examples of this figure is provided in the appendix of this book.

There are twenty-four different quadrilaterals that can be found with the figure, following the rules. However, every class has students who wittingly or unwittingly "bend" the rules by connecting *any* two dots on each diagonal. For instance, see the drawing in figure 6.8.

Even though such a drawing indicates that the student has not fully complied with the condition of connecting dots from each of the four line segments, a fascinating concept has emerged. If

Figure 6.7

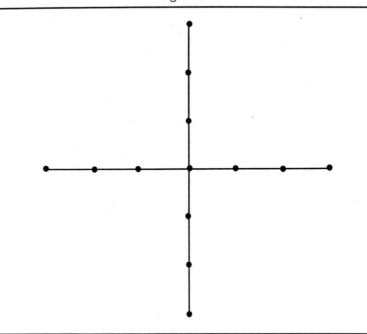

the possibility of such a quadrilateral has not been raised by students prior to this event, now is the moment to address concave versus convex polygons. Students have seen that knowing only *side* lengths can allow angles at the corners (vertices) of quadrilaterals to vary; quadrilaterals can be squeezed together. In fact, they can be squeezed so much that they can "cave in." Since they have four sides, they are quadrilaterals. Most people think only of the traditional form of convex quadrilaterals. If you vary the conditions and allow any two dots on each diagonals to be connected, then many concave quadrilaterals can be found.

Let's return to *convex* quadrilaterals. A good task for students working in pairs is to find as many different convex quadrilaterals as they can by using this device. Provide students with handouts of the line-segment diagonals.

Some students initially may be confused about this task. Why aren't we measuring sides any more? Remind them how diagonals cause a quadrilateral's sides to hold steady without wobbling at the corner angles. Then have a student create one quadrilateral on the board's large version of the diagonals and dots. Ask: How long are the diagonals? Student will be able to tell with no difficulty by counting the distance between vertices on the dotted diagonals. Then ask students to describe the four *triangles* formed by these diagonals. Two of their sides are known from the dotted line segments that are parts of the diagonals (see figure 6.9).

After students have made several examples, have them examine the four triangles formed by the diagonals and sides of

Figure 6.8

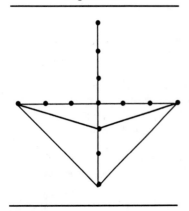

examine the four triangles formed by the diagonals and sides of each quadrilateral. Question: What do all these triangles have in common? Answer: they all have one square corner (a right angle) because that is the way the diagonals are drawn.

Ask students to look at the quadrilateral in figure 6.9. We can exactly describe it by the size of its four triangles. Going clockwise from the top, it has a 1,3 triangle; then another 1,3; then a 2,3; then another 2,3. Yet there is an even simpler way to descri⌣e it. Notice how the sides of adjacent triangles are the same line segment of the diagonal. Thus, instead of describing the quadrilateral by listing the lengths of the triangles' sides, we can simply avoid repeating the lengths of common sides by saying that the quadrilateral in figure 6.9 is 1,3,2,3, formed by intersecting diagonals with those partial lengths. Students may need to be reminded that the order of these four numbers is important.

This numbering system is very helpful in determining repeats that are merely rotations when looking for all the different quadrilaterals that can be formed by this device. Rotations of the same quadrilateral do not count. However, mirror images do.

When all 24 have been found, you should array them all on a wall or give students a handout with them. Working in groups, have students discuss what are the different kinds of quadrilaterals. How might the different types be described? We assume that through good discussion and subsequent explanation students will be able to discern:

- Three different sized squares (a special form of rhombus).
- Three other rhombi in which both diagonals are bisected.
- Nine "kites" in which one diagonal is bisected.
- Three trapezoids that look like isosceles triangles with their tops cut off, parallel to their bases.
- Six quadrilaterals that come in mirror-image pairs; none of their diagonals are bisected and the four triangles formed by diagonals are different. ●

Figure 6.9

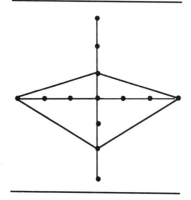

There are many different extensions that build on this initial activity. For instance, students could find all the concave quadrilaterals. There are 9 symmetrical "darts" that look like arrowheads (as in figure 6.8) and 18 others that come in mirror-image pairs.

A quite different extension asks students to explore the 24 convex quadrilaterals for their areas. Remind the students that these are special quadrilaterals chosen because their diagonals form right angles. Therefore, the four triangles that form each quadrilateral can be examined for their areas rather simply. Each triangle has two obvious measurements: one can be the base and the other the height because of the right angle of the diagonal's intersection. Adding up the areas of the four triangles gives the quadrilateral's area. Which quadrilateral has the largest area? Why? Write the area next to each and rank order them. Which have the same area? Why?

Another, perhaps obvious, extension would be to investigate what

Figure 6.10

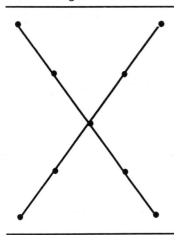

additional quadrilaterals are formed when the diagonals can be extended to a maximum of eight units long (i.e., adding additional dots on the ends of the diagonals). A rather large number of new quadrilaterals can be made using the larger diagonals. These include 1 square, 3 rhombi, 15 kites, 3 trapezoids, and 24 that come in mirror-image pairs, for a total of 46; and these are only the convex quadrilaterals! The appendix includes master sheets for this size.

Students will probably ask at some point, why didn't we find any of the traditional form of rectangle? Because we began with diagonals that were at right angles, we only were able to create a certain number and type of quadrilateral. Therefore, changing the angles at which the diagonals intersect will give different quadrilaterals. Students should draw their own diagonals and then create unusual quadrilaterals from them.

Older students can profit from a structured extension in this vein. Quadrilaterals can be made using isometric dot paper, in which the dots are set in the pattern of equilateral triangles. Give students a handout from the appendix with four unit diagonals intersecting at 60 and 120 degree angles (see figure 6.10). Beginning with this simple device, several interesting wrinkles occur. Two rectangles are found simply by connecting the end points of the diagonals in figure 6.10. Two trapezoids exist. Six other quadrilaterals are found in mirror-image pairs but, most interestingly, one of these pairs is a set of two parallelograms that are not rhombi (see figure 6.11).

If you increase the lengths of the diagonals to six units, a mind-boggling array of quadrilaterals will be found. Areas and lengths of sides could be explored by using the properties of the isometric dot paper, with

Figure 6.11

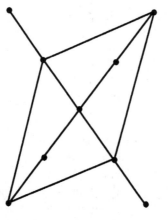
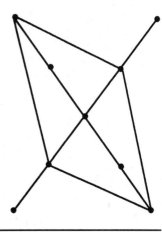

its equilateral triangles from which many relationships can be derived. However, those explorations are rather advanced. Instead, we suggest that students carefully examine the triangles that are formed by the diagonals. How many different triangles can be found? There are ten that can be color coded when these quadrilaterals are displayed in the room.

. . . .

Open-ended Activities in the Classroom

An energetic and creative teacher from Wheaton, Illinois, has evolved several highly interactive activities over the years. Jamie Mulholland's problem-solving activities for her fourth graders have become annual school events of some renown. We will describe them in their well-developed version, realizing that no one would likely try to do them immediately the way this teacher does it after ten years of trial and error. Other teachers have successfully used modified, scaled-down, initial versions of these activities.

Create your own small-scale classroom store by buying many small items (e.g. toys, balloons, pencils, barrettes, stickers, candy, etc.) that students would find interesting. Special close-out sales in stores and garage sales are likely sources of these goodies. Arrange the students into groups and give each group a bag containing a quantity of the same item. Each group gets a different item. For instance, one group may get a bag of 15 whistles that you purchased for $1.99. Another group may get a bag of 27 little candy bars that cost $3.49.

Each group of students must determine the fair price for a single item from the bag, rounded to the nearest cent. They may use calculators, if you so desire. This will be the selling price when they "market" these goods to a class of first graders (who have been given play money coins by their teacher). All items for a group are placed into a clear zip-lock bag with a card that lists the number of items and the individual price. The items for first sale day have been preplanned by the teacher so they will not exceed ten cents per item. First graders are given ten pennies. Your students go to the first-grade classroom and display their wares and sell individual items that the first graders choose to buy. First graders must count out the money to pay for their purchase.

When they return to the classroom, have your students write a description that summarizes the transactions that occurred. For instance: "We had 17 zappers when we started. We asked for 8 cents for each. We sold 6 of them. We have 11 zappers left and 48 cents. This adds up correctly." ●

This kind of mercantilism can occur once a month, as you replenish the goods to be sold and increase their complexity. Sellers will accrue different kinds of items that mix the prices and they can mark down items that are not moving. First graders can progress in the types and amounts of coins that they bring to the sale. Thus, your students will have to make change. Another variation is the White Elephant Sale:

Give each student a bag with the same amount of play money (e.g., 5 one dollar bills, 7 dimes, and 23 pennies). Students are asked to bring in an item they wish to sell, the famous "white elephant." Students set their own asking price that must be less than $5.00. In order to require them to make change, the price of each item must be an uneven amount of dollars (e.g., $4.25).

On the day of the sale, the students are allowed to shop and sell. Often students form partnerships so that one can shop while the other sells both items. The teacher should bring in several items also. These can be sold to students and if anyone forgets to bring in an item of his own, he can sell something for the teacher on a percentage "commission."

It is most valuable to go over the activity at the end of the day and have students write about their transactions and overall experience. It is especially helpful to think about what was learned since the activity will be repeated several times during the year (e.g., the afternoon before a holiday).

Several suggestions from Ms. Mulholland are to have each student make a money box in the week prior to the first white elephant sale. It is more fun when several classes participate. There will be more goods. Adults in the building can be given money to purchase items, thereby keeping the "economy" flowing. Occasionally, the teacher may have to "inflate" the economy by giving students some additional money, especially if some students buy but cannot seem to sell anything. ●

At the end of the year, Ms. Mulholland has a ''restaurant'' run by the fourth and first graders. The fourth graders plan a limited menu for a one-day luncheon. For instance, all diners must get a hot dog but would have a choice among various drinks and chips. The teacher obtains price lists of food and goods to be preordered (buns, meat, drinks, chips, napkins, plates), from local vendors. Groups of fourth graders have to calculate the amount and cost for a particular item that would be ordered. Then all groups must collaborate on the set price to be charged for one meal in order to break even and actually make a small amount of money. Obviously, a key assumption is the number of diners who would come. Therefore, invitations with required responses are sent out to parents and various adults.

One of the most interesting features of this restaurant comes from the need for prepaid orders of some items. Thus, students must raise some initial capital for their venture. Through the cooperation of a local bank vice president, each class negotiates a loan. The going rate of interest is charged over the necessary two weeks and "collateral" is expected. Last year, after much discussion, the class bunny rabbit was offered and accepted as collateral by the bank. The concepts of percentage and interest ($\frac{2}{52}$ of annual interest amount) took on very specific meanings.

On the day of the restaurant luncheon, first and fourth graders are paired. First graders take orders from their assigned tables on a menu checklist. Their fourth-grade partners calculate the bill on a special form, multiplying the cost of a meal by the number of people in the party and adding any extra items that had been requested. Some people may have extra drinks or chips. Students give the bills to the customers, receive payment, and make change.

Each year, the restaurant has more than $500 in transactions. The classes each clear about $50 after expenses and repayment of loans. No collateral has ever been lost.

7

- -
- -
- -
- -
- -

Noncomputational Mathematics

. . . .

Emphasizing Thinking, not Calculating

We have found that years of being battered by computational procedures and abstract symbolism have left many students dazed and fearful of mathematics, particularly of computation. Therefore, we make a strong pitch to them that mathematics is much more than arithmetic, more than computation. To illustrate this idea, we spend significant time engaging them in aspects of mathematics where they need do no calculations and rarely see a number at all: problem-solving activities from two and three-dimensional geometry (on the plane and in space).

We almost always initiate these problems with physical materials. Not only do manipulatives offer essential, concrete representations of ideas, but they also offer marvelous opportunities for visual and spatial thinking in mathematics. We have chosen illustrative activities for this chapter that use readily available materials. You may have to purchase some and others might be simply constructed by you or your students.

Many of the geometrical concepts and topics included in this chapter have related computational aspects. Nonetheless, we encourage you to extend these activities into their computational aspects only after students have had many positive experiences with the noncomputational ideas. Extensions and connections are wonderful if they build on understanding. Teachers invite conceptual and emotional trouble when they require students to jump too soon into computations (e.g., measuring interior angles of regular polygons before students have a feel for what angles and polygons are).

The concepts, problems, and activities of this chapter are remarkably interconnected. We have tried to begin each topic with activities appropriate for younger students (grades 3 and 4). As ideas weave between two and three dimensions, the activities may seem more appropriate for older students (grades 5 and 6). We urge teachers and students not to be misled by unfamiliarity with some of these ideas; people often underestimate their ability to think visually and spatially. With experience, these ideas are quite accessible to students.

Many teachers have seen that it is often the average or below-average mathematics students who excel in visual thinking and analyzing spatial relations. These students may not have fared as well as others in traditional computational mathematics. Yet these newer areas may draw on their perceptual and conceptual strengths. The teacher should not be misled by the above-average students who express some dissatisfaction into believing that these topics are too "hard" for the students.

In fact, a double blessing may occur by wrestling with these topics. Average students may experience their first tastes of success and mathematical power in these noncomputational activities. And the "brighter" students, who have grown accustomed to rapid computation without much thought, to get the one right answer, may truly have to "stop and think" for the first time.

Because some of these topics may be new, we strongly urge the reader of this chapter to make or obtain whatever sets of manipulatives are being described. Even working with photo-reproductions of figures from this chapter (cut and glued to cardboard) is better than merely reading. Although this chapter has more diagrams and drawings than any other in this book, we are painfully aware of the inadequacies of written text and figures to portray the rich complexity of ideas. Maximum benefit is derived from maximum involvement with real materials.

· ·

Geometry of the Plane and Space

The activities in this section are designed to help students conceive of key ideas in two- and three-dimensions. We suggest that you begin by bringing to class several large cubes.

Ask students to examine a cube carefully and write a description of what they see. In discussing their written descriptions, the concepts that you want to establish are *face*, *vertex*, and *edge*. The cube is an example of a polyhedron. The 6 faces are squares, altogether forming 8 vertices and 12 edges.

Next, display some soccer balls and ask students to describe them in terms of their faces. Is it a sphere? No. Show students a true sphere such as a completely smooth rubber ball. How many different surfaces does it have? Only one, and it is not a regular polygon like the pentagons and hexagons of the soccer ball. Although the surface of the soccer ball does not have perfectly flat pentagons and hexagons, it is not one smooth surface like a sphere either. The stitching together of the 12 pentagons and 20 hexagons "pulls" the surfaces a bit so they are not quite flat.

Ask students what the shapes of the pentagonal and hexagonal faces have in common. The lengths of the sides are all the same. When a side from each of two different shapes come together to form an edge, they must be the same length. To some students, this fact will be obvious; to others, a revelation. This kind of visual *analysis* requires experience. Thus, edges are common sides of faces. Each edge is the line formed by exactly two faces coming together. Don't try to have students count the edges and vertices of the soccer ball. The 90 edges and 60 vertices will drive them crazy.

When the sides of 2 polygons come together to form an edge, their respective vertices must also meet. Ask students to describe what is happening at a vertex of the cube. The vertices of 3 squares meet. Is this true for every vertex of the cube? Yes. Ask students to describe what happens at the vertices of the soccer ball. The vertices of 2 hexagons and 1 pentagon meet at every vertex.

Some polyhedra can be formed using only one kind of regular polygon for all its faces (e.g., the cube). These are called *regular* polyhedra. Others can be formed by two or more regular polygons, often in fascinating and complex ways. The soccer ball is an example of polyhedra with several different regular polygons for faces, every vertex the same, and a spherelike symmetry. Such polyhedra are called *semiregular.* ●

After this introduction to the concepts of polyhedron, face, vertex, edge, and polygon, we ask students to work on a series of problems that bounces back and forth between regular polygons and various polyhedra. The general format involves three distinct parts:

1. Manipulating a set of one regular polygon (2 dimensions).
2. Drawing a pictorial representation of what was made with the manipulatives (2 dimensions).
3. Constructing polyhedra based on these sets of manipulatives (3 dimensions).

These three parts require different materials. For activities in the first part, we suggest purchasing vast quantities of plastic triangles, squares, pentagons, and hexagons with sides all the same length (e.g., Pattern Blocks). We believe that making polygons from construction paper is tedious and does not always result in good usable models for the type of activities we will describe. In the second part, we encourage you to use graph paper for recording and drawing. We provide reproducible triangular and hexagonal graph paper in the appendix of this book.

There are many different products available in catalogs for constructing polyhedra. However, the best materials for part 3 of our activities are included in a product called Googolplex, which can be ordered through various catalogs. The pieces include polygonal "frames" and "plates." The frames are the perimeters of triangles, squares, and pentagons; the plates are solid polygons of these shapes that can be fitted into the frames. The sides of all these polygons are equal in length and connector pieces allow the student to hinge these sides of the polygon frames together. Thus, students can move the polygons around on the plane, link their sides together to form an edge, and then fold them up into polyhedra.

The series of activities that follow allow for hours of engaging work. Specific tasks may be spread out over several days or weeks. The materials have such incredible richness that after a certain level of familiarity with essential concepts, they may be set aside for many weeks so that students can return to them later with fresh, renewed interest.

Investigations with Triangles

We suggest beginning with the simplest of geometric shapes, the triangle. Although familiar to students in the primary grades, triangles provide a rich source of concepts.

A rrange the students into pairs and give them a dozen plastic (or wooden) equilateral triangles. Tell them that their task is to investigate the different shapes that can be formed when the triangles are joined together. To begin, all triangles should remain on the surface of the desktop. Triangles are joined by fitting two sides (edges) exactly together. The teacher illustrates this idea by fitting 2 triangles together to form a diamond (technically, a rhombus). Ask students if there is any other way that 2 of these triangles can be joined. The answer is no. Ask them to add a third triangle. How can it be done? Ask students if there is more than one way to join 3 of these triangles. Again, the answer is no; only one way is possible (see figure 7.1).

The teacher should take a moment to rotate the shape upside down and around to the left and right. Ask students if these different rotations produce a different shape. The answer is no.

Three different shapes are possible with 4 triangles (see figure 7.2). As they find these shapes, students should record them on triangular graph paper. Folders for each student to save all papers will greatly facilitate this and future activities.

Ask students to *imagine* folding up each of these shapes along their edges. When folding brings two edges together to meet completely, they would be joined. What three-dimensional figures will result from folding? Many third and fourth graders can correctly visualize the figure in the middle folding up into a pyramid. But what about the other two?

After imagining, students should make and fold these 4

Figure 7.1

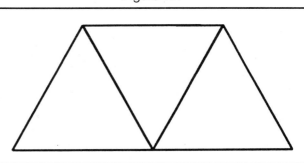

Figure 7.2

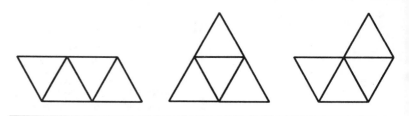

triangle shapes with Googolplex frames. Tape on one side of Pattern Blocks also works. Students are often surprised to find that the 4 triangles on the far left of figure 7.2 also form a pyramid. Of course, by pyramid we mean a *tetrahedron*, one of the regular polyhedra. Adding the Googolplex plates to the frames reveals these faces quite well.

The third shape (on the far right of figure 7.2) folds into what also appears to be a pyramid. The 4 triangles join around the open face of a square. When 4 triangle plates are added to the Googolplex frames, one can clearly see that these 4 triangles do not fold up to be a complete figure. A square frame and plate must be added to complete the square-based pyramid. Ask students to describe the difference between these two pyramids in terms of faces, edges, and vertices. Note that the one with a square base has 1 vertex made of 4 triangles, but the other vertices are composed of 1 square and 2 triangles. In contrast, the tetrahedron contains identical vertices, each with 3 triangles.

Have students fold up two sets of the 4-triangle shape on the far right of figure 7.2. Ask them what could be made if their open, square bases were joined together. They will have formed an 8-sided object: another regular polyhedron, the *octahedron*. You may want to bring in several octahedral dice, available at most hobby shops. Ask students to analyze carefully the vertices of the octahedron. Surprisingly, each vertex is composed of the key piece they started with: 4 joined triangles. How can you start with two sets of 4 triangles and get 6 vertices that each have four triangles? This "magic" occurs when the sets are combined and a pair of triangles is joined with another pair to form a vertex. ●

The next task requires students to find all the ways of linking 5 triangles together.

Before working with manipulatives, ask students to predict how many different ones they will find. Figure 7.3 shows the 4 different shapes.

Students will undoubtedly find two others that are reflections of

. . . .
Figure 7.3

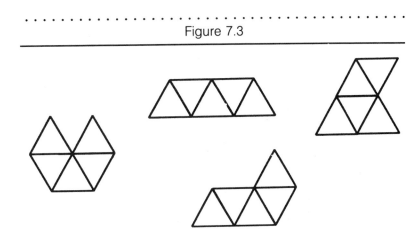

2 shapes. Take a moment to have students examine these reflections. If they are working with solid plastic triangles, they can tape them together and turn the entire shape over. In working with polygons on the plane, we will not consider mirror-image reflections to be different shapes. Ask students to copy the 4 shapes on graph paper.

Ask students to examine the shape on the far left of figure 7.3. Notice how the triangles almost go completely around a circle; only one more would be needed. Ask them to predict what will happen when it is folded up. It makes a little "cap."

Students should use Googolplex triangle frames to make several of these caps. Ask students to describe what they see. How is it like the pyramids previously seen? Five triangles go around an open pentagonal base. Instead of adding a pentagon frame, ask them to put 2 of these caps together at their open pentagonal bases.

How is this shape of 10 triangles like the octahedron and how is it different? Have the pairs of students write down several sentences describing the two figures and answering the question. In discussing their answers, ask students to look carefully at the vertices of the 2 polyhedra. The octahedron always has 4 triangles at a vertex, while the 10-sided figure sometimes has 4 and sometimes 5.

There is another regular polyhedron that can be made with the shapes from 5 triangles, but in a seemingly strange fashion. Have students set aside 2 of these caps. Then make 2 of the 5-in-a-row "strips" from figure 7.3; fold them but do not join any edges. These 20 triangles (2 caps and 2 strips) will form an *icosahedron*, another regular polyhedron. Turn one strip around and join it to the other strip to make one long 10-triangle strip. Then join its ends together (see figure 7.4). Sit this bandlike figure on its base. Note how 5 triangle edges are up and 5 are down, forming open

Figure 7.4

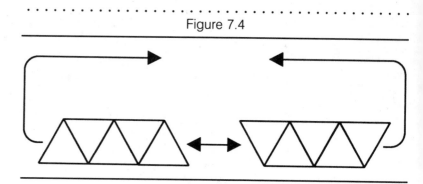

pentagons. The pentagons of the caps can be joined to these pentagons to form the icosahedron.

Ask students to examine carefully the vertices of the icosahedron. Paradoxically, every vertex now appears to be a cap. Five triangles meet at every vertex. As with the octahedron, this surprising feature reaffirms the principal idea behind regular polyhedra: identical vertices. Thus the cap is the major building block of the icosahedron. ●

In subsequent activities, we will illustrate ways to give students the appropriate numbers of the key building block for a given polyhedron and then let them try to construct it. In the next task, we ask students to work with 6 triangles.

Ask students again to predict how many different shapes they will find when joining 6 triangles on the plane. Working with triangles on their desktops they may need to think carefully to discover the 12 different shapes. One way is to add systematically one triangle to every open side of the previous 5-triangle figures. Excluding reflections, the shapes are shown in figure 7.5.

Ask students which ones have mirror images? Those numbered 1 through 7. Some teachers like to ask students to give names to these figures in order to be able to refer to a particular shape easily. Some popular names for them are given in parentheses. Note that number 8 can readily be seen to be a hexagon. Students usually realize that this is the first time that the triangles have gone completely around a point. Have students copy these figures on graph paper.

Ask students which shape will not fold along all its edges (the hexagon). Because the 6 triangles have surrounded the point at their common vertex, all edges cannot be folded up.

These 12 figures are quite versatile for working on the plane but do not fold into anything remarkable. Therefore, we encourage students to make a set of these shapes that will stay together on the plane. Solid plastic triangles can be taped together on both sides.

Figure 7.5

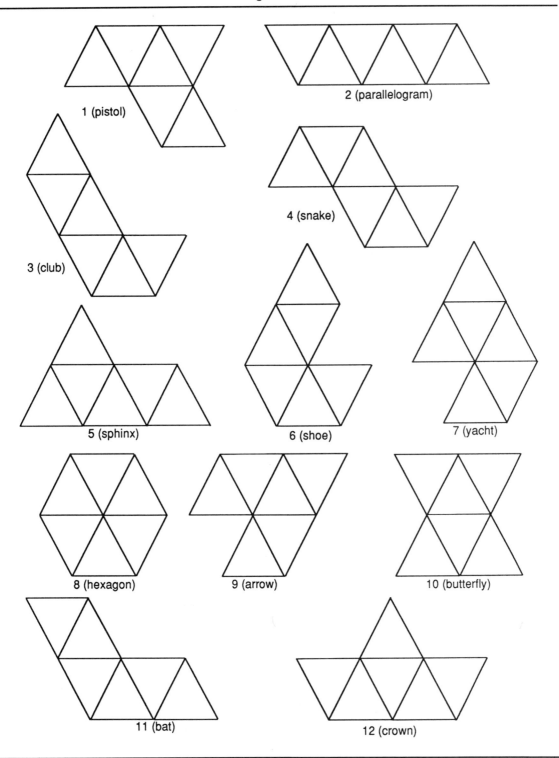

1 (pistol)

2 (parallelogram)

3 (club)

4 (snake)

5 (sphinx)

6 (shoe)

7 (yacht)

8 (hexagon)

9 (arrow)

10 (butterfly)

11 (bat)

12 (crown)

Figure 7.6

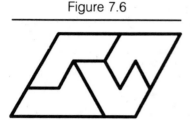

Figure 7.7

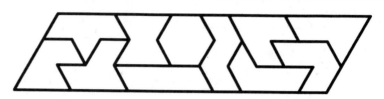

There are many different geometric figures that can be made on the plane by combining these shapes. Students should be allowed some free-play time to explore how these shapes can be fit together. Then we suggest asking students to find parallelograms of different sizes. For instance, the smallest one can be made with just 4 of these pieces (see figure 7.6 for one possible way). Ask students how many triangles are in this figure (24 triangles and 4 of these shapes). If the length of each side of these equilateral triangles were 1 unit, how long are the sides of this parallelogram? It would be: 3 units on one side and 4 units on the other. A unit is the length of one side of a triangle.

Other parallelograms with 3 units on a side are possible and have many solutions: 3 by 5, 3 by 6, 3 by 7, 3 by 8, 3 by 9, and 3 by 10. The 3 by 3 is impossible; the 3 by 11 is difficult; we give a solution in figure 7.7. A solution to the 3 by 12 has never been found.

There is only one possible parallelogram with 2 units on a side: the 2 by 6. It is difficult to find unless you tell students to use the sphinx, bat, arrow, and yacht.

Another good parallelogram is the 4 by 9; it has many solutions. Figure 7.8 shows one. The 5-by-6 parallelogram also has many solutions.

An interesting rhombus that requires all 12 shapes is the 6-by-6 rhombus. See figure 7.9 for a solution.

Figure 7.8

. . . .

Figure 7.9

Other interesting and difficult arrangements of the 6 triangle shapes can be found in Gardner (1971) and Mottershead (1977).

If students are trying to find a particular parallelogram, we usually provide a handout with the desired perimeter drawn. Most third graders need to arrange the pieces within such a boundary. Whenever students find a solution to a particular problem, they should record it on triangular graph paper for peers and posterity. Since multiple solutions are often found, students can be challenged to determine (through visual analysis) if they have found a "new" solution. ●

The term *tessellate* means to tile (completely cover) a surface with a pattern of shapes with no overlaps and no gaps. Mathematicians and artists of many cultures have investigated various geometric tessellations. "Regular" tessellations use one regular polygon to tile the plane. The simplest regular tessellation is the equilateral triangle. Have students examine the triangular graph paper. Note what happens at every vertex: six triangles come together.

Any triangle can be repeated infinitely to tile the plane. Have the students explore this remarkable fact by making a set of a dozen or so congruent triangles from cardboard. Any triangle will do, as long as each is congruent to the others. Tell students to line up their triangles on the desk, oriented identically. Note one particular vertex and mark this vertex of each triangle with a colored dot. Then choose one of the other vertices and mark it with two dots on each triangle (dots of two different colors will also work nicely).

Ask them to try to tessellate with these triangles, keeping sides of common length together. When they do find tessellations, ask them to describe each vertex of the pattern. The vertices of 6 of these triangles will come together in curious fashion (see figure 7.10).

Two of each size angle will be present (i.e., one dot, two dots, and unmarked). Furthermore students may see that the same angles are opposite each other and the 3 different angles in a row (one dot, two dots, and unmarked) form a straight line. If students have begun to study angular measure, they may realize that the common vertex of the 6 angles go around a point that is a full 360 degrees. These 3 different angles sum to 180 degrees, forming a straight line, because they are the 3 interior angles of the triangle. Therefore, any triangles can be arranged on the plane to tessellate in this fashion.

With a basic understanding of tessellation, students can be asked to return to the various triangle sets (2, 3, 4, 5, and 6 triangle shapes) to determine if copies of a particular shape will tessellate. They all will, but finding the patterns of tessellation for some is quite a feat. All tessellations should be recorded on graph paper. ●

In summary, these activities with triangles illustrate how students can work with a particular polygon on the plane and in space by doing the following:

- Finding all the different shapes made by joining a number of this polygon.
- Noting which of these shapes had mirror-image reflections.
- Joining shapes together to make larger polygons (e.g., parallelograms).
- Tessellating (tiling the plane) with a shape.
- Recording findings to all of the above on graph paper.
- Folding various shapes to make polyhedra.

We encourage students to engage in these processes through appropriate activities with the other polygons. The next three sections briefly illustrate the use of squares, pentagons, and hexagons.

. . . .
Figure 7.10

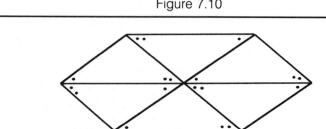

Investigations with Squares

Fortunately for the teacher, there is a wealth of resource material available for working with squares on the plane. A classic book by Solomon Golomb, *Polyominoes* (1965), contains an incredible amount of information about ways of linking squares at their edges. Obviously there is but 1 *domino* —2 joined squares. There are two ways to join 3 squares, shown in figure 7.11.

Ask students to imagine what would happen if the 3 linked squares were folded on their edges. The straight shape could join edges in a "prism" with 3 squares and 2 triangles as open bases. The right-angle shape will fold into a vertex of a cube, the most familiar regular polyhedron.

Golomb recently proposed a deceptively simple problem. Have students tape together squares to make 11 right-angle shapes. Along with 2 individual squares, can these 11 shapes make a 5-by-7 rectangle? Yes, but not as readily as one might imagine. Figure 7.12 shows two possibilities.

Have students find and make all 5 of the 4-square shapes, shown in figure 7.13.

Since 5 shapes have a total of 20 squares, ask students if they can be fitted together to form a 4-by-5 rectangle. How about a 2-by-10 rectangle? Since they cannot be done, don't let students get too frustrated. Instead, they can be introduced to a powerful technique that shows why not. Have students shade alternating squares on graph paper and then cut out the 5 different 4-square shapes. They will see that each shape has only 2 shaded squares except the *T* shape, which will have either 1 or 3 shaded. Because of the arrangement of its 4 squares, the *T* shape must contain an odd number of shaded squares.

Ask students to shade alternative squares of the 4-by-5 and 2-by-10 rectangles on graph paper. They will discover that they have an equal number of shaded and unshaded squares. Therefore, these 4-square shapes cannot form these rectangles. The shading technique is simple but powerful, and can be used on many problems that ask if a particular set of polygons can be arranged to fill a certain area.

The 4-square shapes can readily fit into a 5-by-5 grid of squares. Obviously there would be 5 squares left over. Therefore, ask students to find various ways to do so with a condition: the 5 extra squares must not touch each other. ●

The following activities involve students in work with pentominoes. Pentominoes have been studied extensively by Golomb and many mathematicans because of their incredible versatility. They are commercially available from catalogs along with various resource books.

Figure 7.11

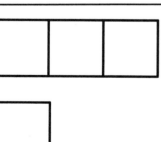

Figure 7.12

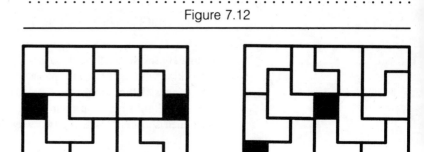

Ask the students to find all 12 pentominoes and record them on graph paper (see figure 7.14). Ask them next to *imagine* folding up each pentomino on its edges. What shapes will be formed? The straight pentomino (no. 1) will have 2 pentagonal openings that could be filled with Googolplex frames, making a prism. The no. 2 pentomino has a large square that prevents all edges from being folded. Many students realize that no. 3 will fold up into a "box," a cube with an open face. Ask them if other pentominoes will form a box. There are 8 altogether.

Figure 7.13

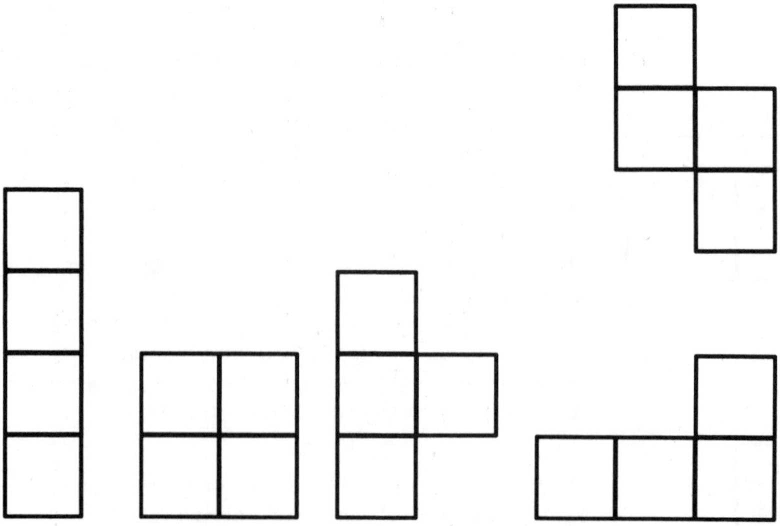

. . . .

Figure 7.14

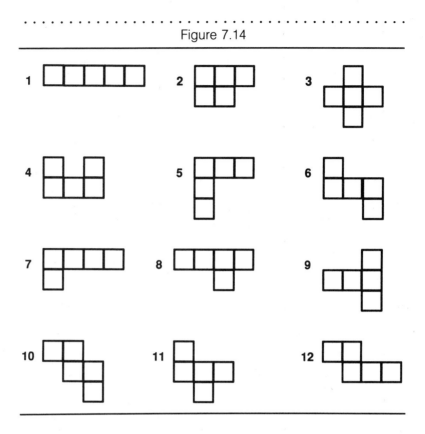

Students should make their predictions, then create the pentominoes from Googolplex, and do the actual folding. Besides no. 3, pentominoes numbered 6 through 12 will fold to a box.

Since the 12 pentominoes total 60 squares, a good question for students is, What rectangles are possible using all 12 shapes? The 6-by-10, 5-by-12, and 4-by-15 rectangles increase in order of difficulty. The 3-by-20 rectangle is possible but exceptionally difficult. Figure 7.15 shows one of 368 solutions for the 4 by 15 and one of the two basic solutions for the 3 by 20. Students should always record their solutions on graph paper and check to see if they have found a different solution from others in the class.

Younger students should start their rectangle explorations with smaller rectangles using only some of the pentominoes. There are many ways to create the 3 by 5, 4 by 5, and 5 by 5. Two 5-by-6 rectangles can be formed by the two halves of the set (see figure 7.16). Obviously these two rectangles can be rotated and joined to form both the 5-by-12 or the 6-by-10 rectangles. Other possible rectangles are 2 by 10, 4 by 10, 5 by 8, 5 by 9, 5 by 10, and 5 by 11.

The twelve pentominoes can also be placed on an 8-by-8 grid, the dimensions of a standard checkerboard. Obviously 4

Figure 7.15

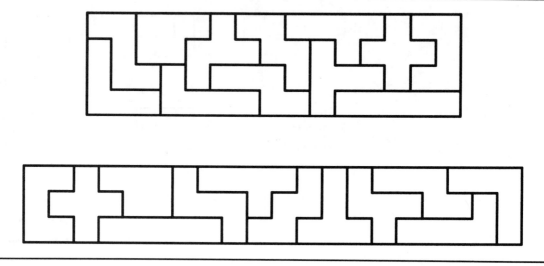

squares would not be covered. Two good problems are to find ways of doing so with either the 4 squares not touching at all or joined in a square. Figures 7.17 and 7.18 show one possibility for each. ●

Here are two good activities for younger students working in pairs with one set of pentominoes:

Provide the students with an 8-by-8 grid on graph paper with the squares the same size as each square of the pentominoes. Students alternate selecting 1 of the pentominoes until each has 6. Then they take turns placing 1 of their pentominoes on the checkerboard, covering exactly 5 of the

Figure 7.16

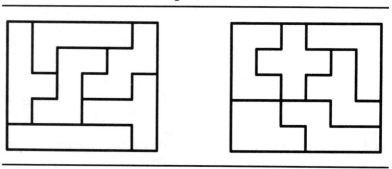

Figure 7.17

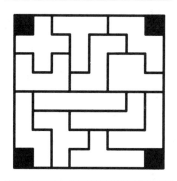

squares. The object of the game is for the students to try to place their 6 pentominoes so that eventually their partners are unable to place any more of theirs.

The other task is quite simple: with their partners not looking, the students select any 3 of the pentominoes, fit them together, and draw their perimeter on paper. The "solution" is recorded on a sheet of graph paper and the 3 pieces are returned to the pile of 12. The partners must then try to create a way to fill this perimeter with any 3 pentominoes. Students often find different solutions. Doing this activity many times brings students insight into which arrangements are easy to find and which are more difficult. The number of pieces can be increased; challenges or tournaments can be held. ●

Each of the twelve pentominoes will tessellate. Give students a dozen or more of the same shape and let them try to tile the plane. Some tessellation patterns are quite simple, others are more unusual. See figure 7.19 for three examples. Continuing the work with squares leads naturally to finding the ways of joining 6 squares.

A sk your students to explore ways of combining 6 squares. This is quite a challenge since there are 35 possible ways. Students usually need a good procedure like systematically adding one square to various edges of the pentominoes.

Recording what has been found is essential. Even third-grade students, sharing what they have found, are usually able to find them all. The major difficulty is excluding rotations and reflections that appear to be different. Students will often claim to have found 40. Careful examination reveals that 5 are actually rotations or reflections of others. Figure 7.20 shows the 35 *hexominoes*. ●

Once students have drawn them on graph paper, they should visualize folding these shapes. One key question is, which of these will fold up into a cube? After they make their predictions, students should make the 6-square shapes out of Googolplex frames and find the ones that can fold into a cube.

Figure 7.18

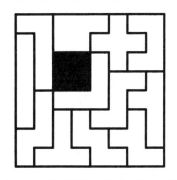

Only 11 of these 6-square shapes can form a cube. They are numbered 18 through 28 in figure 7.20. Ask students to describe these 11; what do they see within this set? Six of them can be described as having a strip of 4 squares in a row with additional squares attached to the either side of the strip. Students can readily see how these form a cube (e.g., the strip makes the sides and the other 2 form the top and bottom). The other 5 shapes have "jagged" sides that make the results of folding quite hard to visualize.

Older students could tackle the following problems: Ask the students to *think* about what rectangles might be made from the entire set of these 6-square shapes. Thirty-five sets of 6 squares each would yield a total of 210 squares. Rectangles might have the following dimensions:

· ·

Figure 7.19

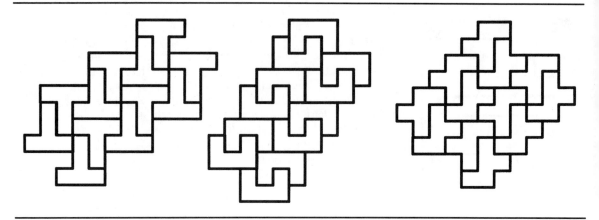

2 by 105
3 by 70
5 by 42
6 by 35
7 by 30
10 by 21
14 by 15

Unfortunately, all are impossible. After the wealth of rectangles from the pentominoes, this fact seems so unlikely that students may not believe you. We do not like to frustrate students by asking them to try to make these large rectangles. Instead we pose the question: Why are these rectangles impossible?

Students who have understood the strategy of alternating colors can apply it to the problem. Ask students to shade alternate squares of the 6-square shapes on their graph paper. Those numbered 1 through 24 in figure 7.20 will yield 3 colored squares each. Those 11 shapes numbered 25 through 35 must have 4 of one color and 2 of another. Therefore, there will always be extra squares of one color or the other when all 35 shapes are used.

Assign different groups of students to draw these various rectangles and shade their alternate squares. Ask them to report on their findings. All rectangles require 105 each of shaded and unshaded squares. Now ask students to figure out how to get 105 shaded squares from their 6-square shapes. It cannot be done; the first 24 shapes can each give 3 shaded squares (for a total of 72). The 11 remaining shapes would thus have to contribute 33 shaded squares to make the 105. But no mixture of 2 and 4 shaded squares could give 33.

Therefore, before students try to construct a particular figure with the entire set, they should do a coloring check. Only if the figure is shown to have more squares of one color than the other

Figure 7.20

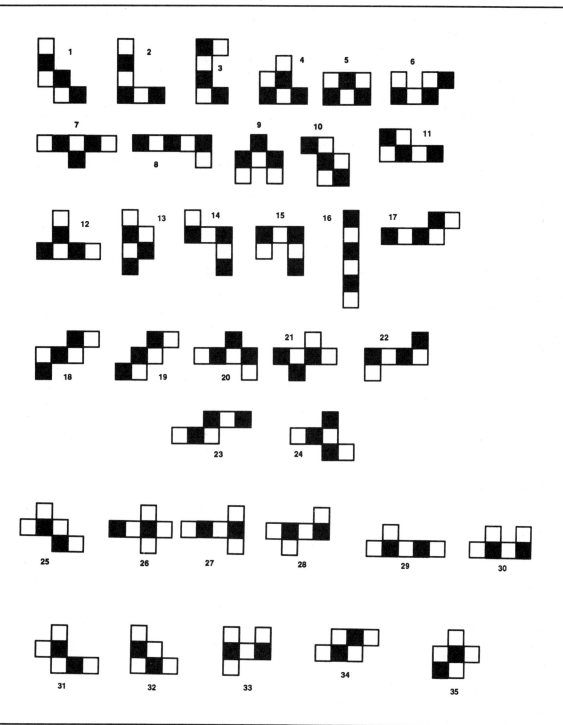

will it be possible. A good numerical problem for older students would be to try different ways of shading the special 11 6-square shapes to determine how many extra squares of one color are possible: 2, 6, 10, 14, 18, or 22.

Each of the individual 6-square shapes will tessellate. Students can exchange pieces they have made so that each can have many congruent pieces of the same shape. Record various tessellations found. ●

Investigations with Pentagons

It is not necessary to go through an entire set of analogous activities with pentagons. We suggest a simpler set of problems.

F irst, ask students to try to tessellate a set of regular pentagons. They will find that 3 pentagons go around a point but leave a gap that cannot be filled by pentagons (see figure 7.21). Ask students to make 4 sets of these 3 joined pentagons from Googolplex. Then fold up each into a kind of basket. Each basket is an essential building block for what comes next.

Now ask students to try to fit these 4 baskets together. The result is surprising: a regular polyhedron of 12 faces. It is the last regular polyhedron, the *dodecahedron*. Be on the lookout for dodecahedron calendars in which each pentagonal face is a different month. Dodecahedron dice are available in hobby shops. We suggest bringing a quantity to class for students to examine. Ask them to describe what they see, especially noting how each vertex is comprised of 3 pentagons (the little basket). They should also see that there is a top and bottom face, thereby making the dodecagon a useful die. ●

Who says pentagons don't tessellate? In order to clarify what is meant by regular tessellation you may want to produce a very unusual polygon. Figure 7.22 shows an irregular pentagon with unequal interior angles but equal sides. Five rotations of this same pentagon are given. One of these orientations may deceive you into believing that it is a regular pentagon.

P hotocopy a quantity of these rotations, glue them to cardboard, laminate them, or cover them with clear adhesive plastic. Do not discuss any of the irregular pentagon's properties with students. It can be tessellated into the highly unusual and appealing pattern shown in figure 7.23. Ask students to try to find a way of tiling the plane with a dozen or more of these pentagons. When this pattern is found, ask students to write a description of what they see. What do you see?

Figure 7.21

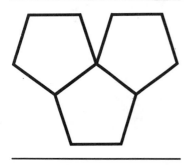

Figure 7.22

Figure 7.23

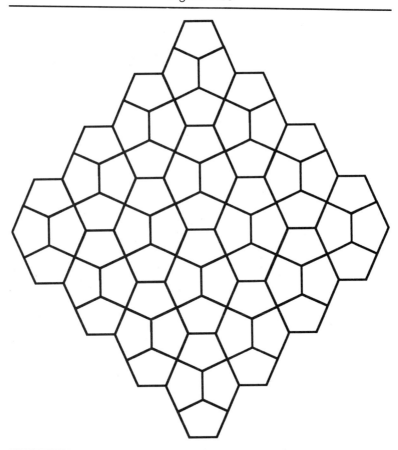

Examine the vertices of the tessellation. Note how some vertices have angles from 4 different pentagons joined, while others have angles from 3. Ask students what can they hypothesize about these angles. They may place pentagons next to one another or on top of one another to compare the sizes of the angles.

Our intent is not to require students to develop formal proofs about this irregular pentagon or its tessellation. Instead, we want some good conjectures and reasoning. Some reasonable conjectures about the pentagon are as follows:

- Its five sides are equal in length.
- It is symmetrical; it has no mirror image.
- It has 3 different angles or 2 pairs of equal angles.
- The lone angle is the largest of the 3.

These ideas alone can provide an excellent start for analyzing this irregular pentagon and its tessellation. Have students mark the 3 different angles with 3 different colored dots. You may provide colored dot stickers for this purpose. Ask students what they now see. They should be able to see the following:

- The four angles that come together in the tessellation are equal and right angles (90°).
- These right angles are always joined together; they never join with the other 2 angles at a vertex.
- At other vertices of the tessellation, one of the lone large angles joins 2 of the other size angles.

Ask students to describe what makes this tessellation work. If they have not perceived it by now, they may begin to see how 4 of these pentagons form an irregular hexagon, shaped somewhat like a coffin. In fact, one can see vertical coffins and then blink only to see horizontal coffins. You might provide students with a photocopy of figure 7.23 and ask them to use 4 different colors to shade in alternating vertical (or horizontal) hexagons. Four colors are needed so that no two hexagons of the same color will touch. These irregular hexagons tessellate very nicely.

Ask students to find another pattern to this tessellation. Another way to "see" it requires focusing on how 4 pentagons combine at their right angle vertices to form a kind of pinwheel. This time students can use 2 colors to shade alternate pinwheels to see this pattern. Ask students: How would you describe the pinwheel? It is a concave, 12-sided figure that also tessellates quite nicely. ●

This tessellation allows an important idea to emerge concerning tiling. Tessellations can be "composed" and "decomposed" at will. Often the way to create a tessellation based on a single, particular shape is to compose a large shape that more obviously tessellates from several of the individual pieces. Conversely, exotic tessellations can be created by systematically cutting up (decomposing) the individual pieces of a simple or boring tessellation. Many resource books on tessellations are available that illustrate how to turn the square tessellations of graph paper into more interesting tessellated shapes by decomposing the squares.

Investigations with Hexagons

The next task is for students to determine ways of joining regular hexagons at their edges. There is one way to join 2 hexagons and three ways to join 3 hexagons (see figure 7.24). The 4 joined hexagons become more interesting. See figure 7.25 for the 7 different shapes.

Ask students to find the possible combinations and record their shapes on the hexagonal graph paper in the appendix.

We do not ask students to fold hexagons. No regular polyhedra made only of hexagons exist. However, there are some unusual polyhedra that use hexagons (e.g., the soccer ball of 20 hexagons and 12 pentagons).

Obviously, fitting together hexagons on the plane will form some kind of "honeycomb," the hexagonal tessellation.

Figure 7.24

Figure 7.25

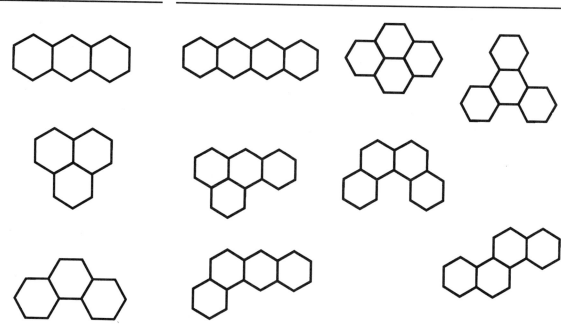

Figure 7.26

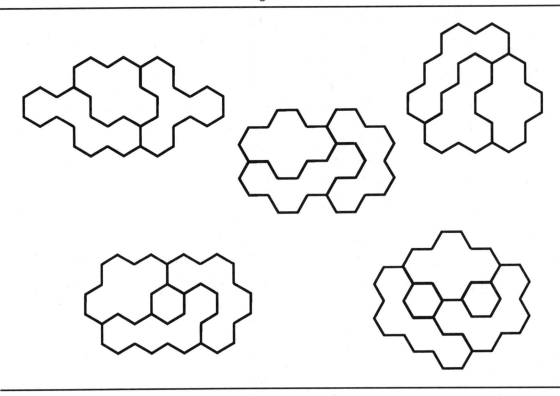

Figure 7.27

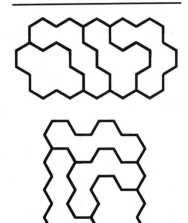

Technically, there will be no actual rectangles, triangles, rhombi, and so forth. Yet there are some fascinating symmetrical shapes that can be formed by the 4-hexagon shapes that are the hexagonal versions of such figures. Students should tape hexagon pattern blocks together to make these shapes. You can provide drawings of the perimeter of various figures or shade them on hexagonal graph paper. Students could also generate their own interesting shapes with 3 or more of these shapes. We suggest below some shapes with symmetrical or geometric features.

The symmetrical shapes in figure 7.26 can each be formed by joining 3 of the 4-hexagon shapes. Note that 1 shape has a hole in the middle and another has two holes. Many solutions are possible. Figure 7.27 shows two rectangular shapes that can be made with 4 of the 4-hexagon shapes.

Working with all 7 4-hexagon shapes is somewhat more difficult. Figure 7.28 shows some possibilities. The long rectangle is very difficult.

Students often try to make a triangle (with 7 hexagons on each side) from the 7 shapes. It is impossible even though the number of hexagons needed would be 28, the same as the total of

Figure 7.28

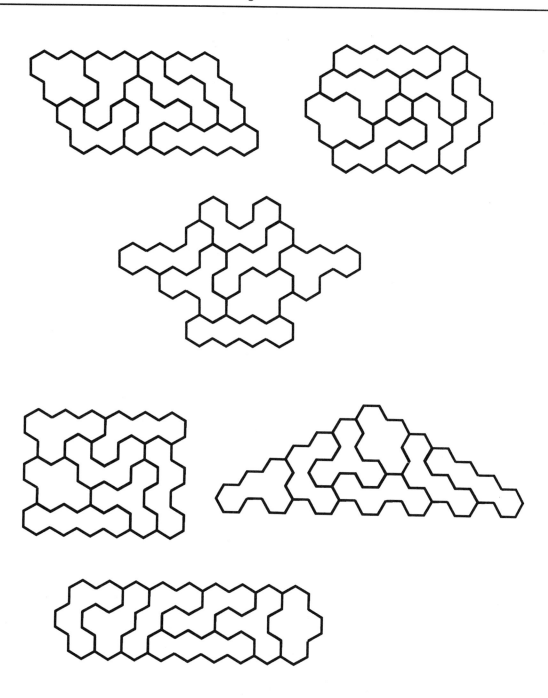

Figure 7.29

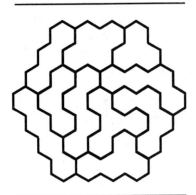

7. Also, it is not possible to make large hexagons from only 4-hexagon shapes; ask the students to think about why. A counting strategy would show that a hexagon would need 1, 7, 19, or 37. Even if the center hexagon were a hole, 6, 18, or 36 hexagons would be needed.

However, if students were to make the 3 3-hexagon shapes of figure 7.24, they could be combined with the 7 4-hexagon shapes of figure 7.25 for a total of 37 hexagons. Will they make a large hexagon? Yes; one solution is shown in figure 7.29. ●

Investigations Combining Polygons

There are many wonderful handbooks, book chapters, and resource guides for helping children understand and work with tessellations. Our intent is to illustrate ways of interrelating ideas in two and three dimensions through problem-solving activities.

Recall that a regular tessellation involves tiling the plane with one regular polygon; only the equilateral triangle, square, and hexagon will accomplish this feat. However, mixing together several regular polygons can also tile the plane. A key distinction that mathematicians make about tessellations involves the vertices where the common edges of polygons come together at a point: does the same set of shapes or angles move in cyclical order around that point? Those tessellations that meet this criterion of the same patterns of shapes around each vertex are called *semi regular*. There are only 8 of them.

Ask students to work with a set of equilateral triangles and squares, all of which have sides of the same length. Thus, common edges can be readily joined. Ask students to tile the plane with sets of these two polygons. Have the class find as many different ways of doing so as possible.

Recording solutions is important but can be a bit tricky. Students can trace the perimeters of individual pieces. Another method is to draw the tessellation using templates of hollow squares and triangles for drawing.

Students should determine which tessellations are actually different from one another. Rotations often appear to be different when they are not. Figures 7.30 and 7.31 show tessellations of triangles and squares.

Ask students to examine carefully the various vertices of each tessellation they have found. Both tessellations in figure 7.30 have 3 triangles and 2 squares at the vertices. All vertices of the one on

Figure 7.30

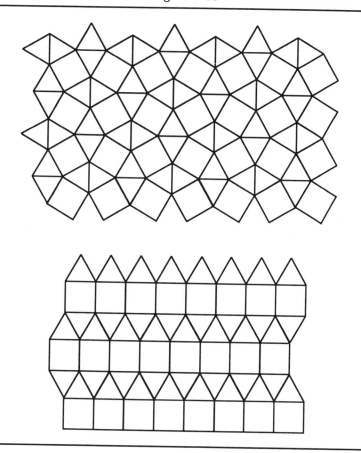

Figure 7.31

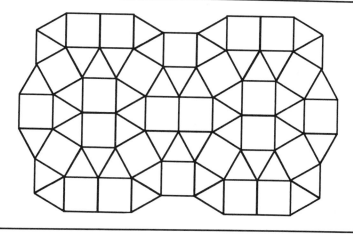

Figure 7.32

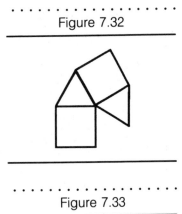

Figure 7.33

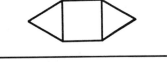

Figure 7.34

4 of these

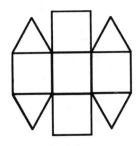

1 of these

1 of these

top are in the same sequence: triangle, triangle, square, triangle, square; or simply, 3,3,4,3,4. The other has vertices of 3,3,3,4,4. Therefore, they are both semiregular tessellations.

In contrast, the tessellation in figure 7.31 has two different types of vertices; some are 3,3,4,3,4 and others are 3,3,3,4,4. Therefore it is not a semiregular tessellation; it is simply an elegant, unusual tessellation. ●

There are three interesting *polyhedra* formed with faces of triangles and squares. To find them, we give students their basic building blocks: the essential pattern that each vertex of the polyhedra contains.

Begin by giving students a picture of the shape in figure 7.32. We ask students to imagine folding up the 2 squares and 2 triangles. When joined, they constitute the regular pattern of polygons at the vertex.

The problem for students is then to use 2 of these shapes plus 2 of the shapes in figure 7.33 to create a polyhedron that will contain 8 triangles and 6 squares. Students should make 2 of each of these shapes with Googolplex and then try to create the polyhedron.

Younger students can create this polyhedron. However, some may need to actually *see* an example of the polyhedron in order to analyze it visually and imagine how to form their pieces into it. We heartily recommend that the teacher make an example of all the unfamiliar polyhedra in this chapter.

The second polyhedron requires 8 triangles and 18 squares. The regular pattern of the vertices is 3 squares and 1 triangle. Students should make the pieces shown in figure 7.34, then fold and join them. The problem is to form them into the polyhedron. Note that they must make 4 pieces that contain the basic building block of 3 squares and 1 triangle at a vertex. The other piece that looks a bit like a cap also shows this criterion, but in a different way. Remind students that one additional square will be needed to complete the polyhedron. When completed, students should be able to see two strips or bands of squares going around the polyhedron. If not, tell them to rotate the cap piece.

Another polyhedron requires 32 triangles and 6 squares. The basic building block is the common vertex of 4 triangles and 1 square; 5 such pieces must be made, folded, and joined (see figure 7.35). Two strips of 4 triangles each are need as well as one piece of a square surrounded by 4 triangles. These pieces should be made and folded but not joined until the 5 basic pieces have been joined to one another. For instance, the lone piece (square surrounded by triangles) could be completely folded and sides joined together into a square-based pyramid, but that would never fit into the surface of a larger polyhedron.

Ask students if the plane can be tiled by some combination of hexagons and triangles. Give them a quantity of pattern blocks of

Figure 7.35

 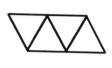 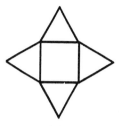

5 of these   2 of these   1 of these

these 2 polygons and charge them with trying to find a
semiregular tessellation. There are only 2, shown in figure 7.36.
One has a common vertex of 3,6,3,6. The other has 3,3,3,3,6.

None of the other tessellations of triangles and hexagons have
only one common pattern at each vertex. For instance, note how
the tessellation in figure 7.37 has two different patterns at the
vertices (3,3,6,6 and 3,6,3,6).

Can triangles and hexagons be joined to form a polyhedron?
Figure 7.38 presents a fairly simple challenge to students. The
building block at each vertex is 2 hexagons and a triangle. A total
of 4 triangles and 4 hexagons are needed to make the
polyhedron. Googolplex does not have hexagons, but they can be
made by joining six Googolplex triangle frames. The resulting
polyhedron has 8 faces; it looks like a tetrahedron with its vertices
sliced off. ●

Figure 7.36

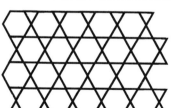

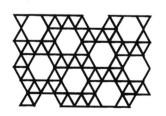

Figure 7.37

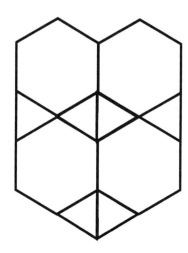

Figure 7.38

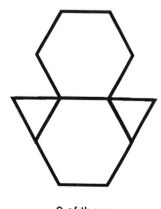

2 of these

Figure 7.39

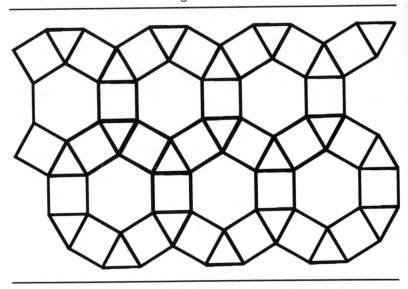

Tessellating hexagons, triangles, *and* squares on the plane can yield several fascinating patterns, only one of which is semiregular.

G ive students a quantity of these 3 polygons and ask them to find various tessellations. Figure 7.39 shows the only semiregular one, with triangle, square, hexagon, and triangle meeting at each vertex (3,4,6,4). Figures 7.40 and 7.41 show two

Figure 7.40

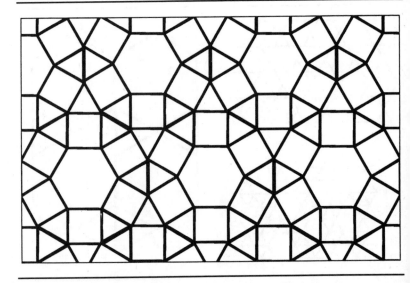

Figure 7.41

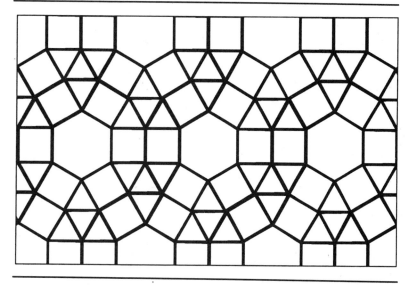

other lovely tessellations having some vertices without hexagons at all. ●

The following activities involve polyhedra.

There is an interesting polyhedron formed with squares and hexagons. The fundamental vertex is composed of 1 square and 2 hexagons. Altogether 6 squares and 8 hexagons are needed. Figure 7.42 shows how Googolplex pieces (using 6 triangles to form each hexagon) can be initially linked for students to try to create this polyhedron. Can they make it?

Figure 7.42

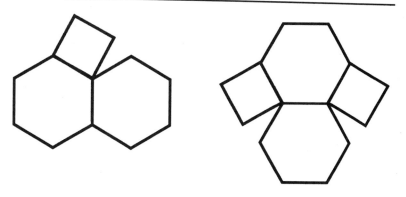

2 of each

Figure 7.43

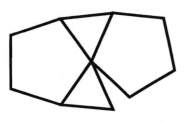

5 of these

Two other polyhedra offer excellent challenges to students. Both involve regular pentagons. In the first polyhedron, 2 pentagons and 2 triangles meet at a point to form the common vertex. Students will need a total of 20 triangles and 12 pentagons from Googolplex pieces. Figure 7.43 shows how 5 of the fundamental shapes as well as 2 additional shapes are needed.

The other polyhedron is the popular soccer ball: 12 pentagons and 20 hexagons are combined using the common vertex of 2 hexagons and 1 pentagon. Have students make 10 of the fundamental pieces shown in figure 7.44. Using these plus 2 additional squares, can they make the soccer ball? ●

Figure 7.44

2 of these

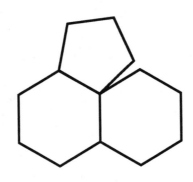

10 of these

2 of these

Investigations with Isosceles Right Triangles

Figure 7.45

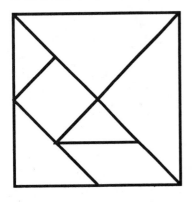

Much has been written about the Chinese *tangrams*—with some dating as far back as 1800. Many resource books are available that show a host of figures that can be made with the 7 pieces, sets of which are readily available in hard plastic. Figure 7.45 shows the traditional arrangement of all 7 into a large square.

In the following activities, students investigate the "essence" of the tangram.

A sk students to analyze the 7 shapes. Compare and contrast them. What do they see? The smallest shape is a triangle; there are 2 of them. By matching sides, students can demonstrate that they are isosceles right triangles.

Ask students to compare these triangles to the other tangram pieces. Fit together their long sides and they form a square, congruent to the square piece in the tangram. Fitting together at their other sides, they will form either the parallelogram or the middle-sized triangle of the tangram. Finally, how do the 2 small triangles compare to the large triangles of the tangram? Four little ones can be arranged to make the large triangle. Thus, a total of 16 of these small triangles have been joined in particular ways to form the 7 tangram pieces.

Whenever students are contemplating the creation of some figure with tangram pieces, we encourage them to analyze their task in terms of the 16 small triangles that must be present. For instance, a problem in many resource books ask students to make a square of any size out of any size out of 2 tangram pieces, then any 3, any 4, any 5, or any 6. Obviously, all 7 can form a square. The catch is that there is no way that 6 pieces can form a square. Ask students to determine why not. By conceiving of the task in terms of these 16 small triangles, older students can usually come up with some good explanations.

Here is what older students can realize: the isosceles right triangles can make squares in two ways: with either hypotenueses (long sides) or their short sides as the perimeter of the square (see figure 7.46).

Using 6 tangram pieces means ignoring one piece, thus eliminating either 1, 2, or 4 of the small triangles. Therefore, a 6-piece square would have to contain either 15, 14, or 12 small triangles.

Squares can be made with either 2 or 4 triangles. Using these as building blocks for larger squares would require totals of either 8 or 16 small triangles. There are no other sizes of squares within the reach of the tangrams (see figure 7.46). Thus, squares with 12, 14, or 15 small triangles are not possible.

. . . .

Figure 7.46

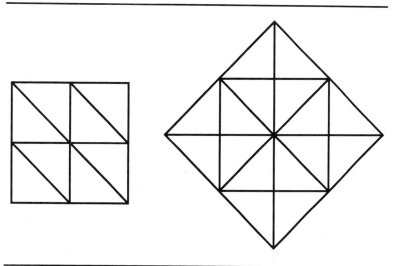

Figure 7.47

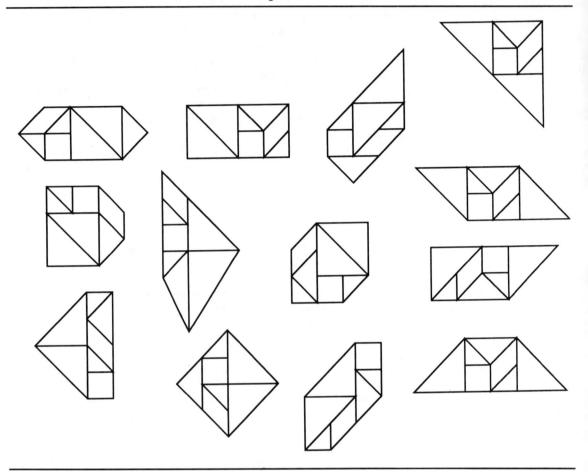

Using similar reasoning students can be challenged to create triangles, rectangles, parallelograms, and trapezoids using different numbers of pieces. Ask them to determine which ones are possible.

A related and equally challenging problem to pose to students is finding all the convex polygons (regular or irregular) that can be made by using all 7 pieces. There are 13 different possibilities, not including reflections (see figure 7.47).

If you want to extend students' thinking into more computational directions, ask students to conceive of the square tangram piece (2 triangles) as one square unit of measure. Then ask the following questions:

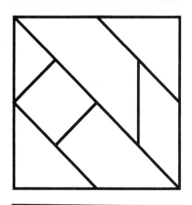

Figure 7.48

- What is the area of each other piece?
- Can quadrilaterals be formed that have areas of 1.5, 2, 2.5, and so forth, increasing by .5 up to 4 square units?
- Can a trapezoid be formed that is ¾ the area of the large square made from all 7 pieces? How about a parallelogram of the same area? ●

There is another set of shapes bearing a remarkable resemblance to the 7-piece tangram. Figure 7.48 shows the seven Sei Shonagon pieces from eighteenth-century Japan, described in Gardner (1988).

Just as with the tangram, the Sei Shonagon pieces are also based on a total of 16 of the small isosceles right triangles. By taping together various tangram pieces from several sets, the 7 Shonagon pieces can be made. Obviously, its total area, the large square, is the same as the tangram.

Ask students to take 2 tangram sets and discard the 4 large triangles; they must work with the remaining 10 pieces. Then give them the drawing of the Shonagon pieces in figure 7.48 and ask them to find the simplest way of taping these 10 pieces together to make the 7 Shonagon pieces.

The Shonagon pieces can be arranged into a square in a different way than figure 7.48, unlike the tangram pieces that can form a square in only one way. Also, the Shonagon pieces can form an even larger square with a central square hole (another feat impossible for the tangram). Figure 7.49 shows these two solutions. Finding them are excellent tasks for students.

Figure 7.49

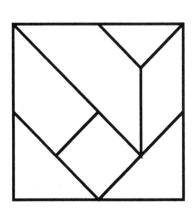

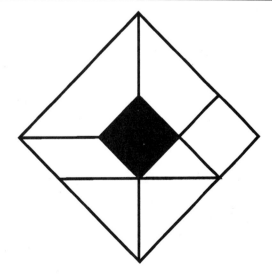

· ·

Figure 7.50

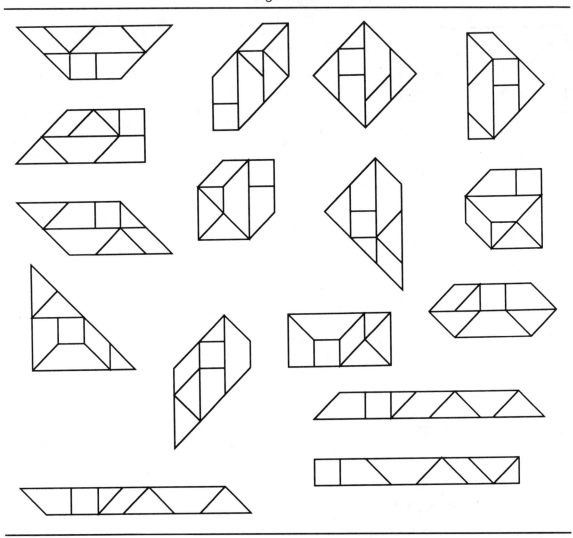

No popular books exist using the Shonagon pieces, therefore you and your students can explore uncharted territory. As in the tangrams, ask students to find:

- All the regular convex polygons of various sizes using from two to seven of Shonagon pieces.
- All the convex polygons that are possible with the seven pieces. (Hint: since the arrangement in Figure 7.48 is halved by the diagonal, the two halves can be moved and reconnected in several ways.)
- Which ones are congruent between the tangram and Shonagon sets?

Figure 7.51

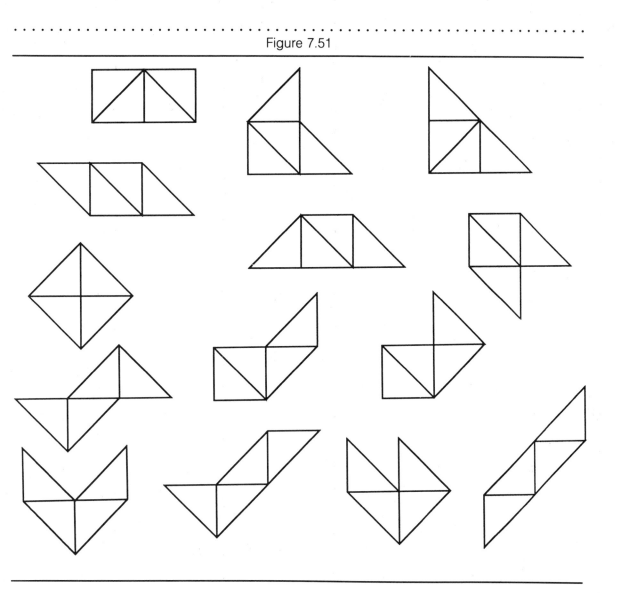

Our students have found sixteen different convex polygons formed by the Shonagon pieces (see figure 7.50). Of particular interest are several long, thin figures with the height of the small square piece (rectangle, parallelogram, and trapezoid); they are not possible with the tangram because of its two large triangles.

In one sense the tangram and Sei Shonagon shapes can be seen as particular pieces from a larger set formed by joining these small isosceles right triangles. How many different ways can 2, 3, or 4 of them be joined? Two of these triangles can be readily seen in the square, parallelogram, and middle-sized triangle of the tangram. Armed with four of the small triangles from gathered from two sets of tangrams, students should try to find all the ways to join 3 triangles (4 ways). Then they should try to find all the ways to join 4 of the triangles (14 ways shown in figure 7.51). ●

These 14 shapes are commercially available from Creative Publications under the name "SuperTangrams." Many different rectangles can be made with them, but also many that appear possible are not. Distinguishing between those made with short-sided versus long-sided squares (as shown in 7.46) is a good analytical device for older students.

Working with Cubes in Space

What would it mean to tessellate in space? The most versatile three-dimensional figure for completely filling space is obviously the cube. Many wonderful activities for building three-dimensional shapes with cubes have been developed. Wooden and plastic cubes abound in catalogs. Some of these can be readily joined at their faces (such as Multilink cubes); others may be taped.

To begin, ask students to join cubes at their faces to find the two ways to join 3 cubes; obviously there is only one way to join 2 cubes. Three cubes form either a 3-in-a-row piece or the L-shaped tricube (see figure 7.52).

Can we use L-shaped tricubes to make larger cubes? If the smallest cube is the "unit" cube (1 by 1 by 1), then the next would be the 2-sided cube (2 by 2 by 2), requiring 8 cubes. Thus, tricubes, by themselves, cannot form the 2-sided cube because they come in sets of 3. But 2 of them plus 1 of the double cubes can make this larger cube quite simply. Next, ask students to describe the ways of combining 2 tricubes. One way is a rectangle (1 by 2 by 3) flat on the plane.

Figure 7.52

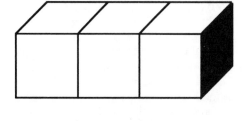
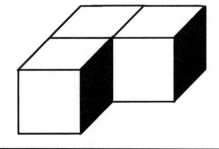

· ·
Figure 7.53

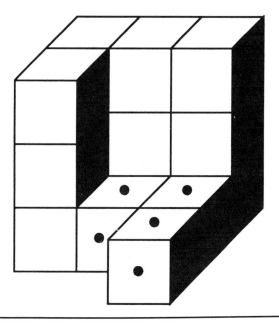

Can L-shaped tricubes form a large 3-sided cube (3 by 3 by 3) that requires 27 cubes? It can be done with 9 tricubes, but it is tricky unless students grasp the idea of *pairing* 2 tricubes into the flat rectangle. The technique of pairing cube shapes to make larger, more readily conceivable and usable shapes will occur frequently. It is a powerful principle analogous to composing in tessellations on the plane.

Figure 7.53 attempts the somewhat difficult task of representing on paper the key feature of how the tricubes can form the larger cube in space. Two of the 6-piece rectangles (formed by 2 tricubes) are standing vertically behind 1 tricube that is lying flat (marked with dots). If 2 more tricubes are stacked on top of this one, then the remaining tricubes can be combined into another rectangle to fit vertically into place. ●

In the next set of activities students will make tetracubes, shapes formed by 4 joined cubes. There are 8 of these, shown in figure 7.54.

Have students tape together individual cubes or connect Multilink cubes so that they can rotate these shapes in space, handling them easily. Ask them to compare and contrast these tetracubes. Five can lie flat on the plane; 2 of these are "regular,"

Figure 7.54

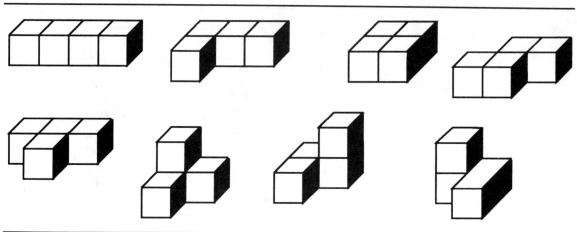

the rectangle and the square. Of the 3 shapes that cannot lie flat and must extend upwards, one pair is a mirror-image reflection. An important idea to emphasize at this point is that we excluded reflections when dealing with shapes on the plane because they could be turned over to use either side. However, we have a different situation with these cubes. Ask students to "turn over" one of the mirror-pair tetracubes. There is no way that we can orient this shape in space to be identical to its twin. Therefore, we must treat these two as different shapes; related, but different, nonetheless.

We have found it quite valuable to have students match the tetracubes they have made with the pictorial representations in figure 7.54. These two-dimensional drawings of three-dimensional shapes are often remarkably difficult for students. Yet with experience, they can conceive of these drawings. Despite other ways to draw cubes in space, we prefer shading one side, as if light were coming from one direction. The real objects are solid and they do cast shadows. You may even want to shine a lamp on these shapes to demonstrate this feature.

We do not advise asking students to try to draw pictures of cubical shapes. Even older students have great difficulty doing so. Work in space with manipulatives and visualizing drawings are quite sufficient.

A technique that greatly aids visualization is to make each of the tetracubes out of a different color. When they are combined into larger structures, this coloring helps a person discern how the structure was made. Even when making the 3-sided cube from 9 tricubes, using 9 different colors greatly helps someone see what was done. Multilink cubes come in 10 colors.

Ask students if they can make larger cubes from the tetracubes. The 2-sided cube requires 8 total cubes. Can any 2 of these tetracubes be combined to do so? No, although students will try mightily to do so. On the other hand, ask small groups of students to share tetracubes and ask, "Can two identical tetracubes form the two-sided cube?" Four cannot, but 4 can. Students can easily see that 4 of the 5 that lie flat cannot because they extend beyond the 2-by-2 bottom of the 2-sided cube. Obviously, 2 square tetracubes need only lie on top of one another. The other 3 tetracubes marvelously fit together with their identical shape to form the larger cube.

The 8 tetracubes (32 unit cubes, in total), cannot be combined into a 3-sided cube that requires 27 cubes. However, they can form a 2-by-4-by-4 rectangular solid. They also will make 2 congruent 2-by-2-by-4 rectangular solids. Ask students to try to find these solids. ●

Another excellent problem, posed by mathematician John Horton Conway, runs as follows:

Ask students to make a 3-sided cube from 6 of the *square* tetracubes plus 3 individual cubes. Figure 7.55 shows how 2 square tetracubes can be placed vertically into an L shape and another can lie flat into the L (note the dotted tetracube). An *X* on one of the single cubes shows where it is placed to complete the bottom of the large cube. Interestingly, with a single cube in the center of the large cube, the mirror image of the shape in figure 7.55 can be rotated to complete the large cube. ●

Undoubtedly, the most famous of all tetracube constructions is the Soma cube devised by mathematician Piet Hein. The 7 Soma pieces include the L-shaped tricube and the 6 irregular tetracubes (the rectangle and the square are excluded). Sets of Soma cube pieces are commercially available with many suggested constructions. Students can make their own tricube and tetracube pieces and then try to construct the 3-sided cube. It is readily attainable with persistence; there are more than 230 different solutions, not counting rotations and reflections.

Creating a set of the 29 different pentacubes is quite a challenge. However, if the task is broken down a bit it is within reach of fifth or sixth graders.

Ask the students to recall the 12 pentominoes (5 squares). Squares have no "height"; ask students to conceive of the pentominoes being made from cubes instead of squares. Thus, students can begin by creating 12 of the 29 pentacubes from already familiar shapes. These are the only pentacubes that lie flat on the plane.

Figure 7.55

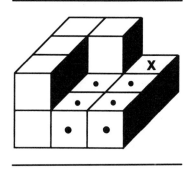

Figure 7.56

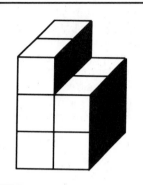

The other 17 pentacubes can be found by systematically adding one cube in various places to the tetracubes. Students will find that 5 of them are symmetrical with no mirror image, while the other 12 are actually 6 mirror-image pairs. Students should find these 17 pentacubes and sort them into these categories.

An excellent introductory problem involves the 12 pentacubes that form 6 mirror-image pairs. Ask students to combine these 12 pentacubes two at a time into various shapes. What can be made? Combining mirror pairs is not nearly as interesting as combining other sets of 2. Most students are delighted to discover that 4 congruent "high chairs" can be formed (see figure 7.56).

Creative Publications markets a set of 25 of the pentacubes as 3-D Pentominoes. Why 25 instead of the full set of 29? How many cubes are included in 25 pentacubes: 125. Just the right amount to make a 5-sided cube, an extraordinarily difficult task.

There are many constructions possible for older students with the pentacubes. The 12 flat pentacubes (the cube version of pentominoes) can be combined into various rectangular solids; not without great persistence, however. Possible rectangular solids are 2 by 3 by 10, 2 by 5 by 6, and 3 by 4 by 5.

A more solvable problem is the following: using the 8 mirror-pair pentacubes that form the 4 chairs, find a rectangular solid that is 2 by 4 by 5. Give them the hint that the pairing technique we have discussed may be helpful once again. Pairs can form chairs and pairs of chairs can form the rectangular solid.

What mixture of tetracubes and the pentacubes might be used to make the 3-sided cube? Students can wrestle with the essential numbers involved. Twenty-seven total cubes can come only from 3 of each type of cube. There is a nasty little cube problem from a mathematician that gives 3 particular cubes from each set; it has only 2 very difficult solutions. Instead, we suggest asking students to create their own 3-sided cube with any 3 tetracubes and any 3 pentacubes. When they find a pleasing construction, they should make another version with each separate cube shape a different color. They can then tape the entire large cube together and challenge others to reproduce what they made (without removing the tape, of course). ●

Conclusion

This chapter has included a wide range of problems for using manipulatives to enhance visual and spatial thinking. Many of the concepts are only touched upon in the traditional elementary school curriculum. Despite their bare mention, we believe they are not supplementary, but vital and exciting vehicles for mathematical thinking. They should precede, or at least accompany, the topics of computational geometry, enriching and enlivening its study.

8

· ·
· ·
· ·
· ·
· ·

Mathematical Relationships

Throughout this book, we have illustrated many different mathematical relationships. We have stressed the value of students' perceiving and analyzing patterns, both numerical and visual. Students in elementary school need extensive experiences in exploring objects and phenomena to recognize, describe, and generalize patterns and relationships. As students become more sophisticated in their conceptual understanding and problem solving, they can be led into more formal analysis and abstract representations such as equations. In this chapter, we will provide illustrative activities from several interrelated areas of the curriculum: arrangements and probability, ratios and proportions, drawing graphical representations, and functions and equations.

Arrangements and Probability

In our consumer-oriented society, we are faced each day with a wealth of choices, near infinite variations in what we can eat, wear, drive, or do. These choices can be a source for helping students understand key concepts from combinatorial mathematics (the different ways things can be combined or arranged) and probability (the likelihood of encountering certain of these arrangements or conditions). In this section, we will examine some of these concepts. Here is a problem for students that you can pose and allow them to represent in a number of ways.

Imagine a dish that will hold 2 scoops of ice cream of 2 different flavors. You have 3 traditional flavors from which to choose: chocolate, vanilla, and strawberry. How many arrangements of 2 scoops of *different flavors* could you possibly get? Three can be readily seen:

> 1. Vanilla and chocolate
> 2. Vanilla and strawberry
> 3. Chocolate and strawberry

Now imagine that these scoops are placed into a cone in the order they appear above. How many different arrangements can we have of these three flavors of ice cream in cones if it does matter which flavor is on top? In addition to the 6 combinations above, there are 3 more:

> 4. Chocolate and vanilla
> 5. Strawberry and vanilla
> 6. Strawberry and chocolate

Numbers 4, 5, and 6 are different from 1, 2, and 3 because the order is reversed.

In the first situation (putting the scoops into a dish), the order of the 2 scoops does not matter: this is called a *combination*. However, the second situation is different; order is important (number 1 is different from number 4). This is called a *permutation*. Thus there are 3 different combinations of 2 scoops from 3 flavors and 6 different permutations. In dealing with arrangements, students should stop and think about which kind of situation they are in. The key question is, does the order matter?

Problems with ice-cream flavors can be extended into more flavors or more scoops in many creative ways. Students could look for patterns that form as they extend the problems. For instance, with the dish problem, keep 2 scoops constant and ask: How many combinations of 2 different flavors are possible with 1 flavor? With 2 flavors? With 3, 4, 5, and so on? What is the pattern?

Two scoops

Number of flavors	Number of combinations
1	0
2	1
3	3
4	6
5	10
6	15

The number of combinations forms a pattern that should look familiar to students. We saw it in chapter 5 when investigating blocks arranged in a triangular pattern.

What happens if you want a banana split with 3 scoops? Does it matter which flavor is in the middle? If it does, you'll be dealing with permutations and more possibilities than if it doesn't. ●

You can vary the context of these problems by having the students suggest or find things around them that can be arranged in different combinations. How about pizzas? What are the different items that can go on besides cheese? Have your student brainstorm a list. Then you should make up a problem such as the following:

A pizza parlor offers 6 different extras that may be put on their pizzas. How many different combinations of pizzas can you get by putting any 2 of these 6 different extras on a pizza?

Mathematically speaking, this is the same problem as having 6 possible flavors of ice cream and choosing 2 different flavors to put in a dish.

You can vary the pizza problem by asking what all the different ways are to put those 6 items on a pizza: 2 at a time, 3 at a time, and so on. There is a very different pattern to this problem. Let us say that the 6 extras are

        M (mushrooms)
        P (pepperoni)
        O (onions)
        X (extra cheese)
        G (green olives)
        S (sausage)

Adding 2 at a time gives 15 ways:

MP, MO, MX, MG, MS
PO, PX, PG, PS
OX, OG, OS
XG, XS
GS

We must help students to think carefully about what is going on in the situation and not just crank out some numbers. It is especially important for students to ask themselves if order matters. Is MP different from PM? Not with pizzas; they are correctly called "combination" pizzas by many restaurants.

Adding 3 extras at a time gives 20 ways:

MPO, MPX, MPG, MPS, MOX, MOG, MOS, MXG, MXS, MGS
POX, POG, POS, PXG, PXS, PGS
OXG, OGS, OXS
XGS

Four at a time gives 15 ways:

MPOX, MPOG, MPOS, MPXG, MPXS, MPGS, MOXG, MOXS, MOGS, MXGS, POXG, POXS, POGS, PXGS, OXGS

Five at a time gives only 6 ways; in each case 1 of the extras has been left off:

MPOXG, MPOXS, MPOGS, MPXGS, MOXGS, POXGS

Obviously, all 6 at the same time can only occur in one way: MPOXGS

To be complete we can note that there are 6 different ways to have just one of these extras: M, P, O, X, G, S. There is also only one kind of pizza that you can get with no (zero) extras. Therefore a summary table might be as follows:

Number of extras at a time	Number of arrangements
0	1
1	6
2	15
3	20
4	15
5	6
6	1

Notice the numerical pattern increases up to 20, then curiously decreases symmetrically.

A somewhat different problem can help students understand another important concept and how it applies to permutations.

Ask students to write down the names of 4 U.S. cities or vacation spots that they would like to visit. Then ask them: "If you had four one-week vacations during the year (one in each season—fall, winter, spring, summer), how would you arrange these visits?" After they have made their decisions, tell them that the travel agency cannot guarantee that the vacations can be made to the 4 places during those particular seasons. What is another good way to schedule these 4 places in the 4 seasons? Obviously, order does matter. Now the key question: How many different ways could these 4 cities be visited in the 4 seasons?

Students could generate a listing of all the possible arrangements; however, older students who have worked with permutations a bit might be able to see a pattern. In either case, the postactivity discussion should address the following:

- For the first vacation in the fall, any one of the 4 cities may be visited. There are 4 ways that this could happen.
- For the second trip in the winter, any one of the 3 cities may be visited. There are 12 ways that this could happen.

How can there be 12 ways? See the following table that uses Albuquerque (A), Boston (B), Chicago (C), and Denver (D) as the four cities.

Fall Can go to any of the 4	Winter Can go to any of the 3 left	Spring Can go to any of the 2 left	Summer Can go to the one left
If Albuquerque (A), then	⟶ B or ⟶ C or ⟶ D		
If Boston (B) then	⟶ A or ⟶ C or ⟶ D		

	Fall Can go to any of the 4	Winter Can go to any of the 3 left	Spring Can go to any of the 2 left	Summer Can go to the one left
If Chicago (C) then	⟶ A or ⟶ B or ⟶ D			
If Denver (D), then	⟶ A or ⟶ B or ⟶ C			
Total ways: 4	**12**	**??**	**??**	

Ask students to create a table such as this one for their 4 cities and complete the two right-hand columns for Spring and Summer. Ask them, "What pattern do you see?"

This problem illustrates the "fundamental counting principle": the number of ways that several decisions can be made in succession is found by multiplying the numbers of choices that can be made at each decision. In this case, $4 \times 3 \times 2 \times 1 = 24$. There are 24 different orders in which to visit the 4 cities.

Older students could be asked: What would be the effect of adding a fifth city? How many possible arrangements of visits would there be? The number jumps to an astonishing 120 ($5 \times 4 \times 3 \times 2 \times 1$). If a rock band were planning to make a 6-city tour, how many different ways might they do it? There are 720 different possibilities.

Here is a slight, but important shift in questioning. Ask students to think back to the 4 cities in 4 seasons. Imagine that a travel agent made all the flight arrangements, believing that it doesn't matter how the 4 cities were visited across the 4 seasons. If so, then any one of these 24 different arrangements might be made. Ask the students to consider that it *does* matter and that they definitely want to go to Albuquerque in the fall. What are the "chances" that Albuquerque would be scheduled for the fall trip by the travel agent even though he did not intentionally do so?

This question is attempting to build a link between arrangements and probability. The key issue for students is to conceive that there are many different possibilities that could occur and we are interested in only some of them. They need to know what are all the possible outcomes or at least how many of them there can be. Then they need to know how many (or what kinds) of the particular outcome of interest there can be. In this case, there are 24 ways to visit the four cities; therefore, the travel agent may make any one of these 24 different arrangements. Of these, only 6 have Albuquerque as the place to visit in the fall. Therefore, only 6 of the 24 possibilities are what is desired (favorable outcomes).

With younger students, it is inappropriate to get into the

numerical aspects of probability. The natural language for discussing possible outcomes is much more important. Think about the different ways to express the important aspects of the concept:

- Do you think we will be going to Albuquerque in the fall?
- Is it more likely that we will be going to Albuquerque in the fall or during one of the other seasons?
- What are the chances that Albuquerque will be planned for the fall?
- How likely is it that Albuquerque will be planned for the fall?
- How probable is it that Albuquerque will be planned for the fall? ●

Here is another activity that will help students get a grasp of these ideas:

T ell students that, for a holiday treat you will be buying 1 candy bar for each them. Pass around a sign-up sheet with 5 or 6 candy bars that you have already bought in quantity (unbeknownst to them). Tally the sign-up sheet so that students can see a table of how many of each type you intend to "buy." Get that many of each kind and wrap each one separately (aluminum foil is a simple and fast way). Make up stickers with students' names and stick one on each candy bar *at random*.

Tell the students that you wrapped the candy bars before you realized that you had "lost" the list of which kind each student had requested. Tell them that you placed the name tags any which way. Give students the tally sheet showing how many of each kind were bought and ask: Do you think you will get what you asked for? Imagine that the tally sheet showed something like the following:

Choco-delight	9
Piles-a-peanuts	7
Crunchy-wunchy	5
Banana-bonker	3
Licorice-lasso	2
Lemon-zonker	1
Total	27

By asking if they think they'll get what they asked for, the teacher gets at the simplest sense of probability for students to grasp. Do I think I will or will not—yes or no? Some will also feel the sense of not being very sure (certain) about what will happen.

The teacher can next focus on the two ends of the table by asking: Who wanted the Lemon-zonker? Do you think you'll get it? Why or why not? There is only 1 of these candy bars among the 27; thus, there are 26 other candy bars that this student could get. It is not very likely that he will get his Lemon-zonker. Another set of questions could then be used: Who were the 9 students who wanted Choco-delights? Do you think you'll get them? Are you more likely to get them than the person who wanted the Lemon-zonker? Why? Nine of the 27 candy bars are Choco-delights (a third); therefore, it is far more likely that some of these students will get what they requested.

Pass out the candy bars and see what did happen. Let the students trade with one another for what they really wanted. We would not push too hard on the numerical analysis since an initial experiential understanding of the major ideas is what we are after. The next activity will show how the numerical analysis can be accomplished. ●

Montana Red Dog is a card game from the Old West in which students predict whether or not their 4-card hand from a deck of playing cards can beat a fifth card that the teacher turns up. To win, one of the students' cards must be higher *and of the same suit* as the teacher's card. The teacher can use the activity to develop understanding of fractions, percentages, and ratios.

A rrange students into groups of 2 or 3 in order to make 10 groups. The activity works best with a oversized deck of standard playing cards that can be purchased at magic shops or through catalogs. The jokers are removed and the cards in each suit go from a low of 2 to a high of ace. In each *round*, the teacher shuffles and deals 4 cards face down to each group. Thus, 40 cards are dealt and 12 remain with the teacher. Groups may look at their own cards but not at each other's. The teacher's cards must not be shown. Each group will get a turn at trying to beat a different card from the teacher's pile.

In Round One, group members examine their cards and decide how confident they are in beating the teacher's card. By consensus the group decides on one judgment corresponding to a number between 1 and 4. The teacher puts up a sheet of newsprint that lists what each number means:

1. We don't think we can beat it.
2. We think we might beat it.
3. We are pretty sure we can beat it.
4. We are certain we can beat it.

Some teachers call this judgment of confidence "betting" from 1 to 4 points. One group at a time shows its cards to the class and states its judgment. Then the teacher turns over the top card from the deck. Students must hold up a card that can beat the teacher's card, if they have one.

In Round Two, the teacher gives one copy of a handout that has 4 columns headed with each suit with A through 2 in descending order underneath. On this handout each group should draw circles around the 4 cards that they have been dealt (see figure 8.1). Then they count how many cards they can definitely beat in each suit (below a circled card) and write this number underneath the column for that suit. They may need to be reminded that if they have no cards in a suit (and thus no circled cards in that suit), then the number that should be written underneath that column is 0. Students should add the 4 column numbers and write this sum in the lower right-hand corner of the page.

Next students should calculate all the cards that they cannot beat (all cards above the highest circled card in any suits *and* all 13 cards in a suit in which they have no cards). They should write these 4 numbers at the top of the suits columns above the names of the suits, add them, and write this sum in the upper right-hand corner. Students should work as a group using one handout sheet, with members of the group helping with the tasks of counting and adding. One simple check on their totals is that the 2 totals must sum to 48 (the total number of cards in the deck minus their 4).

The first group shows their 4 cards and states their confidence level from 1 to 4. However, before the teacher's card is shown, they must also state to the class how many cards they can beat and how many they cannot. The teacher should record all this information in the following manner:

Team	Can beat	Cannot beat	Total	Confidence	Outcome
XXX	21	27	48	2	

. . . .

Figure 8.1

Spades	Hearts	Diamonds	Clubs
4	13	3	7 = 27 cannot beat
A	A	A	A
K	K	K	K
Q	Q	Q	Q
J	J	Ⓙ	J
⑩	10	10	10
9	9	9	9
8	8	8	Ⓖ 8
7	7	7	⑦
6	6	6	6
⑤	5	5	5
4	4	4	4
3	3	3	3
2	2	2	2
7	0	9	5 = 21 can beat

When the teacher's card is shown, the outcome (W or L) can be recorded.

At the end of Round Two, the teacher should lead a discussion by asking key questions, such as

- Who had the best situation for winning? Why?
- Who had the worst? Why?
- Which groups have about the same number of "can beats" as "cannot beats?" What do you think that means?
- How should these numbers affect what number of confidence (bet) you pick?

At the start of Round Three, cards are dealt and all 10 groups circle their 4 cards. The first group makes its judgment and sees the teacher's card as before. This group and the teacher show the 5 cards involved to the class. Now all other groups can cross off these 5 cards from their sheets and *recalculate* their 2 key numbers (can beat vs. cannot beat).

The next group to compete will be considering 43 unknown cards. The round continues in this fashion with each successive group having 5 less cards to consider. The group name, key numbers, total, confidence level, and outcome should be entered into a chart as before.

The students in tenth group will have the benefit of knowing all the cards that have been shown except the 3 remaining in the teacher's pile. If they are very fortunate, they will be able to beat all 3 cards. Thus, they will be *certain* of the outcome. Of course, an earlier group might also be in a situation of certainty because of the particular cards involved.

In the postround discussion, each group will have a different number of total missing cards. Thus, the answer is not obvious when the teacher asks: Which group had the best chance of winning (e.g., 39 can beats and 4 cannots versus 25 can beats and 3 cannots)? Comparing the possible favorable outcomes to the total as fractions (e.g., $\frac{39}{43}$ vs. $\frac{25}{28}$) and as percentages (90.7% vs. 89.3%) illustrates the power of the latter.

Students can also move from percentages to "odds" by using the 2 columns of can beat and cannot beat as a ratio. For instance, 16 can beat and 32 cannot beat is 33.33% favorable outcomes of the total. It can also be referred to as 16 to 32 or 1 to 2 odds for winning vs. losing. Another common way to refer to this situation is 2 to 1 against winning.

Because the activity nearly always involves situations of *uncertainty*, some groups will lose despite high percentages or will win even with low percentages. With proper discussion, these surprises can also enrich students' conceptual understanding of probabilities. ●

. . . .

Ratio and Proportion

There are many interconnections among the concepts of ratio, proportion, fractions, decimals, and percents. If handled well by the teacher and text, they can greatly assist students' conceptual and procedural understanding. However, connections also can be a source of confusion, especially when the procedures for symbol manipulation are stressed.

Students must grasp that at the heart of these concepts there is a relationship between two things. Fractions express the relationship between a part and the whole. The part may be seen as a size (half of the candy bar) or as a quantity (6 of the 12 jelly beans). When thinking in decimals, one looks at the part/whole relationship in a special way, seeing the whole is terms of tenths, hundredths, and so on. This thinking shifts a bit for percents and the whole is imagined to be 100.

Each of these concepts can be considered to be a special kind of *ratio* in which two things are related to each other. However, the concept of ratio is much broader than part/whole relationships. It can extend to comparing any two things, quantities, or measures, and they do not even have to be the same types of things.

The fundamental multiplicative aspect of ratios is experienced by younger students when noticing how 1 person has 2 eyes, 2 people have 4 eyes, 3 have 6, and so on. When teaching multiplication, teachers use these relationships to build conceptual understanding. Teachers should help students to make charts that show the inherent patterns of these relationships.

Similarly, equivalent amounts of money illustrate both multiplication and ratio relationships. One dollar is 10 dimes; 2 are 20; and so on. One quarter is 5 nickels; 2 are 10; and so on. In this same way, working with the equivalences of various measures is helpful (e.g., 3 feet is 1 yard, 60 seconds is a minute, etc.).

As with money, students need to see how these units retain the basic ratio of their definition through the multiplicative relationship. Younger students need to measure physically and see with their own eyes that 3 feet really is 36 inches, 3 chunks of 12. This is analogous to physically manipulating money, exchanging 5 dimes for 5 groups of 10 pennies, one group at a time.

One of the best ways for students to address ratio is through *scaling*, in which they measure physical objects that vary in size but retain their fundamental shape and hence, relationships (e.g., similar geometric figures). You can start scaling with the following simple activity.

Ask a student to go to lower-left corner of the chalkboard with a centimeter ruler and draw a horizontal straight line that begins at the left side. It can be any length as long as its measure in centimeters is an integer. When completed, ask another student also to begin at the left side of the chalkboard and draw a line a little bit above the first, *twice as long*, going in the same horizontal direction.

Now ask the class: If we repeat this action, each line beginning at the left side, double the length of the preceding one, how many students will it take before the next line cannot be drawn because it would be too long for the board? Have them guess, then proceed ahead with successive doubling by students. Even if the initial line was only 1 centimeter long, drawn horizontally on a 5-meter chalk board, the tenth student could not draw the next line. In discussing the activity later, be sure to point to several pairs of successive lines and ask what the relationship between them is. Repeat this activity with tripling and students may be surprised to see that even with a 1-centimeter start, the seventh student cannot continue. ●

A number of interesting ratio activities can be done with recipes.

For instance, if 2 tablespoons of a drink mix should be mixed with 8 ounces of water, how many spoonfuls would be need if we used 16 ounces? Through working with various recipes and relationships, younger students can see that if you double one of the ingredients, then you should double the others also. Similarly, if we only had 1 tablespoon of drink mix, how much water should be added? Students can usually see that half as much of one ingredient requires half as much of the other (4 ounces). If younger students can't readily see these relationships, then adding the wrong amounts of water to drink mix and tasting will spur some real motivation.

However, fully developed proportional reasoning is not only using multiplicative relationships with the same ingredient or entity. In the situations of drink mix and water just described, the following table summarizes what was concluded.

Spoonfuls of drink mix	Ounces of water
2	8
? (4)	16
1	? (4)

Simple proportional reasoning suggested that doubling the water meant doubling the drink mix; halving the mix meant halving the water. Ask students how much water would be needed if we had 3 spoonfuls of drink mix?

Spoonfuls of drink mix	Ounces of water
2	8
3	?

In this case, increasing the spoonfuls from 2 to 3 creates a problem for students who do not fully grasp what is happening with proportions. Some erroneously reason that adding 1 to the left column means you must add 1 to the right.

In order to help the students realize that the numerical ratio of drink mix to water is 2 to 8 (2:8) or 1 to 4 (1:4), students need to play with some recipes and some charts of the numbers that they found.

Give students the basic relationship of 2:8 and let them figure out what other amounts must be present to keep the same relationship for a variety of amounts that you suggest, all of which are easy to compare within the same column. For instance, consider the following:

Spoonfuls of drink mix	Ounces of water
2	8
?	16
8	?
1	?
?	48

Then ask students to reorganize these 5 examples of the relationship into a new table that starts with 1 spoonful and increases the number of spoonfuls.

Spoonfuls of drink mix	Ounces of water
1	4
2	8
4	16
8	32
12	48

Now students can begin to see that the *pattern* that is at the heart of the relationship is the ratio of drink mix to water. Older students can begin to see that we can think of proportional relationships in several ways. Not only is 4 : 8 as 1 : 2 (water to water in the same relationship as mix to mix), but also 1 : 4 as 2 : 8 (the ratio of mix to water must be the same). Now ask students what amounts of water we would need with 3 spoonfuls. In your discussion, note how 1 : 3 is equivalent to 4 : 12 and 1 : 4 is equivalent to 3 : 12. Then students can determine how much water would be needed for 5, 6, or 7 spoonfuls of drink mix. ●

If students have worked with tangram pieces and other geometric figures and shapes, the following activity will have a strong experiential base.

Collect a variety of squares. Find at least 6 squares of different sizes around the room. With *centimeter* tape measures or rulers, ask students to measure the perimeters of these squares. Older students will realize that they need only measure one side and multiply by 4. For younger students, you can ask them to measure one side and then measure the perimeter and compare the two lengths. Next, have students measure the diagonal of each square.

Make a table similar to the following on the board or on newsprint:

	Length of diagonal	**Length of perimeter**
Square no. 1		

It is helpful for students to create the table so that the squares are ordered from shortest to longest diagonal. Ask students what they see. How are the perimeter and the diagonal related? You may word the question as follows: How many of these diagonals would it take to make the perimeter? In each case the relationship (ratio) is not quite 1 to 3. A little less than 3 of these diagonal lengths would make a perimeter. No matter how big the squares may get, this relationship always appears to be the same.

Younger students do not need to do any calculations; they should simply talk about their estimate of what they have found. Most students can see that the perimeter is never 3 times as big as the diameter. Some may ask, "Is it always the same?" You may ask them, "How can we find out?"

Using a calculator to divide the perimeter by the diagonal is a good idea. The value of using centimeter rulers or tape measures should now be apparent. If the data has been collected as centimeters (and millimeters), then it is in decimal form ready to be entered directly into a calculator (3 centimeters and 5 millimeters is 3.5 centimeters). Be sure to allow for slight errors in measuring these shapes. The constant ratio is about 2.8. Older students may explore why this is (see figure 8.2).

The isosceles right triangle has 2 different lengths for its sides (two short sides and one long, the hypotenuse). Every time we look at a square, we can see 2 of these isosceles right triangles, with the hypotenuse as the diagonal of the square. The relationship between the short side and the hypotenuse is always the same; it is constant, regardless of the actual size of the triangle. Therefore, when we compare the diagonal to the perimeter, the ratio is always 1 long side to 4 short sides. If a short side is 1 centimeter long, then the long side is 1.414. Therefore, the ratio of the diagonal to the perimeter is 1.414 to 4 or about 1 to 2.83.

The next part of the activity requires finding several regular hexagons of different sizes. Pattern blocks may be used. Students may also create hexagons from 6 equilateral triangles. Once again, ask students to measure the lengths of the diagonals (distance between opposite vertices) and the perimeters of each

Figure 8.2

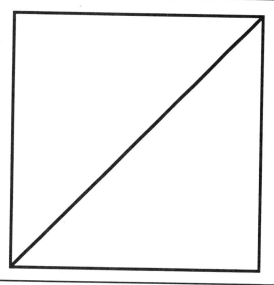

hexagon. When these data are entered into a table comparable to the one for squares, what relationship can be seen? Why? This time students should see in a flash that the diagonal runs along the sides of 2 equilateral triangles. Since the hexagon is formed by 6 of these triangles, the ratio will always be 2 sides to 6 sides (1 : 3) (see figure 8.3).

Finally comes the coup de grace: find 6 or more cylinders of different sizes so that students can measure the circular base with tape measures. Ask them to measure the diameter (essentially, a diagonal) and circumference (the perimeter) of each and enter them into a chart. What is the relationship between these 2 lengths? Even to the eye (and mind) of most third graders, they can see that the relationship is more than 3 times as big. As with the squares, older students can use calculators to compute the ratio. They will find it to be about 3.14. Of course, this is perhaps the most famous ratio students will encounter in elementary school; it even has its own name (pi) and symbol, (π). ●

With this foundation of activities, students will have a strong sense of what is going on and why. Regardless of the size of a circle, the relationship between its diameter and circumference (and hence, its radius and circumference) is always the same. The fact is inherent in the constant ratios among similar shapes.

The concept of π also allows the teacher to discuss another potential confusion for students. If a ratio is the relationship among two numbers (entities, things, quantities), why does the book talk about ratio as a single

Figure 8.3

number, as in the case of π? In real life, we want to find general relationships that are true regardless of the scale. Therefore, we frequently boil down the ratio to the key multiplier. Of course, this multiplier is easier to see when it is an integer (e.g, 5 times as many pennies as nickels) and harder to see when it is an irrational number like π.

If you can provide students with experiences with this multiplicative relationship, they can appreciate that ratios can be expressed as "1 to something" or as "something to 1" (such as the ratio of diameter to circumference is always 1 to 3.1416 . . .). This way of thinking about ratios will be very helpful.

Derived measures

One of the most ignored and frequently misunderstood aspects of ratio is incredibly pervasive in students' lives. Our society is filled with comparisons between two very different kinds of entities so that we cease to consider the two any longer. We speak of distance in feet or miles and time in minutes or hours, but how do we speak of speed? In "gurbs" or "morphs"? No! Speed or velocity does not have its own units of measurement; we depend on two other units (e.g., miles per hour). Why?

Speed is a derived measure in which we relate two other measures in a ratio. We can also refer to it as a *rate*. Many such rates are common in our society and language. The fundamental measures (and their actual quantities) are taken for granted and not reflected upon because of our rich schemata and vast experiences. Instead, we think of the one number of the derived measure. Even younger students have a sense of the "speed limit." But what do the numbers actually refer to? A car may not actually have gone 55 miles in 1 hour: perhaps it really went 11 miles in 12 minutes.

Have students brainstorm and rank order units of measure for length (distance) and time. Then ask them to pair one measure from each list (e.g., miles per hour). Ask them which sound strange (e.g., inches per year)? Which sound familiar (e.g., feet per second)? Are some sensible and others not so? Why? Would we ever speak of millimeters per hour? How many millimeters would a snail travel in an hour? We will return to rate of speed shortly.

Consider the following derived measures; older students should discuss what is going on with some measures that they are familiar with.

- Fuel efficiency (miles per gallon).
- Air pressure for tires (pounds per square inch).
- Wage or salary (dollars per hour or week).
- Typing speed (words per minute).

They should notice that, like velocity, wages and typing speed refer to something relative to time. Ratios look at one measure relative to (in relation to) the other. This point is crucial. Students must have a strong conceptual understanding of each measure, in its own right, and then keep the relationship between the two in mind. Not simple tasks. Consider the following derived measure.

What is "population density"? It is a ratio of population to area. Below is the population density of the fifty states (rounded off to integer values). Ask students to review these data and describe what they see.

How do the students conceive of population? A million people? Ten million people? How many are on their block? In their neighborhood? In their town or city? How do they conceive of area? Square miles? What about miles themselves (long distances)? If these individual measures do not have strong foundations for students, how can the two be juxtaposed? Students often ask: Why does a big state like Texas have a small number for density (54)? What is their conception of "density"? Or "dense"? Will a schema for a forest help? Dense versus sparse collections of trees?

A teacher we know has students study the growth of cities in social studies with a large sheets of paper (3 feet by 4 feet) with grids drawn of one-inch squares (essentially giant graph paper). Each square represents a certain number of feet, constituting a city block. Students are divided into groups and each group is given a sheet of the gridlike graph paper. Natural boundaries of bodies of water and mountains that surround this emerging town/city are drawn on the paper. Over several rounds that represent

---

Population density (people per sq. mile)

State	Density	State	Density	State	Density
Alabama	77	Louisiana	95	Ohio	263
Alaska	1	Maine	36	Oklahoma	44
Arizona	24	Maryland	429	Oregon	27
Arkansas	44	Massachusetts	733	Pennsylvania	264
California	151	Michigan	163	Rhode Island	898
Colorado	28	Minnesota	51	South Carolina	103
Connecticut	638	Mississippi	53	South Dakota	9
Delaware	308	Missouri	71	Tennessee	112
Florida	108	Montana	5	Texas	54
Georgia	94	Nebraska	21	Utah	18
Hawaii	150	Nevada	7	Vermont	55
Idaho	12	New Hampshire	102	Virginia	135
Illinois	205	New Jersey	986	Washington	62
Indiana	153	New Mexico	11	West Virginia	81
Iowa	52	New York	371	Wisconsin	87
Kansas	29	North Carolina	120	Wyoming	5
Kentucky	92	North Dakota	9		

years or decades, the teacher gives each group cubes that represent families. The students must place them on the grid according to various constraints that relate to the societal and geographic concepts she is teaching.

More and more immigrants (cubes) arrive and have less and less land onto which they can move. Eventually, one group of students realizes that the cubes can go on top of one another and they begin to build a city of skyscrapers and high-rise apartment buildings. The population density of urban living is represented by this activity. For each time period, the teacher asks the students to record the number of families, multiply by a factor (say, 5) to get the population, and then divide by a figure representing the area (the number of habitable squares on the grid). Thus, students calculate their own measure of population density. ●

Velocity

Students must grasp that in velocity we are concerned with the rate at which a distance is traveled in a period of time. It is a ratio of distance relative to time. That is a bit abstract, so instead of deductively hitting students with this notion, try sneaking up on them with inductive activities. All you need is a tape measure and a stop watch.

Ask your tallest student (or the one with the biggest feet) to walk a distance of 24 feet across the room in "baby steps," left heel in front of and touching right toe, and so forth. Use the stop watch to time the event. Ask for several more volunteers to repeat this baby-step walk just a little faster than the first student did. Time their walk and record these data.

Record the 8 or 10 sets of distance/time data from the students in a two-column chart. Since the distance was always the same, the successive times recorded should be increasingly shorter if the students were, in fact, walking faster. This idea makes good sense to students, conceptually and logically. It fits with what they just saw and experienced.

Next, play with the numerical, empirical data. Ask how fast was the fastest and how slow was the slowest? Students may answer in terms of the times. Then ask for not the time, but the *speed*. Even though some students may be able to go directly to the idea that one can simply divide the distance measure by the time measure to obtain a measure of velocity, we suggest not doing so. Instead, *talk* about what actually happened (e.g., Harry went 24 feet in about 18 seconds). Then pose some analytical questions, such as: How long did it probably take him to go 12 feet (halfway)? Students see right away that half the distance was traveled in half the time. Measure 12 feet to the halfway point and put a cardboard marker there that says "12 feet in 9 seconds." Repeat questioning for other distances such as 6 feet.

Now a key shift occurs. Instead of cutting distance into parts, we want students to cut up the *time*. Ask the students to take a theoretical time of 16 seconds to walk the 24 feet and cut that into parts, examining the distance you must cover during each time. For instance, if you must go 24 feet in 16 seconds, how far must you go in 8 seconds, then in 4 seconds; these should be the same as when asking for half the distance and then half again. Now can they see what distance you must cover in 2 seconds? One eighth of the time means one-eighth of the distance (3 feet). Mark this distance on the floor from the starting line.

Then ask, "What was the distance covered in one second?" Half again: 1½ feet. The total distance should be marked off into 16 intervals, each 1 second/1½ feet. Then you can try to accomplish the feat of baby stepping 24 feet in 16 seconds.

We have intentionally started the activity with numbers for distance and time that would easily divide into parts, making it possible to get down to the 1-second intervals. All of the cardboard markers from the floor can be copied onto a table on the chalkboard that shows the way that *the same speed* can be described by many different numbers. However, each one is the same ratio. The relationship between the numbers is always the same because the speed was the same. Only after this strong experiential base is built should the *procedure* of dividing the total distance by the total time to get the equivalent of what happened in a 1-second interval be introduced.

Note that the numbers that are used to work empirically with the ratios are "nice" numbers that are easy for students. Also note that we have intentionally used an experiential activity with a relatively slow speed to illustrate the relationship between distance and time so that the speed is almost constant throughout the distance. In other words, acceleration is negligible. Thus, when we mark off the distance into parts of equal length, students can conceive of equal time intervals for each of these distances. ●

Mathematics educator Carole Greenes describes a marvelous question she poses to older students: Can I shoot a marble down the chalkboard tray faster than the speed limit posted in front of the school? The students are intrigued and hotly debate the possibilities. They measure the length of the chalkboard tray and then time with a stopwatch the flight of the marble that she shoots. The students must then convert the rate in feet per second into miles per hour to compare with the speed limit sign. She usually can exceed the speed limit. Here again, students must ignore any acceleration. Most will not even think of it, but some might.

We have been discussing rate (speed or velocity) as a ratio of distance and time. Our approach to helping students think about rate fits with the derived unit of measure for rate and readily conceptualizes questions such as: If I traveled 250 miles in 5 hours, how fast was I going (average rate of speed)? We do *not* suggest using variables or equations to represent this relationship until seventh or eighth grade. When they are introduced, the appropriate algebraic formula would be: $R = D/_T$.

This formula contrasts with one common to textbooks: $R \times T = D$. Most texts try to get students to use this as an all-purpose formula. However, it is only good if one has a well-developed concept of rate. Notice that this formula is most easily used to represent a situation such as: If I go 50 miles per hour for 5 hours, how far will I get?

Of course, these formulas are really different arrangements of the same variables. However, the way they are arranged influences the way students understand them. The first emphasizes the essential ratio relationship. Working with many examples of such ratios will help students build the conceptualization needed to move readily to the formula $R = D/_T$ and then to the more flexible understanding required to work with the traditional formula ($R \times T = D$).

Several fascinating sets of data are available for students to examine rates of speed. Some almanacs list the top speeds of various animals. Here is an excerpt from the *World Almanac and Book of Facts* with the speed given in miles per hour.

Cheetah	70	White-tailed Deer	30
Wildebeest	50	Wart hog	30
Lion	50	Grizzly Bear	30
Quarterhorse	47	Domestic Cat	30
Elk	45	Human	27
Coyote	43	Elephant	25
Gray fox	42	Black Mamba Snake	20
Hyena	40	Squirrel	12
Zebra	40	Pig	11
Greyhound	39	Chicken	9
Rabbit	35	Spider	1.17
Giraffe	32	Tortoise	0.17
Reindeer	32	Snail	0.03

Ask students simply to examine this table and describe what they see or infer. As we have stated in other such data sets, we would ask (if they didn't): How were these data collected? What was actually measured? Did these animals actually "run" for one entire hour and then someone measure how far they had gone? Definitely not. These figures are based on an animal's top speed over about a quarter-mile distance for most of these animals. Have students guess which animals were actually measured at shorter distances for brief time periods: cheetah, lion, elephant, human, snake, spider, tortoise, and snail.

An interesting data collection project for library work might be to find out how fast various creatures of the sea can swim and relate these data to humans in the water. Can humans outswim an otter? ●

Most almanacs also have data on various world records for sports events. For instance, Olympic records over the years have been compiled for running and swimming various distances. Older students may be able to analyze these data. In each case, the winning time is recorded for certain distances. In swimming events, different strokes are given for many of these distances.

Ask your students to consider the data from current world records (all times have been converted to seconds).

	Running		Freestyle	Swimming strokes Breast	Butterfly	Back
100 meters	9.83		48.74	61.65	52.84	55.19
200 meters	19.72		107.44	133.34	116.24	118.14
400 meters	43.86		227.80	—	—	—

Questions for older students might include the following:

- For running: Were the people who set these 3 records running at the same speed? That is, are the running times proportional? (No; twice the distance required more than twice the time for each record.)
- For swimming: Were the people who set the 3 freestyle records swimming at the same speed? (No, again; for the same reason).
- For swimming: Does doubling the distance (100 vs. 200 meters) have the same effect on the times for each of the 4 swimming strokes? (It is close: the times for freestyle and butterfly are 2.20 as long—e.g., 107.44/48.74—and the breast- and backstrokes are 2.16 and 2.14 as long).
- For running vs. swimming: Is there a constant ratio between running and freestyle swimming? (Yes; about 1 to 5. It takes about 5 times as long to swim each of these 3 distances as it does to run. They vary a bit: 4.96, 5.45, and 5.19).

Almanacs also list top speeds and record times for various automobile races (e.g., the Indianapolis and Daytona 500s). Another exploration that may interest some students involves electric or battery powered cars. How fast can they go? How do they compare with these real racing cars? Students need only take appropriate measures of distance and time and calculate the ratio. Then some form of conversion to miles per hour will allow a comparison to other measures. ●

Have your students ever given much thought to videotapes? When they buy a blank videotape in order to record television shows, have they ever read the labels? When they record a show onto the tape, what setting do they use on the videocassette recorder (VCR)? Do they even know that there are three different settings: SP, LP, and EP? What do these letters mean?

Here are some basic facts about the standard VHS videocassette tapes and recorders. A standard VHS T-120 tape will record 120 minutes (2 hours) of programming when the VCR is set at SP (short play). When set at LP (long play) 240 minutes (4 hours) can be recorded, and 360 minutes (6 hours) at EP (extended play). The question is: What is going on with the tape and the VCR at these different settings? How is the VCR able to vary the length of time that the programming is recorded?

When taping at SP (120 minutes), the actual tape is running through the machine very fast, twice as fast as LP (240 minutes). Individual "frames" of pictures are being recorded. Twice as fast means twice as many pictures. Generally speaking, the more frames, the better the clarity of the recording when shown back. Ask students if they have ever compared the quality of the pictures of 6-hour taping (e.g., 3 TV movies) versus the 2-hour taping of just one movie. There usually is a definite difference.

Ask students, "How 'fast' is this VCR recording images at these different settings?" In order to answer, they must have another piece of information. Ask them what else they need to know. Here is the crucial fact: videocasette tapes are 246 meters or 807 feet long. Therefore, the 120-minute setting of SP is recording images onto 246 meters of tape in 120 minutes. Thus, the key ratio is 246:120 or about 2:1 or 2 meters per minute. At that setting in every minute, 2 meters of tape pass through the recording head of the VCR. Therefore, the LP setting of 240 minutes is recording at about 1 meter of tape per minute and EP (360 minutes) at about $\frac{2}{3}$ of a meter per minute. Can students visualize this phenomenon?

Perhaps working with feet and seconds is easier for students. Saying that 807 feet passes through the head in 120 minutes (807:120) means that about 6½ feet go through in 1 minute. That length is the same as 78 inches and the time is 60 seconds. Thus, 78 inches go through in 60 seconds, more than 1 inch per second at SP.

Are these occurrences still hard to visualize? Peggy Goldman, an art teacher in Deerfield, Illinois, uses the following activity to bring these ideas to life:

Get a spool of clear acetate 16-millimeter film for the projector. Arrange students in a long assembly line and unroll the film. Each student has a set of magic markers and may draw a simple image or design on about thirty frames of the film. Goldman urges that each design be a little different from the one on the preceding frame. When the film is rewound and shown, the consecutive images jump and dance. Showing the film at various speeds allows students to see how individual frames are flashed remarkably quickly even at the slowest setting. With a stopwatch,

students can calculate how many seconds their thirty frames took
to show. ●

· ·

Graphing Relationships

Graphing is a powerful tool for mathematical thinking. Just as students
can be helped to shift their thinking and representations from real objects
to tables, so can they shift from tables to graphs. Even younger students
can begin to make simple graphs using the data that they generate or collect
in their activities. The numerical data arrayed in tables can be translated
into a graphical form that will greatly facilitate analysis and understanding
of proportional relationships.

An excellent project for graphing and proportional reasoning is TIMS
(Teaching Integrated Math and Science) developed by Goldberg and Wagreich (1989). A wide variety of activities requires students to use materials
to design and conduct investigations. One of their introductory activities
involves students balancing various combinations of nuts and washers on
an equal-arm balance (or a two-pan scale). Here is a simplified version of
this activity:

Get a large quantity of 3 different sizes of washers (or nuts)
from a hardware or building supply store. Actually any small
objects of different mass will work but the trick is to find 3 different
objects with masses in a "nice" proportional relationship (e.g., 2
grams, 3 grams, and 4 grams). Do not tell the students these
masses.

Give students quantities of these 3 sizes of washers for a
series of experiments. Ask them to determine what quantity of one
kind of washer will balance what quantity of a different kind of
washer. For instance, they might begin with 2 of the large washers
(4 grams each) and be asked to find how many of the small
washers (2 grams each) will be needed to balance them. Then
they continue to experiment with 4 of the large washers, and then
8 of them. These data are recorded onto a table.

Number of large washers	Number of small washers
2	4
4	8
8	16

Next students plot these data points onto a graph with equal-
scale axes and draw a line connecting them. In explaining the
graph and the experiment, encourage students to interpolate from

the graph how many small washers would likely balance one large washer, then 3 (see figure 8.4). They can then empirically verify this prediction with the materials.

Similarly, you can lead students to extrapolate for greater quantities by extending the straight line that connects the data points. Ask them how many large washers would balance 10 small washers. Guide their thinking as they move back and forth between representations and ratios. The graph allows students to move across from 10 small washers to meet the extended line and then straight down to the number of large washers that must be present to produce that data point for the line. The table allows students to see the numbers in the ratios and talk about them: 8 small washers is twice as many as 4 large ones, so the small washers must always be twice as many; or there are always half as many large washers as small ones; and so on.

An analogous process can be used with various comparisons between any two of these washers. The juxtaposition of experimenting with the materials and equal balance arm, arraying data in tables, graphing real data, and predicting (interpolating and

· ·

Figure 8.4

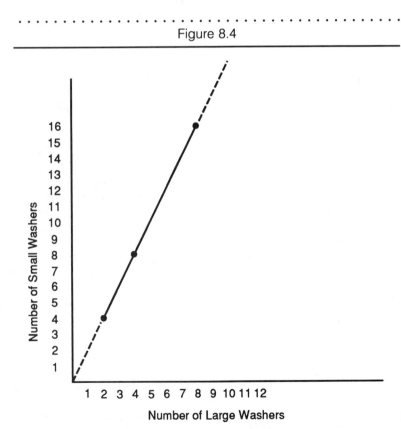

Number of Large Washers

extrapolating) is very powerful. By carefully selecting the masses of the items to give "nice" numbers, the teacher can sequence the development of ideas and complexity of the relationships. For instance, after the initial experimentation, graphing, and discussion, the students could be asked: How many large washers will balance 7 of these washers? Since they have only whole washers (and not 3½), they will not be able to do the actual balancing, but they will understand the relationship. ●

After grounding in the simpler experiments with the easy ratio (e.g., 2 : 4 or 1 : 2) students should be led into experiments that compare various quantities of small to medium (2 : 3) and medium to large (3 : 4). These ratios are less likely to be immediately seen. Doing the experiments, arraying the data in tables, and graphing all work together for students to experience, discuss, and understand the relationships. Creating the tables and predicting other data points obviously give students a lot of motivated practice with multiplication or division. Working with the equal-balance arm or two-pan balance scale also provides a powerful metaphor for equations.

. . . .

Functions

Although the concept of function may conjure up for you all the meaningless symbols of algebra and the tedium of solving equations, it does not have to be so. Despite many rather abstract ways of defining a function, there are many meaningful experiences teachers can provide for students in elementary school that will lay the foundation for the abstractions and symbolic representations of functions that will come later.

The essence of a function is that two sets of numbers are paired in a particular way. Each number in the first set corresponds exactly to one number in the other set. Thus, the value of the second number depends on, or is a function of, the first. For instance, ask students to imagine the machine in figure 8.5. It performs a special function: it changes any number that goes in (the input) into a different number (the output). A particular function machine always changes the input in the same way.

The problem for the students is to determine the rule that this function machine is using. Like any good inductive problem, students need to see lots of raw data. We could show many examples of what the machine might do:

Input	changed to	Output
3	⟶	5
2	⟶	4
6	⟶	8
9	⟶	11

· ·

Figure 8.5

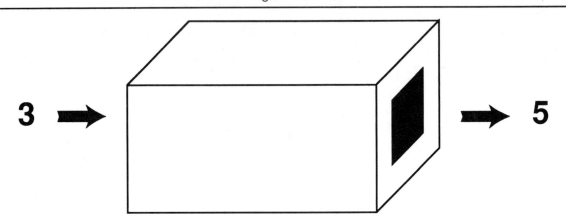

What is the rule that this function machine is using? Add 2 to the input. In order to be a function, for each particular input, only one output is possible.

To help them determine the rule, students can suggest input for you to enter into the function machine. Then you tell them the output. They will quickly see that ordering the input will also order the output in some way, helping them to see the relationship between the two sets.

The teacher can create different function machines to illustrate a variety of patterns, such as multiplicative (input 1, 2, 3, 4 gives output 3, 6, 9, 12); or even multiplicative and additive (input 1, 2, 3, 4 gives output 4, 7, 10, 13—the pattern is multiply the input by 3 and add 1).

An excellent example of an investigation with functions also comes from the TIMS project (Goldberg and Wagreich 1989):

Provide several different kinds of small balls (e.g., superball and tennis ball) to each group of students. Ask them to predict how high these balls will bounce when dropped from a particular height. Then give one type of ball to each group of students and ask them to use a meter stick to measure carefully the height of the *initial* bounce when dropped from specific heights (e.g., 80, 40, and 20 centimeters). The TIMS activities help students to become careful planners of experiments and recorders of data. Students should be encouraged to set up a data table for heights of drops and bounces, take measurements of bounces for each height, and use the average value of the three measurements in subsequent graphing.

The TIMS activities address important issues in the scientific method, especially controlling and manipulating "variables." The drop height of the ball is manipulated and varied, while the bounce height is observed (a dependent variable—it is a *function* of the drop height). Thus, these two variables can be arrayed in a table to show a functional relationship.

Drop height (cm.)	Bounce height (cm.)
20	?
40	?
80	?

Note how in the activity we deliberately choose drop heights that double in order to help younger students develop proportional reasoning in that dimension. Whatever they find as the bounce height at 20 cm., they might expect to find a bounce height twice as high at 40 cm. The heart of the TIMS activities is graphing these data so that students can see the straight-line relationships. These lines will be different for different balls and different surfaces.

Older students can be led to examine carefully the ratios involved. For one particular kind of ball dropped onto the same floor surface, the bounce heights will be in approximately the same ratio to their drop heights. However, this ratio will change with different balls (e.g., superballs will have a higher ratio than tennis balls) and the same ball may have a different drop/bounce height ratio on a different surface (e.g., rug versus wooden floor). ●

. . . .

Number Sentences and Equations

Most textbooks introduce students to number sentences and equations far too early in their development. When confronted with the symbols 8 − 3 = 5, most first graders have not built an adequate conceptualization of these symbols; they must rely on rote memory to parrot correct answers. Teachers need to use many different ways to build an understanding of equivalence. Third graders can readily understand equations when related to the washer and nuts experiments using a two-pan scale.

The teacher does not even need a set of accurate weights to start children on the right conceptual foot. Imagine using a set of small washers of equal mass to balance with another set of objects of equal mass. For instance:

Prepare a collection of identical opaque plastic bottles (e.g., vitamin bottles) that can be filled with equal amounts of sand to give a standard mass equal to 10 washers. With a balance scale, students should establish this equivalence, as they did with washers and nuts.

Next students can determine the mass of various larger, nonstandard objects such as potatoes in terms of their two units of measure: bottles and washers. Thus, a large potato might be balanced with 2 bottles and 3 washers. Pictorial representation of this equivalence can help students build the foundations for equations. By the choice of 10 washers equaling one bottle, a parallel to the decimal system can be made. How many washers does this potato weigh? (2 bottles + 3 washers = 23 washers)

The simple equal-arm balance should not be underestimated for its power to provide a schema for number sentences. Younger students should consider the situation shown in figure 8.6.

On one side of the balance are 2 *known* quantities (2 small bottles that are each equivalent to 10 washers). On the other side are 7 washers and a bigger opaque bottle of *unknown* mass. This simple situation can be used to help students understand several relationships and ideas. What would be the mass of this big bottle in terms of washers? In essence, the question asks: "Seven plus what equals twenty?" Even younger children can "see" that if you want to balance the big bottle with washers, one way is to get it all by itself on one side of the scale with some quantity of washers. To do so, you could take the 7 washers off, but that action or "operation" would make the scale unbalanced. Therefore, you must also take 7 off the other side as well, which would require a substitution of 10 washers for one of the small bottles (or exchanging the 2 small bottles for 20 washers). Have the students perform these actions.

Record in pictorial form what transpired. (The pictures in figure 8.7 show what students usually do in the above situation.) Finally, you may translate these words, actions, and drawings into symbolic form, if appropriate for the students' level. For instance, 1 [Big Bottle] + 7 [washers] = 2 [small bottles]. Since students want to know how many washers the big bottle is equivalent to, this sentence can be translated to 1 [B] + 7 = 20. Taking 7 washers away from each side is thus represented symbolically as 1 [B] = 13. The equal sign (=) will then have a particular referent in their schemata that is more appropriate than the interpretations that students often develop, such as the = in 1 + 4 = 5 means

. . . .

Figure 8.6

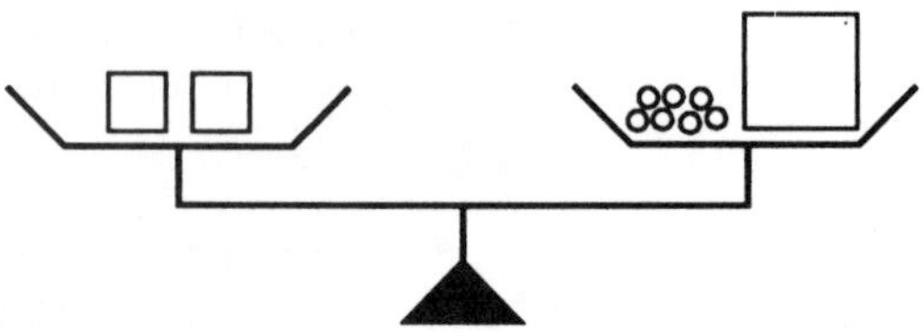

Figure 8.7

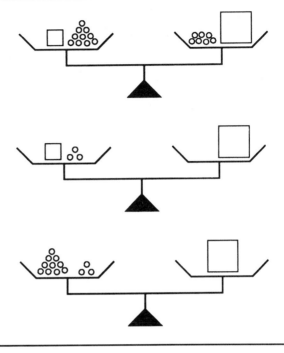

the direction to compute (1 plus 4 makes 5) or that the equal sign separates the "problem" from the "answer."

Repeat these experiments and experiences with several bottles or by varying the mass inside the big bottle. A simple way is simply to put a different number of washers into the opaque big bottle each time. More complex situations can be enacted that require more actions to be taken in order to balance the scales and discover the mass of the big bottle. For instance, students can attack the real situation that we represent below symbolically.

1 [B] + 2 [s b] = 3 [s b] + 5 washers

A more complicated situation would be:

2 [B] = 2[s b] + 8 washers

This situation requires the proportional reasoning that both sides of the balance (equation) could be divided into two equal halves. That is:

2 [B] = 28; therefore [B] + [B] = 14 + 14; therefore [B] = 14 ●

If students can see and manipulate these situations before moving to the pictorial or symbolic forms, they can understand exactly what is going on. Then they can readily conceive of abstractions that are based on real situations.

This chapter has explored many different mathematical relationships. Student were able to directly experience some of these through the senses. For others, the teacher had to stage experiences with phenomena or apparatus. Activities varied in complexity and abstractness, yet each could be expressed symbolically.

As we have stressed throughout this book, it is crucial for you as the teacher to build the proper conceptual and experiential foundation for students before requiring symbol manipulation. The topics in this chapter are frequently presented in textbooks primarily through symbols and procedures. The kinds of problem-solving situations and activities described in this chapter offer a good beginning for understanding. Helping students to ''get a good feel'' for an idea through such experiences before dealing with a textbook may be the best insurance of mathematical success that you can provide.

postscript

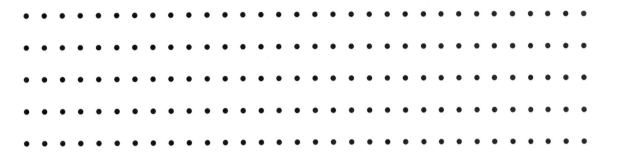

Over the years, students have shown us that they are remarkably capable of appreciating the beauty, richness, power, and usefulness of mathematics. Our concern with both their conceptual understanding *and* their feelings toward mathematics led us to explore linking the domain of mathematics with their worlds. Obviously, others share our excitement with integrating mathematics and the natural phenomena of science; projects such as AIMS and TIMS are attracting teachers and enlivening classrooms across the country. We have barely scratched the surface of possible problem-solving activities that integrate mathematics and social studies. The power of the microcomputer for creating and using graphics, spreadsheets, and data bases has barely begun to be used as a tool for understanding mathematics.

The value of manipulatives and games for all ages of students is now evident. Students more readily recognize and appreciate underlying mathematical concepts when their interests have been tickled. Bright colors, exciting action, and powerful ideas can be blended. Playfulness, creativity, and intellectual curiosity go hand-in-hand.

The domain of mathematics is not static. Computer technology, mathematical software, and discrete mathematics are changing the face of college and high school curricula. Elementary and middle schools can and should build the conceptual foundations for topology (see Hyde and Bizar 1989), chaos theory and fractal geometry (see Barnsley 1988; Gardner 1986). As good as the *Standards* may be, we should not see it as the final word, but rather as the license to create new and exciting possibilities for students to understand, appreciate, and use mathematics.

appendix

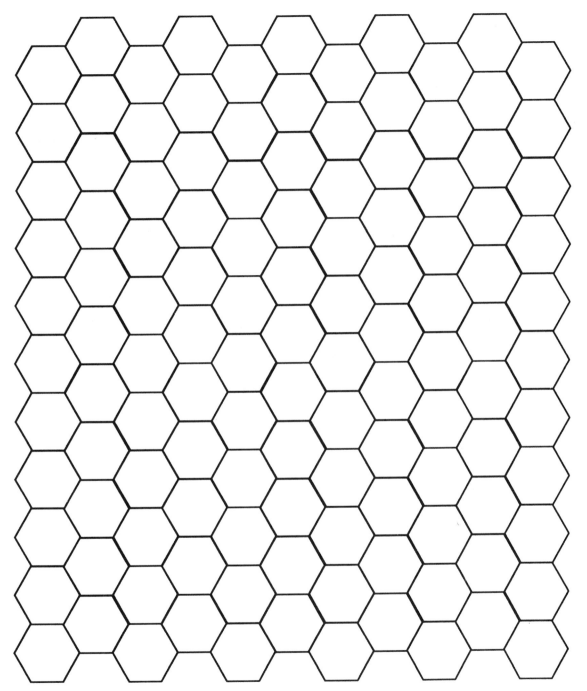

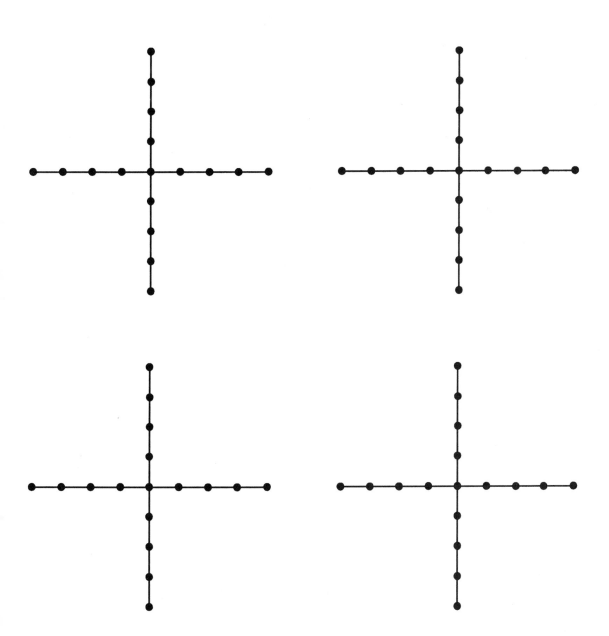

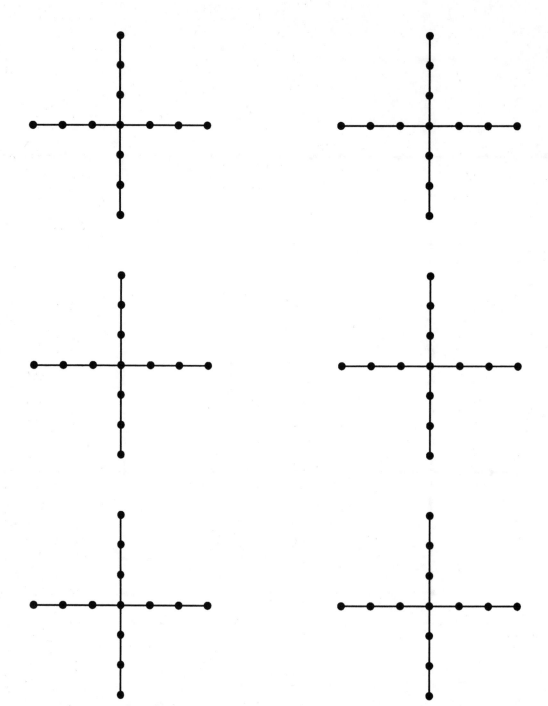

references

Baratta-Lorton, M. 1985. *Mathematics Their Way*. Reading, Mass.: Addison-Wesley.

Barnsley, M. 1988. *Fractals Everywhere*. San Diego: Academic Press.

Cambourne, B., and J. Turbill. 1987. *Coping with Chaos*. Portsmouth, N.H.: Heinemann.

Charles, R., F. Lester, and P. O'Daffer. 1987. *How To Evaluate Progress in Problem Solving*. Reston, Vir.: National Council of Teachers of Mathematics.

Charles, R. I., & E. A. Silver, eds. 1988. *The Teaching and Assessing of Mathematical Problem Solving*. Reston, Va.: National Council of Teachers of Mathematics.

Gardner, M. 1961. *The Second Scientific American Book of Mathematical Puzzles & Diversions*. New York: Simon and Schuster.

———. 1971. *Martin Gardner's Sixth Book of Mathematical Games from Scientific American*. New York: Scribner's.

———. 1986. *From Penrose Tiles to Trapdoor Ciphers*. New York; W. H. Freeman.

———. 1988. *Time Travel and Other Mathematical Bewilderments*. New York: W. H. Freeman.

Goldberg, H., and P. Wagreich. 1989. "Focus on Integrating Science and Math." *Science and Children*. 26 (February):22–24.

Golomb, S. W. 1965. *Polyominoes*. New York: Scribner's.

Greenes, C., L. Schulman and R. Spungin. 1989. *Thinkermath: Developing Number Sense and Arithmetic Skills*. Sunnyvale, Calif.: Creative Publications.

Hyde, A. A., and S. V. Turner. 1988. *Math Explorations in Logo for Grades 5–8*. Evanston, Ill.: National College of Education.

Hyde, A. A., and M. Bizar. 1989. *Thinking in Context: Teaching Cognitive Processes across the Elementary School Curriculum.* New York: Longman.

Johnson, D. W., and R. T. Johnson. 1987. *Learning Together and Alone: Cooperation, Competition, and Individualization.* Englewood Cliffs, N.J.: Prentice-Hall.

Lappan, G., and P. W. Schram. 1989. "Communication and Reasoning: Critical Dimensions of Sense Making in Mathematics." In Trafton 1989.

Lesh, R., and J. S. Zawojewski. 1988. "Problem Solving." In *Teaching Mathematics in Grades K–8: Research Based Methods*, ed. T. R. Post. Boston: Allyn & Bacon.

Lindquist, M. M. 1989. "It's Time To Change." In Trafton, 1989.

Mottershead, L. 1977. *Metamorphosis: A Source Book of Mathematical Discovery.* Sydney, Australia: John Wiley.

National Council of Teachers of Mathematics. 1989. *Curriculum and Evaluation Standards for School Mathematics.* Reston, Va.: National Council of Teachers of Mathematics.

Papert, S. 1980. *Mindstorms: Children, Computers, and Powerful Ideas.* New York: Basic Books.

Reys, R. E., P. R. Trafton, B. Reys, and J. Zawojewski. 1986. Calif.: *Computational Estimation (Grades 6–8).* Palo Alto, Calif.: Dale Seymour.

Schoenfeld, A. H. 1987. "A Brief and Biased History of Problem Solving." In *Teaching and Learning: A Problem Solving Focus*, ed. F. R. Curcio. Reston, Va.: National Council of Teachers of Mathematics.

Schmuck, R. A., and P. A. Schmuck. 1988. *Group Processes in the Classroom.* Dubuque, Iowa: Wm. C. Brown.

Slavin, R., ed. 1985. *Learning To Cooperate, Cooperating To Learn.* New York: Plenum.

Trafton, P. R., ed. 1989. *New Directions for Elementary School Mathematics.* (1989 Yearbook) Reston, Va.: National Council of Teachers of Mathematics.

The World Almanac and Book of Facts. 1988. New York: World Almanac.

problems/
activities
index

general index

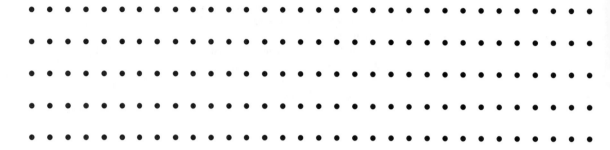

Page numbers in boldface type represent related problems and/or activities.